Fodor's

EIGHTH
New
EDITION

Philadelphia & the Pennsylvania Dutch Country

D0666872

Fodor's Travel Publications, Inc.
New York • Toronto • London • Sydney • Auckland

Grateful acknowledgment is made to Paul Fussell for permission to reprint "The Search for Intelligent Life" from PHILADELPHIA Magazine. Copyright © 1988 by Paul Fussell.

**Fodor's Philadelphia &
the Pennsylvania Dutch Country**

Editor: Katherine Kane, Melanie Roth
Area Editors: Rathe Miller, Michael Schwager
Editorial Contributors: Suzanne De Galan, Rathe Miller, Marcy Pritchard, Michael Schwager, M.T. Schwartzman
Art Director: Fabrizio La Rocca
Cartographer: David Lindroth
Illustrator: Karl Tanner
Cover Photograph: Peter Beck/Uniphoto

Design: Vignelli Associates

Special Sales

Contents

Maps

Foreword

Although every care has been taken to ensure the accuracy of the information in this guide, the passage of time will always bring change, and consequently, the publisher cannot accept responsibility for errors that may occur.

All prices and opening times quoted here are based on information supplied to us at press time. Hours and admission fees may change, however, and the prudent traveler will avoid inconvenience by calling ahead.

Fodor's wants to hear about your travel experiences, both pleasant and unpleasant. When a hotel or restaurant fails to live up to its billing, let us know and we will investigate the complaint and revise our entries where the facts warrant it.

Send your letters to the editors of Fodor's Travel Publications, 201 E. 50th Street, New York, NY 10022.

Highlights and Fodor's Choice

Highlights

The highlight of Philadelphia's Welcome America celebration during the summer of 1993 was the opening of the Pennsylvania Convention Center. It marked the beginning of a revitalized Philadelphia hosting more out-of-town guests than ever before. Finished on time and on budget, the $522 million complex has 435,000 square feet of exhibit space. The main exhibit hall stretched over two square city blocks and could hold seven football fields. Vice President Al Gore cut the ribbon, and there was much talk of a revived city economy. It is already affecting the surrounding area: New stores and restaurants have opened in the neighborhood, and there's more life on the streets after dark. Within a month of its opening, 120 citywide conventions had already been booked, with estimates of more than 800,000 visitors and $350 million of direct economic impact.

The transformation of the old Reading Railroad train shed is the city's next project. Scheduled for completion in March 1994, the Victorian-era terminal, the largest remaining single-span terminal in the world, will be converted into a grand hall with exhibit space and a ballroom.

The construction of a Marriott Hotel in the convention-center area will add 1,200 much-needed hotel rooms by January 1995. Plans for 1994 and 1995 include spending $12 million more to widen streets and beautify 22 blocks around the convention center.

Philadelphia's Independence Hall has also received attention. Federal funds have scaffolding up and repairs underway to building-threatening deterioration. The site is so popular that it was kept open daily till 9 PM throughout the summer of '93. It was a first-time-ever experiment that if successful will be continued.

Six other buildings in Independence National Historical Park that had been closed because of funding difficulties or disrepair are again open.

Philadelphia wants to "own" the fourth of July and definitely acquired a piece of it in '93. Capping the Welcome America festivities on Independence Day, President Bill Clinton joined in the presentation of the Philadelphia Liberty Medal to African National Congress President Nelson Mandela and South African President F.W. de Klerk.

Along South Broad Street, the idea for the Avenue of the Arts is taking shape. Tagged at about $200 million, there are plans to create a new jazz hall, a creative-arts school, a performing-arts center, and a theater and rehearsal space. The centerpiece will be a new $90 million concert hall for the Philadelphia Orchestra.

Lovers of classical music and the Philadelphia Orchestra are adjusting to the passing of the baton from music director Ricardo Muti to Wolfgang Sawallisch. Muti will make occasional appearances as conductor laureate.

The Pennsylvania Ballet, under the direction of Christopher D'Amboise, is back on its toes after a near-demise in 1991.

Controversy sizzles at the Barnes Foundation, the finest collection of Impressionist art outside Paris. Critics charged that the new president of the board, Richard Glanton, out for personal power and prestige, cooked up a multimillion-dollar repair budget to justify a world tour of selected paintings. The repairs and tour will keep the museum closed until at least mid-1995.

The Greater Philadelphia Film Office continues to attract the production of feature films to the city. Recently the office reeled in Jonathan Demme's *Philadelphia*, starring Tom Hanks and Denzel Washington, and *Two Bits*, starring Al Pacino. Also set here is the pilot for a new network TV series, "Philly Heat," starring Peter Boyle. With luck, the men's room at 30th Street Station may see yet another movie murder as it did in both *Blowout* and *Witness*.

The newest attractions at America's oldest zoo are two rare white lions, the only ones in America, and the one-acre, $6 million Carnivore Kingdom. The state-of-the art natural habitat has a mixture of species—among them snow leopards, jaguars, pelicans and pandas—in a simulated mountainscape with waterfalls and wild plants.

In Camden, across the Delaware River from Penn's Landing, is the New Jersey State Aquarium. Opened in 1992, it's an enjoyable 10-minute ferry ride to 3,000 fishes, crustaceans, and other sealife. The 760,000-gallon main tank is the second largest in the country, and there's a smaller petting tank stocked with sharks and rays.

Even if you don't like bugs you'll enjoy the new Insectarium, a museum-zoo with more than 1,500 species, which joins the city's scores of small museums ranging from the bizarre to the elegant.

Philadelphia's Delaware River waterfront is experiencing an entertainment boom. In the past few years, more than a dozen new clubs and restaurants have opened along the river, with a water taxi ferrying revelers between the clubs. Delaware Avenue along Penn's Landing has been renamed Christopher Columbus Boulevard, but there is sentiment to change it back. Across town at the Schuykill River, there is a movement to change the name of Kelly Drive back to East River Drive, restoring the nomenclatural symmetry with West River Drive.

South Street, the city's main entertainment strip, may have grown too popular for its own good. Hordes of youths clog the thoroughfare, blaring radios and driving away more sedate patrons. Main Street, Manayunk, in the north-west part of the city, has become what South Street used to be. Popular but not inundated, the shops, restaurants, and clubs stay open late, and you can enjoy a peaceful stroll along the street or the Manayunk Canal. There's even a yuppie pool hall that plays jazz in the background and has never had a fight.

In Old City, more than 25 galleries remain open into the evening on "First Friday." Art lovers stroll from gallery to gallery, sipping wine, munching cheese, and creating a re-fined street-party atmosphere. Art students dressed in black abound. The Wednesday "Make It a Night" program, which debuted in 1992, has had moderate success. Stores and galleries stay open late, and prices are reduced for parking, public transportation, some restaurants, and movie theaters. The extended shopping hours hook up with events: for example, during the week-long Mellon PSFS Jazz Festival, Wednesday night heard jazz, blues, and Dixieland from live bands scattered around the Walnut Street shopping area.

In 1991, the national recession and cutbacks in federal dol-lars, combined with Philadelphia's own brand of corrup-tion, mismanagement, shortsighted unions and patronage, had led the city to the brink of bankruptcy. Now Philadel-phia has the sense of a city on the way up. It's cleaner, safer, and on the brink of solvency. In 1993, the city govern-ment enacted what may be its first honestly balanced bud-get in memory. The city's bond rating has improved from junk status to nearly investment grade. A big part of the change is the mayor, Ed Rendell, who took office in 1992. He's charged up the city, received good reviews from both the local and national media, and unlike previous mayors has been able to work with city council.

The opening of the convention center has resulted in a greater police presence downtown, especially around the convention center, the Benjamin Franklin Parkway and historic sites. Besides patrol cars, you'll notice cops on foot, on horseback and, new to Philly, on bicycles. The Police De-partment has also initiated a new taxi enforcement unit, which will cut down on the ripoffs by unlicensed as well as licensed hacks. Police stationed at strategic locations will check cab drivers' licenses and fares. You'll also see new dark-blue signs directing visitors to museums, tourist sites and parking lots. For security and hospitality, maps are given out free at hotels. They show "safe" routes from ho-tels to the convention center, with Community Service Representatives along the routes. New entities, such as the Center City District and the South Street/Headhouse Dis-trict, supplement the normal city services, sweeping the sidewalks, answering questions, assisting visitors. East of City Hall, you'll see the privately funded Market East Mar-shals, patrolling in their distinctive green jackets.

At 30th Street Station, two dozen new stores in the South Concourse make waiting for a train a more pleasant experience. The $100 million restoration of Philadelphia's principal train station includes The Market at 30th Street, with bakeries, restaurants, bars, a gourmet coffee stand, flower shop, and bookstore. The improvements have not detracted from the sense that you're in a *real* train station.

At the airport, USAir and the city announced another improvement program, this one a $320 million, three-year plan for renovations to concourses and terminals and for a new runway.

One of the city's finest freebies has reopened: the observation deck at the top of City Hall tower, at the foot of the Billy Penn statue. Go up and see him sometime.

The city now has five luxury hotels, two of which have received both the Mobil Guide five-star and the AAA Guide five-diamond ratings. You don't have to stay there to enjoy them—you can sip tea at the Mary Cassatt Room in the Rittenhouse; dance in Founders, a 19th-story restaurant with a panaromic view in the Hotel Atop the Bellevue; or enjoy a jazz trio in the elegant Swann Lounge at the Four Seasons.

And Newmarket, the once-bustling wooden-and-glass upscale minimall at the foot of South Street, is showing signs of life. Plans have been announced for a $15 million arts and entertainment complex in the space, which has been moribund for a decade.

Now the bad news: Philadelphia has suffered the fate of most major American cities. Crime is a problem. Cars parked downtown overnight are routinely vandalized or stolen. The city continues to fight the battle of the homeless, 90% of whom are men in their 20s and 30s, panhandling, lying on sidewalks, and intimidating tourists and citizens alike. The city moved a colony of them from Logan Circle on the Benjamin Franklin Parkway and is now dislodging them from their subway station shantytown at 13th and Market.

One result of these urban conditions is middle-class flight to the suburbs. The erosion of the economic base and the decline in the city's quality of life set in motion a downward spiral. Many Philadelphians who have no strong reason to stay in the city and who have the means to leave, do so. But many do stay, love the city, and enjoy its pleasures. And as a visitor, chances are you'll experience Philadelphia at its best.

Fodor's Choice

No two people will agree on what makes a perfect vacation, but it's fun and helpful to know what others think. We hope you'll have a chance to experience some of Fodor's Choices yourself while visiting Philadelphia. For detailed information about each entry, refer to the appropriate chapters in this guidebook.

Special Moments

The steps of the Philadelphia Museum of Art at dawn

Walking Forbidden Drive along Wissahickon Creek

Feeding time for the big cats at the zoo

Independence Hall any time

Taste Treats

Bassett's butterscotch-vanilla ice cream at Reading Terminal Market

Fresh soft pretzels with mustard from street-corner vendors

The Peking duck specialty of the house at Joe's

Frozen yogurt at Scoop De Ville

Tastykakes anywhere

The pressed lobster at Le Bec-Fin

Off the Beaten Track

Bryn Athyn Cathedral

Laurel Hill Cemetry

After Hours

Jazz at Zanzibar Blue

Cheeseteaks at Pat's (9th St. and Passyunk Ave.) at 3AM

The view of Boathouse Row, the Waterworks, and the Philadelphia Museum of Art from West River Drive

Club-hopping by river taxi along the Delaware River waterfront

Walking around Independence National Historical Park

Hotels

Four Seasons (*Very Expensive*)

Hotel Atop the Bellevue (*Very Expensive*)

The Rittenhouse (*Very Expensive*)

Adam's Mark (*Expensive*)

Ramada Suites–Convention Center (*Moderate*)

Restaurants

The Fountain (*Very Expensive*)

Le Bec-Fin (*Very Expensive*)

Susanna Foo (*Very Expensive*)

Osteria Romana (*Expensive*)

Marrakesh (*Moderate*)

Roller's (*Moderate*)

Tokio (*Moderate*)

Thai Garden East (*Inexpensive*)

Van's Garden (*Inexpensive*)

Brandywine Valley

Longwood Gardens

Brandywine River Museum

Winterthur Museum and Gardens

Bucks County

Fonthill, Henry Chapman Mercer's concrete castle, and the Mercer Museum, both in Doylestown

Floating down the Delaware River in an inner tube rented from Bucks County River Tubing

Exploring River Road north of New Hope and staying overnight at a bed-and-breakfast

Lancaster County

A visit to a farmers market: the Central Market in downtown Lancaster or the Green Dragon Farmers Market and Auction in Ephrata

A drive along the back-country roads between Routes 23 and 340 to see the Amish farms and roadside stands

Lunch at a Pennsylvania Dutch restaurant

An overnight stay at a Mennonite farm

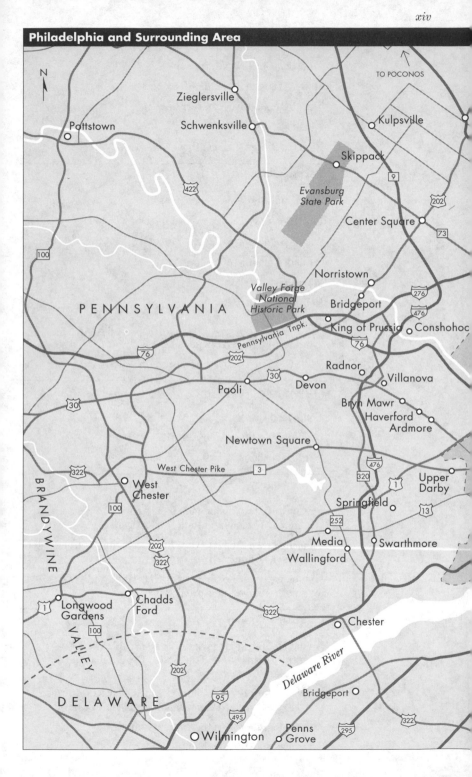

Philadelphia and Surrounding Area

N

TO POCONOS

Zieglersville

Schwenksville

Pattstown

Kulpsville

Skippack

9

202

Evansburg
State Park

Center Square

73

100

Norristown

Valley Forge
National
Historic Park

Bridgeport

276

PENNSYLVANIA

Pennsylvania Tnpk.

King of Prussia

476

Conshohoc

76

202

76

Radnor

30

Devon

Villanova

Paoli

Bryn Mawr

Haverford
Ardmore

30

Newtown Square

BRANDYWINE

West Chester Pike

3

476

West
Chester

322

320

1

Upper
Darby

100

Springfield

13

252

202

Media

Swarthmore

322

Wallingford

Longwood
Gardens

Chadds
Ford

322

Chester

1

100

VALLEY

Delaware River

202

DELAWARE

95

Bridgeport

495

Penns
Grove

295

322

Wilmington

Chalfont

Washington Crossing

[95]

Warrington

[232]

Trenton

Montgomeryville

[611]

Yardley

Newtown

[1]

Warminster

Richboro

[1]

Horsham

[132]

[532]

Southampton

[309]

[276]

Feasterville

[13]

Willow Grove

Fort Washington

Bryn Athyn

Pennsylvania

Tnpk.

[95]

Abington

Jenkintown

Burlington

hocken

Cheltenham

The Wissahickon

[1]

[13]

Delaware River

[541]

[73]

Riverside

Schuylkill River

[1] [13]

[130]

Bala-Cynwyd

[611]

[95]

Fairmount Park

Betsy Ross Br.

[76]

PHILADELPHIA

[73]

[38]

Ben Franklin Br.

Pennsauken

[291]

Camden

[676]

Cherry Hill

[295]

[70]

Walt Whitman Br.

Gloucester City

Marlton

NEW JERSEY

✈ Philadelphia International Airport

[30]

Woodbury

[130]

New Jersey Tnpk.

0   10 miles

0   15 km

Philadelphia

Poplar St.

Parrish St.

Aspen St.

Brown St.

George St.

Vineyard St.

TO GERMANTOWN,
TEMPLE UNIVERSITY,
CHESTNUT HILL

Parrish St.

Ridge Ave.

Rte. 611

28th St.

27th St.

26th St.

25th St.

24th St.

23rd St.

Corinthian Ave.

19th St.

North St.

Wallace St.

Fairmount Ave.

Mt. Vernon St.

*Fairmount
Park*

Green St.

Brandywine St.

Spring Garden St.

**Philadelphia
Museum of Art**

Buttonwood St.

Buttonwo

18th St.

Hamilton St.

**Rodin
Museum**

Benjamin Franklin Parkway

Callowhill St.

Broad St.

76

30

Schuylkill River

676 30

Tours 3 and 4

17th St.

*Logan
Circle*

Franklin Institute

Race St.

Broad St. Subway

Phil
Conve
Reading T

**Academy
of Natural
Sciences**

Cherry St.

23rd St.

19th St.

Arch St.

**Suburban
Station**

**30th St.
Station**

John F. Kennedy Blvd.

Market-Frankford Subway

30th St.

Subway-Surface

Market St.

City Hall

13th St.

Juniper St.

Broad St.

Broad St. Subway

TO U.
OF
PENN.

TO
AIRPORT

Airport Train (R1)

76

Ludlow St.

Chestnut St.

Sansom St.

21st St.

Walnut St.

20th St.

*Rittenhouse
Square*

16th St.

Locust St.

Locust St.

15th St.

Schuylkill River

Spruce St.

19th St.

25th St.

24th St.

Pine St.

Lombard St.

Schuylkill Ave.

N

22nd St.

South St.

Bainbridge St.

Rte. 611

Grays Ferry Ave.

Pemberton St.

Fitzwater St.

23rd St.

Catharine St.

Webster St.

0 ——— 440 yards

0 ——— 400 meters

Christian St.

Carpenter St.

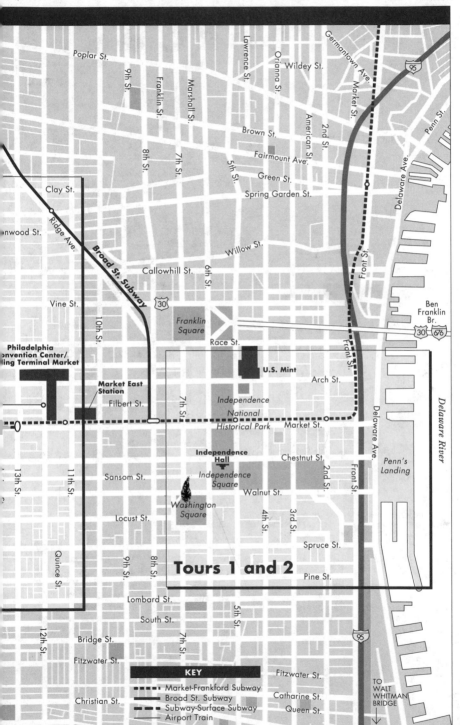

Poplar St.

9th St.

Lawrence St.

Orianna St.

Wildey St.

Germantown Ave.

I-95

Franklin St.

Marshall St.

Brown St.

American St.

2nd St.

Market St.

Fairmount Ave.

Green St.

Penn St.

8th St.

7th St.

5th St.

Spring Garden St.

Delaware Ave.

Clay St.

Ridge Ave.

nwood St.

Broad St. Subway

Willow St.

Front St.

Vine St.

Callowhill St.

6th St.

10th St.

30

Franklin Square

Ben Franklin Br.

Race St.

30 76

Philadelphia onvention Center/ ling Terminal Market

Market East Station

Filbert St.

7th St.

U.S. Mint

Arch St.

Front St.

Delaware Ave.

Independence National Historical Park

Market St.

Delaware River

Independence Hall

Chestnut St.

Penn's Landing

13th St.

11th St.

Sansom St.

8th St.

Independence Square

Walnut St.

2nd St.

Front St.

Locust St.

9th St.

Washington Square

4th St.

3rd St.

Spruce St.

12th St.

Quince St.

Tours 1 and 2

Pine St.

Lombard St.

South St.

5th St.

95

Bridge St.

7th St.

Fitzwater St.

KEY

Fitzwater St.

TO WALT WHITMAN BRIDGE ↓

Christian St.

Catharine St.

Queen St.

- - - - Market-Frankford Subway
────── Broad St. Subway
═══════ Subway-Surface Subway
────── Airport Train

World Time Zones

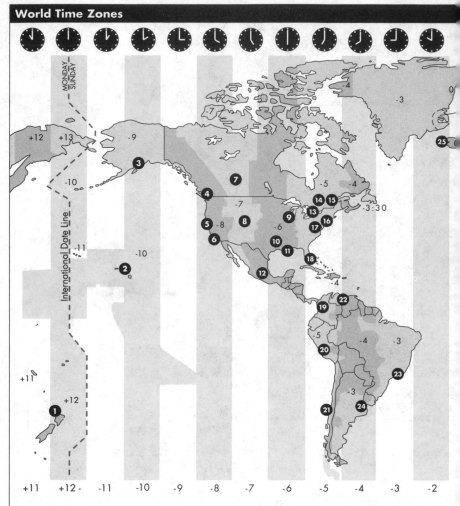

Numbers below vertical bands relate each zone to Greenwich Mean Time (0 hrs.).
Local times frequently differ from these general indications,
as indicated by light-face numbers on map.

Algiers, **29**	Berlin, **34**	Delhi, **48**	Istanbul, **40**
Anchorage, **3**	Bogotá, **19**	Denver, **8**	Jerusalem, **42**
Athens, **41**	Budapest, **37**	Djakarta, **53**	Johannesburg, **44**
Auckland, **1**	Buenos Aires, **24**	Dublin, **26**	Lima, **20**
Baghdad, **46**	Caracas, **22**	Edmonton, **7**	Lisbon, **28**
Bangkok, **50**	Chicago, **9**	Hong Kong, **56**	London (Greenwich), **27**
Beijing, **54**	Copenhagen, **33**	Honolulu, **2**	Los Angeles, **6**
	Dallas, **10**		Madrid, **38**
			Manila, **57**

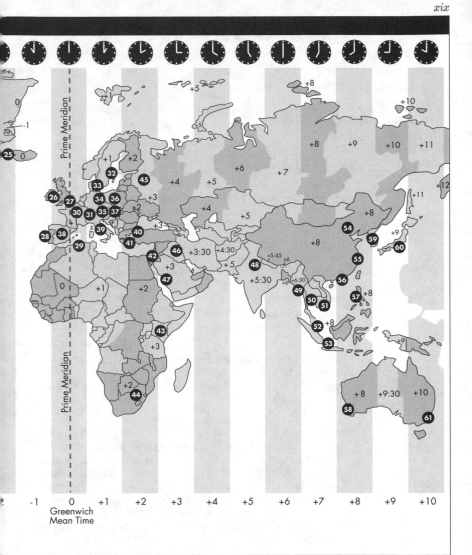

Introduction

By Chuck Stone

*A senior editor of
the* Philadelphia
Daily News,
*Chuck Stone is
professor of
English at the
University of
Delaware.*

Yo, World!

Which is not a mere "hello," but a run-them-all-together
salutation of "Hithere," "Howareya," and "Have-a-good-
day."

Philadelphians claim credit for "Yo" as a greeting, although
they concede it wasn't in vogue when Quaker William Penn
founded Philadelphia or when the city's most distinguished
citizen, Benjamin Franklin, prowled the streets in pensive
solutide. Instead, a muscle-bound movie here may be the
source of its popularity.

In the movie *Rocky*, Philadelphians shout "Yo, Rocky!" as
the underdog boxer jogs over some of the city's cobbled
streets, through the open-air Italian market, up the Benjamin Franklin parkway ("America's Champs Elysées"), and
up the expansive steps of the Philadelphia Art Museum.
Reaching the top, he raises his arms in a "V" in sweet antici-
pation of victory.

Today, many visitors try to imitate Rocky's dash up the 98
steps of this sandstone-color Greco-Roman building before
entering to browse through its fabled art treasures. That
irony is only one of the many examples of Philadelphia's *au-
dacious uniqueness*.

Philadelphia is a fountainhead of superlatives cherished by
both historians and tourists: the world's largest city-owned
park, Fairmount Park; the oldest art school in America, the
Pennsylvania Academy of Fine Arts; the first U.S. medical
school to admit women, Women's Medical College of Pennsylvania; the oldest natural-science museum, the Academy
of Natural Sciences; the oldest U.S. opera house still in use,
the Academy of Music; the first library in America to circu-
late books, the Library Company founded by Benjamin
Franklin; the world's largest sculpture atop a building, the
statue of William Penn atop City Hall; the oldest black
newspaper in America, the *Philadelphia Tribune;* the oldest African Methodist Episcopal church, Mother Bethel
AME; and the nation's oldest street of continuous occupation, Elfreth's Alley, a narrow, one-block street of 33 Colonial homes in Center City (downtown).

All of these buildings still breathe architectural vitality. Or
as that popular song cheerfully promises, "Everything old
is new again."

But if love is a many-splendored thing, the name, Philadelphia, is a many-storied legend.

The "Philadelphia Lawyer," long a symbol of legal genius,
was probably invented when a gout-ravaged, white-haired

Philadelphian, Andrew Hamilton, successfully defended Peter Zenger in the nation's first libel case. The plaintiff was New York governor William Cosby (no relation, of course, to a famous and cherished Philadelphia son, Bill Cosby).

The Philadelphia Story amused theatergoers with its inside peek at upper-class eccentricities.

The Philadelphia Negro, by W.E.B. duBois, set a standard for sociological research.

Philadelphia Cream Cheese enhances hors d'oeuvres (although the name alone doesn't claim to titillate taste buds).

And Philadelphians still yearn to make the world forget W.C. Fields's suggested impudence for his epitaph: "On the whole, I'd rather be in Philadelphia."

Classical-music lovers around the world pay homage to the Philadelphia Orchestra for its buoyant interpretations of Tchaikovsky. During the winter, the orchestra delights its fans in the Academy of Music's chandeliered splendor, a building modeled after La Scala Opera House. When summer comes, the orchestra moves to Fairmount Park's outdoor Frederic Mann Music Center, where music lovers can lie on blankets under the stars and soar with the classics.

Musical diversity is a Philadelphia tradition.

Jazz still reflects the swinging sassiness of three Philadelphia jazz greats, Dizzy Gillespie, Stan Getz, and John Coltrane.

Popular music went through a golden period when South Philadelphia's "Golden Boys"—Frankie Avalon, Fabian, Jimmy Darren, and Bobby Rydell—seduced a whole generation into swooning to their love songs.

"Philly Sounds" still transform contemporary music with Teddy Pendergrass, the Ojays, the Stylistics, and the irrepressible Patti LaBelle, who can blow a hole in your soul every time she belts out a tune.

If Americans have "danced by the light of the moon," they owe that terpischorean pleasure to a Philadelphian. South Philadelphian Chubby Checker popularized the "Twist"— and America's sacroiliacs have never been the same since.

Contrary to a Boston myth, the Philadelphia metropolitan area houses the nation's largest number of institutions of higher education, including a University for the Arts. *Parade Magazine* nominated Philadelphia's Central High School as one of the nation's 12 best high schools.

Given this explosive creativity, it's easy to understand why no city has nurtured the arts more lovingly. Visitors can share that affection when they visit the majestic Free Library with its Parthenon-like facade, the famed Rodin Museum, and the Pennsylvania Academy of the Fine Arts, a spectacular urban maharaja's palace.

But this "Athens of America" has also encouraged commerce to be an equally dominant force.

Four of the city's most distinctive buildings are the ovalfront Philadelphia Merchants Exchange (1832) that majestically adjoins a cobblestones street, the huge glass-paned dome that capacious Memorial Hall wears like a Victorian dowager's tiara, Independence Blue Cross's blue-glass-tinted headquarters, and the stately City Hall, an exquisite example of Second French Empire style.

Visitors to the nation's capital may have noticed the City Hall's architectural twin, the Executive Office Building, across the street from the White House.

I ronically, this City Hall also became as excuse for resisting progress. An unspoken rule decreed that no building could be constructed higher than City Hall with its statue of William Penn on top. Eventually, Philadelphia's plow-resisting mentality succumbed to American ingenuity. Today, Liberty Place, the Mellon Bank Center, and four new skyscrapers have virtually doubled the height of the city's skyline.

In the wintertime, Philadelphians follow convention. They lunch indoors. But when summer arrives, they lunch in their ubiquitous park. Fairmount Park winds through the city, an urban oasis from smoke-clogged, noisy traffic jams. Visitors can relax in its verdant serenity with noon-day picnics, softball tournaments, and family barbecues. A meandering Schuylkill River through the park also attracts a daily stream of neighborhood anglers and rowers from the city's 13 rowing clubs.

Because Quaker William Penn founded Philadelphia, Quakers quickly dominated the city's early political and commercial life. The Quarker City influence has diminished, but the memory lingers. Today, the nation's most enduring exercise in multiethnicity flavors the city's political and social life.

Although all of the city's founding fathers were WASPs, Philadelphia soon opened its arms to the world "tired . . . huddled masses, yearning to be free." Successive waves of immigrants swarmed into Philadelphia as they did into New York City.

Mention the name of a neighborhood and Philadelphians will candidly identify its ethnic abundance: Italian South Philadelphia, black North Philadelphia, Irish Olney, Jewish Northeast, Puerto Rican Hunting Park, Chestnut Hill WASPs, Center City Chinatown, Vietnamese West Philadelphia, Polish Port Richmond, and Ukrainian Nicetown. Each enclave's lifestyles and restaurants exalt is ethnic heritage.

At the same time, the city's peoplescape is changing. Recently arrived yuppies are gentrifying black and Puerto Rican low-income neighborhoods within walking distance of Center City office buildings and the art museum. The relentless survival of ethnic neighborhoods, however, unfrocks a won't-lie-down-and-die spirit behind the city's name.

William Penn chose the name "Philadelphia," a Greek word for "brotherly love." He hoped it would fill expectations for his "Holy Experiment"—"you shall be governed by laws of your own making, and live a free, and if you will, a sober and industrious people."

Since 1682, Philadelphia has diligently met all of those goals, even if the great journalist Lincoln Steffens dubbed it in 1903 "the worst-governed city in the country."

But Philadelphians have been forced to cope with the reality that their "City of Brotherly Love" is no more brotherly—nor even sisterly—than any other American city. Philadelphia has endured its share of white-black confrontations, other interethnic battles (early Colonialists roaming the streets, beating up the Germans and Quakers), and electoral decisions decided solely on race.

When the controversial ex-cop and colorful mayor Frank L. Rizzo held office, the Italian-American community provided his staunchest electoral base.

When the city's first black mayor, W. Wilson Goode, made a more perverse kind of history by approving the bombing of a neighborhood, black voters supported his reelection with 98% of their vote, even though an entire city block of black homes was incinerated and 11 blacks (including five children) were killed.

Every city should enjoy an interlude of greatness. Between 1949 and 1962 Richardson Dilworth and Joseph Clark dominated the city's politics, and "For one brief moment there was Camelot." Although the "Dilworth-Clark Renaisance" lasted only 13 years, it set a standard by which Philadelphia is still judged. These men dared to envision a people who would owe a higher loyalty to their city than their neighborhoods.

But Philadelphia's neighborhoods have triumphed because they are more than houses on a street. They are daily celebrations of life where families still sit on the marble steps of sentry-like rowhouses and gossip as the sun sets. They lounge in their bucolic backyards behind 12-room flagstone houses, attend religious services in Colonial-period churches, or just hang out on the street corner. "Yo, Angelo, your mother's lookin' for ya. Dinner's ready."

A *Washington Post* feature installed Philadelphia in the Culinary Hall of Fame with this observations of stunning authority: "There are four kinds of cuisine, Italian, French,

Chinese and Philadelphia." Not only with the truth set you free, it will emancipate your taste buds. Succulent crabs are served in joyous heaps at world-famed Bookbinder's, Walt's, or DiNardo's. Cheesesteaks (as Philadelphian as the Liberty Bell), barbecue ribs (that will remind Southerners of home), hoagies (subs or hero sandwiches), pepper pot soup, Jewish deli corned beef, and Philadelphia's ubiquitous mustard-smeared pretzles cover the city's foodscape like a midwinter blizzard.

For food shopping, either the Reading Terminal Market in a cavernous railroad shed with its Amish farmers and Asian proprietors, or the outdoor Italian Market with barrel-by-carton sidewalk displays of fruits, vegetables, and exotic foods offer great money-saving values.

And then there's South Street, a one-thoroughfare adventure that combines the fascinations of New York's Greenwich Village and San Francisco's Ghirardelli Square. As Philadelphia *Daily News* writer Kathy Sheehan summed it up: "South Street must be the only street in America where, in one trip, you can do your laundry, watch live Jello-O wrestling, and buy a bridal gown, used books, natural foods, crazy hats, a mattress and box spring, wind-up toys, toilet paper, a VCR, key chains ▀▀ ▀▀▀▀▀, Central American art, a box of wood screws, fresh flowers, used clothing, a fountain pen, window shades, water ice, margaritas, mint juleps, rolling papers, healing crystals, and Halloween masks."

Along the east bank of the Schuylkill River, boathouses are contoured by strings of white lights that brighten the dark night. It's a year-round festival of lights.

As the seasons change, so do the sports teams. Philadelphia's Eagles, the Flyers, the Phillies and the 76ers are supported by fanatically loyal fans. How fanatic? "Philadelphia fans will boo Santa Claus," a national news magazine once groused.

On New Year's Day, while Americans are recovering from night-before revelry and blearily watching football bowl games, energetic Philadelphians strut into the national limelight with the Mummers, gaudily plumated string bands. After kicking up their frisky heels in an all-day parade of skits and dances, they dissolve into all-night neighborhood revelries.

But with all of Philadelphia's festive enticements, *caveat peregrinator* (let the tourist beware). As with any big city, Philadelphia does have a crime problem, although the efficiency of the PAVies might lead you to believe that illegal parking is the city's most serious offense.

PAVies (Parking Authority Vultures) will ticket your car if you pause one minute on a street to buy a hotdog or pick up a package. If you're parked in a "No stopping" zone, your car stands a good chance of being towed. Unsuspecting tourists have filled the columns of letters-to-the-editor with tales of horror because they erroneously assumed that the Philadelphia Parking Authority fanatics would exercise a reciprocal civility respected in their hometowns. In Philadelphia, PAVies don't. Beware of these ticket-writing zealots.

Yo, America!

Check out your "Cradle of Liberty" with its Independence Hall, Liberty Bell, Art Museum, cheesesteaks, Reading Terminal Market, ethnic neighborhoods, cobbled streets, hoagies, Center City boutiques, theaters, buoyant classical music, jazz nightclubs, the South Street cornucopia, and the neighborhood streets teeming with life.

As the rock groups at two simultaneous Live Aid concerts in London and Philadelphia sang, "We are the world, We are the children." In Philadelphia, we are the neighborhoods, we are the people—just like all of America.

1 Essential Information

Before You Go

Visitor Information

For free information on travel to Philadelphia and its environs, contact the **Philadelphia Convention and Visitors Bureau** (1515 Market St., Suite 2020, Philadelphia 19102, tel. 215/636–3300), the **Philadelphia Visitors Center** (16th St. and John F. Kennedy Blvd., Philadelphia 19102, tel. 215/636–1666 or 800/321–9563), and the **Pennsylvania Division of Travel Marketing** (453 Forum Bldg., Harrisburg 17120, tel. 717/787–5453 or 800/847–4872).

Tips for British Travelers

Government Tourist Office
Contact the **United States Travel and Tourism Administration** (Box 1EN, London WIA 1EN, tel. 071/495–4466).

Passports and Visas
British subjects need a valid 10-year passport. A visa is not necessary unless (1) you are planning to stay more than 90 days; (2) your trip is for purposes other than vacation; (3) you have at some time been refused a visa, or refused admission to, the United States, or have been required to leave by the U.S. Immigration and Naturalization Service; or (4) you do not have a return or onward ticket. You will need to fill out the Visa Waiver Form 1–94W, supplied by the airline.

To apply for a visa or for more information, call the U.S. Embassy's Visa Information Line (tel. 0891/200–290; calls cost 48p per minute or 36p per minute cheap rate). If you qualify for visa-free travel but want a visa anyway, you must apply in writing, enclosing an SAE, to the U.S. Embassy's Visa Branch (5 Upper Grosvenor St., London W1A 2JB), or, for residents of Northern Ireland, to the U.S. Consulate General (Queen's House, Queen St., Belfast BT1 6EO). Submit a completed Nonimmigrant Visa Application (Form 156), a valid passport, a photograph, and evidence of your intended departure from the United States after a temporary visit. If you require a visa, call 0891/234–224 to schedule an interview.

Customs
British visitors aged 21 or over may import the following into the United States: 200 cigarettes or 50 cigars or 2 kilograms of tobacco; one U.S. liter of alcohol; gifts to the value of $100. Restricted items include meat products, seeds, plants, and fruits. Never carry illegal drugs.

Insurance
Most tour operators, travel agents, and insurance agents sell specialized policies covering accident, medical expenses, personal liability, trip cancellation, and loss or theft of personal property. Some policies include coverage for delayed departure and legal expenses, winter-sports, accidents, or motoring abroad. You can also purchase an annual travel-insurance policy valid for every trip you make, during the year in which it's purchased (usually only trips of less than 90 days). Before you leave, make sure you will be covered if you have a pre-existing medical condition or are pregnant; your insurers may not pay for routine or continuing treatment, or may require a note from your doctor certifying your fitness to travel.

The **Association of British Insurers,** a trade association representing 450 insurance companies, advises extra medical coverage for visitors to the United States.

For advice by phone or a free booklet, "Holiday Insurance," that sets out what to expect from a holiday-insurance policy and gives price guidelines, contact the Association of British Insurers (51 Gresham St., London EC2V 7HQ, tel. 071/600–3333; 30 Gordon St., Glasgow G1 3PU, tel. 041/226–3905; Scottish Provincial Bldg., Donegall Sq. W, Belfast BT1 6JE, tel. 0232/249176; call for other locations).

Tour Operators Tour operators offering packages to Philadelphia include **Albany Travel (Manchester) Ltd.** (Central Buildings, 211 Deansgate, Manchester M2 5QR, tel. 061/833–0202), **Cosmosair** (Ground Floor, Dale House, Tiviot Dale, Stockport, Cheshire SK1 1TB, tel. 061/480–5799), **Jetsave** (Sussex House, London Rd., East Grinstead, W. Sussex RH19 1LD, tel. 0342/32823), **Kuoni Travel** (Kuoni House, Dorking, Surrey RH5 4AZ, tel. 0306/740888), and **Speedbird** (Pacific House, Hazelwick Ave., Three Bridges, Crawley, West Sussex RH10 1NP, tel. 0293/611611).

Hints for Travelers with Disabilities Main information sources include the **Royal Association for Disability and Rehabilitation** (RADAR, 25 Mortimer St., London W1N 8AB, tel. 071/637–5400), which publishes travel information for the disabled in Britain, and **Mobility International** (228 Borough High St., London SE1 1JX, tel. 071/403–5688), the headquarters of an international membership organization that serves as a clearinghouse of travel information for people with disabilities.

When to Go

Like other northern American cities, Philadelphia can be uncomfortably hot and humid in the summer and freezing cold in winter (winter snowfall averages 21 inches). However, any time is right to enjoy the special pleasures offered throughout the year. For sports fans, the schedule is packed with exciting competition year-round. **Spring** brings cherry blossoms, followed by azaleas, tulips, and dogwood. The city shows off with its Easter Parade and open-house tours. In **summer**, the Philadelphia Orchestra gives free concerts at the Mann Music Center, and free performances abound at Penn's Landing and other outdoor plazas. The Freedom Festival celebrates the nation's birth with hot-air-balloon races, restaurant extravaganzas, and special ceremonies. **Autumn** offers Super Sunday, a giant block party, numerous parades, and the Army-Navy football classic. And **winter** is highlighted by the spectacular Mummer's Parade on New Year's Day; the orchestra, theater, and ballet seasons; and the famous Philadelphia Flower Show.

Climate The following are average daily maximum and minimum temperatures for Philadelphia.

Jan.	40F	4C	May	72F	22C	Sept.	76F	24C
	27	- 3		54	12		61	16
Feb.	41F	5C	June	81F	27C	Oct.	67F	19C
	27	- 3		63	17		50	10
Mar.	49F	9C	July	85F	29C	Nov.	54F	12C
	34	- 1		68	20		40	- 4
Apr.	61F	16C	Aug.	83F	28C	Dec.	43F	6C
	43	6		67	19		31	- 1

Information Sources For current weather conditions for cities in the United States and abroad, plus the local time and helpful travel tips, call the **Weather Channel Connection** (tel. 900/932–8437; 95¢ per minute) from a touch-tone phone.

Festivals and Seasonal Events

For exact date and other information about the following events, contact the **Philadelphia Visitors Center** (*see* Visitor Information, *above*).

Jan. 1: Mummer's Parade is an all-day event during which some 30,000 sequined and feathered paraders—members of string bands, "fancies," "brigades," and comics—march north on Broad Street to City Hall.

Feb.: Black History Month features exhibits, lectures, and music at the Afro-American Historical and Cultural Museum, plus a number of other events around the city. *Afro-American Historical and Cultural Museum, 7th and Arch Sts., Philadelphia 19106, tel. 215/574–0380.*

Feb.: Philadelphia Boat Show displays more than 500 yachts, sailboats, and powerboats. *Philadelphia Civic Center, 34th St. and Civic Center Blvd., Philadelphia 19104, tel. 215/823–7400.*

Feb.: Mummer's String Band Show of Shows is a chance to see what you missed on New Year's Day. *Philadelphia Civic Center, 34th St. and Civic Center Blvd., Philadelphia 19104, tel. 215/823–7400.*

Late Feb.: U.S. Pro Indoor Tennis Championships attracts many of the world's top men tennis pros. *The Spectrum, Broad St. and Pattison Ave., Philadelphia 19148, tel. 215/336–3600.*

Feb.–May: Chinese New Year celebrations include 10-course banquets Tuesday through Sunday night beginning at 6:30 PM. Chefs come from China to prepare the feast. *Chinese Cultural Center, 125 N. 10th St., Philadelphia 19107, tel. 215/923–6767.*

Mar.: St. Patrick's Day Parade brings the wearing of the green to Benjamin Franklin Parkway.

Mar.: Philadelphia Flower Show, the nation's largest indoor flower show, features acres of exhibits. *Philadelphia Civic Center, 34th St. and Civic Center Blvd., Philadelphia 19104, tel. 215/625–8250.*

Mar.: The Book and the Cook teams the city's best chefs and the world's top cookbook authors in a four-day event. Meet the authors and sample their dishes. For information, contact the Visitors Center (tel. 215/636–1666).

Mar.–June: American Music Theater Festival presents opera, musical comedy, cabaret-style revues, children's programs, and experimental works at indoor and outdoor theaters around the city. *Tel. 215/557–9140.*

Apr.: Philadelphia Antiques Show offers museum-quality antiques, lectures, and appraisals to benefit the Hospital of the University of Pennsylvania. *103rd Engineers Armory, 33rd St. above Market St., Philadelphia 19104, tel. 215/387–3500.*

Apr.: Easter Promenade features a parade down South Street with music, entertainment, celebrities, and a fashion contest. *8th and South Sts., tel. 215/238–0402.*

Late Apr.: Penn Relays is one of the world's oldest and largest amateur track meets. *Franklin Field, 33rd and Spruce Sts., Philadelphia 19104, tel. 215/898–6154.*

Late Apr.: St. Walpurgis Night Festival, the traditional Swedish welcome to spring, offers food, song, dance, and bonfires.

American Swedish Historical Museum, 1900 Pattison Ave., Philadelphia 19145, tel. 215/389–1776.

May: Philadelphia Open House is a two-week period during which selected private homes, gardens, and historic buildings in neighborhoods around the city—including Society Hill, Germantown, and the Main Line—open their doors to the public. *Tel. 215/928–1188.*

May: Dad Vail Regatta is the largest collegiate rowing event in the country. Up to 500 shells from over 100 colleges race on a 2,000-meter course on the Schuylkill River along Kelly Drive in Fairmount Park. *Tel. 215/636–1666 or 215/248–2600.*

Third Thursday in May: Rittenhouse Square Flower Market for 80 years has held this one-day sale of plants, flowers, and food, including the traditional candy lemon stick in a fresh lemon. *18th and Walnut Sts., tel. 215/525–7182.*

Late May: Jambalaya Jam celebrates New Orleans with such specialties as pralines, gumbo, jambalaya, and other Creole and Cajun food favorites; bands playing ragtime, Dixieland, and jazz music; and Louisiana crafts. *On the Great Plaza at Penn's Landing, tel. 215/923–4992.*

Late May–early June: Devon Horse Show and Country Fair, first held in 1896, is a nine-day event in which top riders compete for more than $200,000 in prize money. *Devon Fairgrounds, U.S. 30, Devon 19333, tel. 215/964–0550.*

June: Rittenhouse Square Fine Arts Annual, America's oldest (1931) and largest outdoor juried art show, exhibits paintings and sculpture by more than 100 Delaware Valley artists. *Rittenhouse Sq., 18th and Walnut Sts., tel. 215/636–1666.*

First weekend in June: Elfreth's Alley Days features open houses on America's oldest continuously occupied street, along with food, fife-and-drum music, and Colonial crafts. *Elfreth's Alley, between Front, 2nd, Arch, and Race Sts., tel. 215/574–0560.*

June: Mellon Jazz Festival presents music from local talent to the top names in jazz in a week-long series of concerts (many free) at locations around town. *Tel. 215/625–0291.*

June: CoreStates Pro Cycling Championship, the country's premier bicycle race, attracts the world's top cyclists. *Tel. 215/636–1666.*

June–Aug.: Head House Crafts Fair. More than 40 artisans exhibiting jewelry, stained glass, leather, and quilts on summer weekends from noon to midnight Saturday, noon to 6 PM Sunday. *2nd and Pine Sts., tel. 215/790–7400.*

June–Aug.: Philadelphia Orchestra's Summer Season brings outdoor concerts with free lawn seating. *Mann Music Center, 52nd St. and Parkside Ave., Philadelphia 19131, tel. 215/878–7707 or 215/567–0707.*

July: Freedom Festival. The city celebrates the nation's birth with several days of parades (including the Mummers), hot-air-balloon races, a drum-and-bugle competition, Independence Day ceremonies at Independence Hall, and the Old City Outdoor Restaurant Festival. It all culminates in a grand old-fashioned July 4 fireworks display. *Tel. 215/636–1666.*

July: Riverblues is a weekend waterfront festival featuring the top names in blues. *On the Great Plaza at Penn's Landing, tel. 215/636–1666.*

Late Aug.: Philadelphia Folk Festival, America's oldest continuous folk festival, consists of three days of concerts and workshops. Performers featured range from the relatively new and unknown to folk superstars. There's also food, crafts, folk dancing, impromptu jam sessions, and sing-alongs. Many "folk-ies" camp out on the grounds. *Old Pool Farm, Schwenksville 19473, tel. 215/242–0150.*

Sept.: International In-Water Boat Show, the largest in-water boat show on the East Coast, fills the 10-acre basin in Penn's Landing with yachts and other pleasure craft. *Penn's Landing, tel. 215/449–9910.*

Sept.: Philadelphia Distance Run is the country's premier half-marathon with more than 7,000 runners completing a 13.1-mile course through the streets of downtown and along the Schuyl-kill River. *Tel. 215/685–0052.*

Last Saturday in Sept.: Von Steuben Day Parade, along Ben-jamin Franklin Parkway, honors the general who trained the Continental soldiers at Valley Forge. *Tel. 215/636–1666.*

Oct.: Pulaski Day Parade. The Polish American Congress hon-ors a hero of the Revolutionary War, the Polish general known as the "father of the American Cavalry," with a parade up Broad Street. *Tel. 215/636–1666.*

Oct.: Super Sunday is Philadelphia's largest block party with food, entertainment, rides, games, more than 400 exhibit booths, and as many as 250,000 guests. *Benjamin Franklin Parkway, tel. 215/299–1044.*

Second Monday in Oct.: Columbus Day Parade includes both a parade on South Broad Street and a festival at Marconi Plaza. *Tel. 215/636–1666.*

Early Nov.: Philadelphia Craft Show is three days of exhibits by 100 craftspeople from around the country. *103rd Engineers Ar-mory, 33rd St. above Market St., tel. 215/636–1666.*

Nov.: Fairmount Park Marathon draws several thousand run-ners for the 26.2-mile race along the Schuylkill River. Plans are tentative for 1994. *Tel. 215/685–0052.*

Nov. or Dec: Dog Show. The Kennel Club of Philadelphia spon-sors this event, which draws more than 3,000 entries. *Phila-delphia Civic Center, 34th St. and Civic Center Blvd., Philadelphia 19104, tel. 215/823–7400.*

Late Nov.: Thanksgiving Day Parade features thousands of marchers, floats, and local personalities. The finale is the arriv-al of Santa Claus, ushering in the Christmas shopping season. *Benjamin Franklin Pkwy., tel. 215/636–1666.*

Dec.: Christmas Tours of Historic Houses take visitors around historic Fairmount Park and Germantown houses decorated with Christmas finery. *Tel. 215/763–8100 or 215/848–1777.*

Dec.: John Wanamaker's Light Show is a gala display with pipe-organ music held hourly in the Grand Court of the department store. *Wanamaker's, 13th and Market Sts., tel. 215/422–2450.*

Dec.: The Nutcracker. The Pennsylvania Ballet's production of the Tchaikovsky classic is a Philadelphia Yuletide tradition. *Academy of Music, Broad and Locust Sts., tel. 215/893–1935.*

Dec. 25: Washington Crossing the Delaware. More than 200 par-ticipants with four 40-foot replicas of Durham boats, re-enact the events of Christmas Day 1776, when George Washington and his troops took the Hessian camp at Trenton by surprise. *Washington Crossing Historic Park, Washington Crossing 18977, tel. 215/493–4076.*

What to Pack

Clothing Pack light because porters and luggage trolleys are hard to find. Philadelphia is a fairly casual city, although men will need a jacket and tie in some of the better restaurants. Jeans and sneakers or other casual clothing are fine for sightseeing. You'll need a heavy coat for winter, which can be cold and snowy. Summers are hot and humid, but you'll need a shawl or jacket for air-conditioned restaurants. Many areas are best explored on foot, so bring good walking shoes.

Miscellaneous Bring an extra pair of eyeglasses or contact lenses. If you have a health problem that may require you to purchase a prescription drug, pack enough to last the duration of the trip. And don't forget to pack a list of the addresses of offices that supply refunds for lost or stolen traveler's checks.

Luggage Regulations Free baggage allowances on an airline depend on the airline, the route, and the class of your ticket. In general, on domestic flights you are entitled to check two bags—neither exceeding 62 inches, or 158 centimeters (length + width + height), or weighing more than 70 pounds (32 kilograms). A third piece may be brought aboard as a carryon; its total dimensions are generally limited to less than 45 inches (114 centimeters), so it will fit easily under the seat in front of you or in the overhead compartment. There are variations, so ask in advance. The single rule, a Federal Aviation Administration safety regulation that pertains to carry-on baggage on U.S. airlines, requires that carryons be properly stowed and allows the airline to limit allowances and tailor them to different aircraft and operational conditions. Charges for excess, oversize, or overweight pieces vary, so inquire before you pack.

Safeguarding Your Luggage Before leaving home, itemize your bags' contents and their worth; this list will help you estimate the extent of your loss if your bags go astray. To minimize that risk, tag them inside and out with your name, address, and phone number. (If you use your home address, cover it so that potential thieves can't see it.) At check-in, make sure that the tag attached by baggage handlers bears the correct three-letter code for your destination. If your bags do not arrive with you, or if you detect damage, do not leave the airport until you've filed a written report with the airline.

Insurance In the event of loss, damage, or theft on domestic flights, airlines limit their liability to $1,250 per passenger. Excess-valuation insurance can be bought directly from the airline at check-in but leaves your bags vulnerable on the ground. Your own homeowner's policy may fill the gap; or you may want special luggage insurance. Sources include **The Travelers Companies** (1 Tower Sq., Hartford, CT 06183, tel. 203/277–0111 or 800/243–3174) and **Wallach and Company, Inc.** (107 W. Federal St., Box 480, Middleburg, VA 22117, tel. 703/687–3166 or 800/237–6615).

Traveler's Checks

Although you will want plenty of cash when visiting small cities or rural areas, traveler's checks are usually preferable. The most widely recognized are **American Express, Citicorp, Thomas Cook,** and **Visa,** which are sold by major commercial banks. American Express also issues *Traveler's Cheques for Two,* which can be counter-signed and used by you or your traveling companion. Thomas Cook checks are free when bought direct; the others cost 1%–2% of the checks' face value. Always record the numbers of checks as you spend them, and keep this list separate from the checks.

Getting Money from Home

Cash Machines Automated-teller machines (ATMs) are proliferating; many are tied to international networks such as **Cirrus** and **Plus.** You can use your bank card at ATMs away from home to withdraw money from an account and get cash advances on a credit-card account (providing your card has been programmed with a personal identification number, or PIN). Check in advance on limits on withdrawals and cash advances within specified periods. Remember that on cash advances you are charged interest from the day you get the money from ATMs as well as from [tellers. And note that transaction fees for ATM withdrawals outside your home turf will probably be higher than for withdrawals at home.

For specific Cirrus locations in the United States and Canada, call 800/424–7787 (for U.S. Plus locations, 800/843–7587), and press the area code and first three digits of the number you're calling from (or the calling area where you want an ATM).

American Express Cardholder Services The company's **Express Cash** system lets you withdraw cash and/or traveler's checks from a worldwide network of 57,000 American Express dispensers and participating bank ATMs. You must *enroll first* (call 800/227–4669 for a form and allow two weeks for processing). Withdrawals are charged not to your card but to a designated bank account. You can withdraw up to $1,000 per seven-day period on the basic card, more if your card is gold or platinum. There is a 2% fee (minimum $2.50, maximum $10) for each cash transaction, and a 1% fee for traveler's checks (except for the platinum card), which are available only from American Express dispensers.

At AmEx offices, cardholders can also cash personal checks for up to $1,000 in any seven-day period; of this $200 can be in cash, more if available, with the balance paid in traveler's checks, for which all but platinum cardholders pay a 1% fee. Higher limits apply to the gold and platinum cards.

Wiring Money You don't have to be a cardholder to send or receive an **American Express MoneyGram** for up to $10,000. To send one, go to an American Express MoneyGram agent, pay up to $1,000 with a credit card and anything over that in cash, and phone a transaction reference number to your intended recipient, who needs only present identification and the reference number to the nearest MoneyGram agent to pick up the cash. There are MoneyGram agents in more than 60 countries (call 800/543–4080 for locations). Fees range from 5% to 10%, depending on the amount and how you pay. You can't use American Express, which is really a convenience card—only Discover, MasterCard, and Visa credit cards.

You can also use **Western Union.** To wire money, take either cash or a check to the nearest office. (Or you can call and use a credit card.) Fees are roughly 5%–10%. Money sent from the United States or Canada will be available for pick up at agent locations in Philadelphia within minutes. There are approximately 20,000 agents worldwide (call 800/325–6000 for locations).

Traveling with Cameras and Camcorders

About Film and Cameras If your camera is new or if you haven't used it for a while, shoot and develop a few rolls of film before leaving home. Pack some lens tissue and an extra battery for your built-in light meter, and invest in an inexpensive skylight filter, to both protect your lens and provide some definition in hazy shots. Store film in a cool, dry place—never in the car's glove compartment or on the shelf under the rear window.

Films above ISO 400 are more sensitive to damage from airport security X-rays than others; very high speed films, ISO 1,000 and above, are exceedingly vulnerable. To protect your film, don't put it in checked luggage; carry it with you in a plastic bag and ask for a hand inspection. Such requests are honored at American airports. Don't depend on a lead-lined bag to protect film in checked luggage—the airline may very well turn up the dosage of radiation to see what you've got in there. Airport metal detectors do not harm film, although you'll set off the alarm if you walk through one with a roll in your pocket. Call the Kodak Information Center (tel. 800/242–2424) for details.

About Camcorders Before your trip, put new or long-unused camcorders through their paces, and practice panning and zooming. Invest in a skylight filter to protect the lens, and check the lithium battery that lights up the LCD (liquid crystal display) modes. As for the rechargeable nickel-cadmium batteries that are the camera's power source, take along an extra pair, so while you're using your camcorder you'll have one battery ready and another recharging.

About Videotape Unlike still-camera film, videotape is not damaged by X-rays. However, it may well be harmed by the magnetic field of a walk-through metal detector. Airport security personnel may want you to turn the camcorder on to prove that that's what it is, so make sure the battery is charged when you get to the airport.

Car Rentals

All major car-rental companies are represented in Philadelphia, including **Avis** (tel. 800/331–1212, 800/879–2847 in Canada); **Budget** (tel. 800/527–0700); **Dollar** (tel. 800/800–4000); **Hertz** (tel. 800/654–3131, 800/263-0600 in Canada); and **National** (tel. 800/227–7368). Lower-price companies include **Enterprise** (tel. 215/521–3700). In cities, unlimited-mileage rates range from about $35 per day for an economy car to about $50 for a large car; weekly unlimited-mileage rates range from $140 to $270.

Extra Charges Picking up the car in one city or state and leaving it in another may entail drop-off charges or one-way service fees, which can be substantial. The cost of a collision or loss-damage waiver (*see below*) can be high, also.

Cutting Costs If you know you will want a car for more than a day or two, you can save by planning ahead. Major international companies have programs that discount their standard rates by 15%–30% if you make the reservation before departure (anywhere from two to 14 days), rent for a minimum number of days (typically three or four), and prepay the rental. Ask about these advance-purchase schemes when you call for information. More economical rentals are those that come as part of fly/drive or other packages, even those as bare-bones as the rental plus an airline ticket.

Other sources of savings are the companies that operate as wholesalers—companies that do not own their own fleets but rent in bulk from those that do and offer advantageous rates to their customers. Rentals through such companies must be arranged and paid for in advance. Among them is **Auto Europe** (Box 1097, Camden, ME 04843, tel. 207/236–8235 or 800/223–5555, 800/458–9503 in Canada). You won't see these wholesalers' deals advertised; they're even better in summer, when business travel is down. Always ask if unlimited mileage is available. Find out about any required deposits, cancellation penalties, and drop-off charges, and confirm the cost of the CDW.

One last tip: Remember to fill the tank when you turn in the vehicle, to avoid being charged for refueling at what you'll swear is the most expensive pump in town.

Insurance and Collision Damage Waiver The standard rental contract includes liability coverage (for damage to public property, injury to pedestrians, etc.) and coverage for the car against fire, theft (not included in certain countries), and collision damage with a deductible—most commonly $2,000–$3,000, occasionally more. In the case of an accident, you are responsible for the deductible amount unless you've purchased the collision damage waiver (CDW), which costs an average $12 a day, although this varies depending on what you've rented, where, and from whom.

Because this adds up quickly, you may be inclined to say "no thanks"—and that's certainly your option, although the rental agent may not tell you so. Note before you decline that deductibles are occasionally high enough that totaling a car would make you responsible for its full value. Planning ahead will help you make the right decision. By all means, find out if your own insurance covers damage to a rental car while traveling (not simply a car to drive when yours is in for repairs). And check whether charging car rentals to any of your credit cards will get you a CDW at no charge. In many states, laws mandate that renters be told what the CDW costs, that it's optional, and that their own auto insurance may provide the same protection.

Traveling with Children

Publications
Newsletter *Family Travel Times,* published 10 times a year by **Travel With Your Children** (TWYCH, 45 W. 18th St., 7th Floor Tower, New York, NY 10011, tel. 212/206–0688; annual subscription $55), covers destinations, types of vacations, and modes of travel.

Books *Great Vacations with Your Kids,* by Dorothy Jordon and Marjorie Cohen ($13; Penguin USA, 120 Woodbine St., Bergenfield, NJ 07621, tel. 800/253–6476), and *Traveling with Children—And Enjoying It,* by Arlene K. Butler ($11.95 plus $3 shipping per book; Globe Pequot Press, Box 833, Old Saybrook, CT 06475, tel. 800/243–0495, or 800/962–0973 in CT) help plan your trip with children, from toddlers to teens.

Tour Operators **GrandTravel** (6900 Wisconsin Ave., Suite 706, Chevy Chase, MD 20815, tel. 301/986–0790 or 800/247–7651) offers international and domestic tours for grandparents traveling with their grandchildren. The catalogue, as charmingly written and illus-

trated as a children's book, positively invites armchair traveling with lap-sitters aboard. **Rascals in Paradise** (650 5th St.,
Suite 505, San Francisco, CA 94107, tel. 415/978–9800 or 800/
872–7225) specializes in programs for families.

Getting There On domestic flights, children under 2 not occupying a seat trav-
Air Fares el free, and older children currently travel on the "lowest appli-
cable" adult fare.

Baggage The adult baggage allowance applies for children paying half or
more of the adult fare. Check with the airline for particulars.

Safety Seats The FAA recommends the use of safety seats aloft and details
approved models in the free leaflet **"Child/Infant Safety Seats
Recommended for Use in Aircraft"** (available from the Federal
Aviation Administration, APA–200, 800 Independence Ave.
SW, Washington, DC 20591, tel. 202/267–3479). Airline policy
varies. U.S. carriers must allow FAA-approved models, but
because these seats are strapped into a regular passenger seat,
they may require that parents buy a ticket even for an infant
under 2 who would otherwise ride free.

Facilities Aloft Airlines do provide other facilities and services for children,
such as children's meals and freestanding bassinets (to those
sitting in seats on the bulkhead, where there's enough legroom
to accommodate them). Make your request when reserving.
The annual February/March issue of *Family Travel Times*
gives details of the children's services of dozens of airlines ($10;
see above). "Kids and Teens in Flight" (free from the U.S. Department of Transportation, tel. 202/366–2220) offers tips for
children flying alone.

Hotels **The Four Seasons Hotel Philadelphia** (1 Logan Sq., Philadelphia 19103, tel. 215/963–1500) allows children under 17 to
stay free in their parents' room, runs holiday tea parties for
kids, and provides a *Family Activities and Children's Services*
brochure for guests. The **Guest Quarters Suite Hotels** in the
Philadelphia area (tel. 800/424–2900) offer the luxury of two-
room suites with kitchen facilities plus children's menus in the
restaurants; children under 18 stay free in their parents' suite.
Most **Days Inn** hotels (tel. 800/325–2525) charge only a nominal
fee for children under 18 and allow kids 12 and under to eat free.

Baby-sitting Make arrangements with the hotel concierge or housekeeper,
Services or contact **Rocking Horse Child-Care Center** (6th and Walnut
Sts., Curtis Center, Suite 25 LL, Philadelphia 19106, tel. 215/
592–8257), which offers part- and full-time care for children
ages 6 weeks to 10 years.

Hints for Travelers with Disabilities

Organizations Several organizations provide travel information for people
with disabilities, usually for a membership fee, and some pub-
lish newsletters and bulletins. Among them are the **Information Center for Individuals with Disabilities** (Fort Point Pl., 27–
43 Wormwood St., Boston, MA 02210, tel. 617/727–5540 or 800/
462–5015 in MA between 11 and 4, or leave message; TDD/TTY
tel. 617/345–9743); **Mobility International USA** (Box 3551,
Eugene, OR 97403, voice and TDD tel. 503/343–1284), the U.S.
branch of an international organization based in Britain (*see below*) and present in 30 countries; **MossRehab Hospital Travel Information Service** (1200 W. Tabor Rd., Philadelphia, PA 19141,
tel. 215/456–9603, TDD tel. 215/456–9602); the **Society for the**

Advancement of Travel for the Handicapped (SATH, 347 5th Ave., Suite 610, New York, NY 10016, tel. 212/447–7284, fax 212/725–8253); the **Travel Industry and Disabled Exchange** (TIDE, 5435 Donna Ave., Tarzana, CA 91356, tel. 818/368–5648); and **Travelin' Talk** (Box 3534, Clarksville, TN 37043, tel. 615/552–6670).

Travel Agencies and Tour Operators **Directions Unlimited** (720 N. Bedford Rd., Bedford Hills, NY 10507, tel. 914/241–1700), a travel agency, has expertise in tours and cruises for the disabled. **Evergreen Travel Service** (4114 198th St. SW, Suite 13, Lynnwood, WA 98036, tel. 206/776–1184 or 800/435–2288) operates Wings on Wheels Tours for those in wheelchairs, White Cane Tours for the blind, and tours for the deaf and makes group and independent arrangements for travelers with any disability. **Flying Wheels Travel** (143 W. Bridge St., Box 382, Owatonna, MN 55060, tel. 800/535–6790 or 800/722–9351 in MN), a tour operator and travel agency, arranges international tours, cruises, and independent travel itineraries for people with mobility disabilities. **Nautilus,** at the same address as TIDE (*see above*), packages tours for the disabled internationally.

Publications In addition to the fact sheets, newsletters, and books mentioned above are several free publications available from the Consumer Information Center (Pueblo, CO 81009): "New Horizons for the Air Traveler with a Disability," a U.S. Department of Transportation booklet describing changes resulting from the 1986 Air Carrier Access Act and those still to come from the 1990 Americans with Disabilities Act (include Department 608Y in the address), and the Airport Operators Council's *Access Travel: Airports* (Dept. 5804), which describes facilities and services for the disabled at more than 500 airports worldwide.

Twin Peaks Press (Box 129, Vancouver, WA 98666, tel. 206/694–2462 or 800/637–2256) publishes the *Directory of Travel Agencies for the Disabled* ($19.95), listing more than 370 agencies worldwide; *Travel for the Disabled* ($19.95), listing some 500 access guides and accessible places worldwide; the *Directory of Accessible Van Rentals* ($9.95) for campers and RV travelers worldwide; and *Wheelchair Vagabond* ($14.95), a collection of personal travel tips. Add $2 per book for shipping. The Sierra Club publishes *Easy Access to National Parks* ($16 plus $3 shipping; 730 Polk St., San Francisco, CA 94109, tel. 415/776–2211).

Hints for Older Travelers

Organizations The **American Association of Retired Persons** (AARP, 601 E St. NW, Washington, DC 20049, tel. 202/434–2277) provides independent travelers the Purchase Privilege Program, which offers discounts on hotels, car rentals, and sightseeing, and the AARP Motoring Plan, provided by Amoco, which furnishes domestic trip-routing information and emergency road-service aid for an annual fee of $39.95 per person or couple ($59.95 for a premium version). AARP also arranges group tours, cruises, and apartment living through AARP Travel Experience from American Express (400 Pinnacle Way, Suite 450, Norcross, GA 30071, tel. 800/927–0111); these can be booked through travel agents, except for the cruises, which must be booked directly (tel. 800/745–4567). AARP membership is open to those 50 and over; annual dues are $8 per person or couple.

Two other membership organizations offer discounts on lodgings, car rentals, and other travel products, along with such nontravel perks as magazines and newsletters. The **National Council of Senior Citizens** (1331 F St. NW, Washington, DC 20004, tel. 202/347–8800) is a nonprofit advocacy group with some 5,000 local clubs across the United States; membership costs $12 per person or couple annually. **Mature Outlook** (6001 N. Clark St., Chicago, IL 60660, tel. 800/336–6330), a Sears Roebuck & Co. subsidiary with 800,000 members, charges $9.95 for an annual membership.

Note: When using any senior-citizen identification card for reduced hotel rates, mention it when booking, not when checking out. At restaurants, show your card before you're seated; discounts may be limited to certain menus, days, or hours. If you are renting a car, ask about promotional rates that might improve on your senior-citizen discount.

Educational Travel **Elderhostel** (75 Federal St., 3rd floor, Boston, MA 02110, tel. 617/426–7788) is a nonprofit organization that has offered inexpensive study programs for people 60 and older since 1975. Programs are held at more than 1,800 educational institutions in the United States, Canada, and 45 other countries; courses cover everything from marine science to Greek myths and cowboy poetry. Participants generally attend lectures in the morning and spend the afternoon sightseeing or on field trips; they live in dorms on the host campuses. Fees for programs in the United States and Canada, which usually last one week, run about $300, not including transportation.

Tour Operators **Saga International Holidays** (222 Berkeley St., Boston, MA 02116, tel. 800/343–0273), which specializes in group travel for people over 60, offers a selection of variously priced tours and cruises covering five continents. If you want to take your grandchildren, look into **GrandTravel** (*see* Traveling with Children, *above*).

Further Reading

Walking Tours of Historic Philadelphia, by John Francis Marion, is the best book of its kind. The Foundation for Architecture's *Philadelphia Architecture: A Guide to the City* contains maps, photos, biographies of noted Philadelphia architects, and detailed descriptions of almost 400 sites. *Sculpture of a City,* produced by the Fairmount Park Art Association, contains informative text and beautiful photos. *Philadelphia's Outdoor Art: A Walking Tour,* by Roslyn F. Brenner, is an excellent guide to the more than 50 works of art along Benjamin Franklin Parkway. *Public Art in Philadelphia,* by Penny Balkin Bach, is the most comprehensive work on the subject. *1787: The Day to Day Story of the Constitutional Convention* and Catherine Drinker Bowen's *Miracle at Philadelphia* tell the story of the Constitution.

For biographies of seven Philadelphians, read *Philadelphia: Patricians and Philistines, 1900 to 1950,* by John Lukacs. *Principato,* by Tom McHale, is a family saga set in Philadelphia.

Other selections are *Country Walks Near Philadelphia,* by Alan Fisher; *Philadelphia One-Day Trip Book,* by Jane Ochevhausen Smith; *Philadelphia Preserved,* by Richard Webster; *Philadelphia—A Dream for the Keeping,* by John Guinther; *Bed & Breakfasts and Country Inns: Mid-Atlantic Region* by Fodor's Travel Publications; *The Philadelphia Trivia Quiz,* by Bernard M. Stiefel; and *Philadelphia with Children,* by Elizabeth Gephart.

In fiction, *God's Pocket,* by Pete Dexter; *South Street,* by David Bradley; and *Payback* and *Final Fear* by Philip Harper, all capture some of the grittier aspects of Philadelphia.

Arriving and Departing

By Plane

Flights are either nonstop, direct, or connecting. A **nonstop** flight requires no change of plane and makes no stops. A **direct** flight stops at least once and can involve a change of plane, although the flight number remains the same; if the first leg is late, the second waits. This is not the case with a **connecting** flight, which involves a different plane and a different flight number.

Airports and Airlines Philadelphia International Airport (tel. 215/492–3181) is located in the southwest part of the city, 8 miles from downtown. It's served by **American** (tel. 800/433–7300), **Continental** (tel. 800/525–0280), **Delta** (tel. 800/221–1212), **TWA** (tel. 800/221–2000), **Midwest** (tel. 800/452–2022), **Mohawk** (tel. 880/252–2144), **Northwest** (tel. 800/225–2525), **United** (tel. 800/241–6522), and **USAir** (tel. 800/231–3131). International carriers are **Air Jamaica** (tel. 800/523–5585), **British Airways** (tel. 800/247–9297), and **Swissair** (tel. 800/221–4750).

Cutting Flight Costs The Sunday travel section of most newspapers is a good source of deals. When booking, particularly through an unfamiliar company, call the Better Business Bureau to find out whether any complaints have been registered against the company, pay with a credit card if you can, and consider trip-cancellation and default insurance.

Promotional Airfares All the less expensive fares, called promotional or discount fares, are round-trip and involve restrictions. The exact nature of the restrictions depends on the airline, the route, and the season and on whether travel is domestic or international, but you must usually buy the ticket—commonly called an APEX (advance purchase excursion) when it's for international travel—in advance (seven, 14, or 21 days are usual). You must also respect certain minimum- and maximum-stay requirements (for instance, over a Saturday night or at least seven and no more than 30, 45, or 90 days), and you must be willing to pay penalties for changes. Airlines generally allow some changes for a fee. But the cheaper the fare, the more likely the ticket is to be nonrefundable; it would take a death in the family for the airline to give you any of your money back if you had to cancel. The lowest fares are also subject to availability; because only a certain percentage of the plane's total seats will be sold at that price, they may go quickly.

Consolidators Consolidators or bulk-fare operators—also known as bucket shops—buy blocks of seats on scheduled flights that airlines anticipate they won't be able to sell. They pay wholesale prices, add a markup, and resell the seats to travel agents or directly to the public at prices that still undercut the airline's promotional or discount fares. You pay more than on a charter but ordinarily less than for an APEX ticket, and, even when there is not much of a price difference, the ticket usually comes without the advance-purchase restriction. Moreover, although tickets are marked nonrefundable so you can't turn them in to the airline for a full-fare refund, some consolidators sometimes give you your money back. Carefully read the fine print detailing penalties for changes and cancellations. If you doubt the reliability of a company, call the airline once you've made your booking and confirm that you do, indeed, have a reservation on the flight.

The biggest U.S. consolidator, C.L. Thomson Express, sells only to travel agents. Well-established consolidators selling to the public include **UniTravel** (Box 12485, St. Louis, MO 63132, tel. 314/569–0900 or 800/325–2222); **Council Charter** (205 E. 42nd St., New York, NY 10017, tel. 212/661–0311 or 800/800–8222), a division of the Council on International Educational Exchange and a longtime charter operator now functioning more as a consolidator; and **Travac** (989 6th Ave., New York, NY 10018, tel. 212/563–3303 or 800/872–8800), also a former charterer.

Charter Flights Charters usually have the lowest fares and the most restrictions. Departures are limited and seldom on time, and you can lose all or most of your money if you cancel. (Generally, the closer to departure you cancel, the more you lose, although sometimes you will be charged only a small fee if you supply a substitute passenger.) The charterer, on the other hand, may legally cancel the flight for any reason up to 10 days before departure; within 10 days of departure, the flight may be canceled only if it becomes physically impossible to operate it. The charterer may also revise the itinerary or increase the price after you have bought the ticket, but if the new arrangement constitutes a "major change," you have the right to a refund. Before buying a charter ticket, read the fine print for the company's refund policy and details on major changes. Money for charter flights is usually paid into a bank escrow account, the name of which should be on the contract. If you don't pay by credit card, make your check payable to the escrow account (unless you're dealing with a travel agent, in which case, his or her check should be payable to the escrow account). The Department of Transportation's Consumer Affairs Office (I–25, Washington, DC 20590, tel. 202/366–2220) can answer questions on charters and send you its "Plane Talk: Public Charter Flights" information sheet.

Charter operators may offer flights alone or with ground arrangements that constitute a charter package. Well-established charter operators include **Council Charter** (205 E. 42nd St., New York, NY 10017, tel. 212/661–0311 or 800/800–8222), now largely a consolidator, despite its name, and **Travel Charter** (1120 E. Long Lake Rd., Troy, MI 48098, tel. 313/528–3500 or 800/521–5267), with Midwestern departures. **DER Tours** (Box 1606, Des Plains, IL 60017, tel. 800/782–2424), a charterer and consolidator, sells through travel agents.

Discount Travel Travel clubs offer their members unsold space on airplanes,
Clubs cruise ships, and package tours at nearly the last minute and at
well below the original cost. Suppliers thus receive some reve-
nue for their "leftovers," and members get a bargain. Membership generally includes a regular bulletin or access to a toll-free
telephone hot line giving details of available trips departing
anywhere from three or four days to several months in the future. Packages tend to be more common than flights alone, so if
airfares are your only interest, read the literature before join-
ing. Reductions on hotels are also available. Clubs include **Discount Travel International** (114 Forrest Ave., Suite 203,
Narberth, PA 19072, tel. 215/668–71E4; $45 annually, single or
family), **Moment's Notice** (425 Madison Ave., New York, NY
10017, tel. 212/486–0503; $45 annually, single or family), **Trav-
elers Advantage** (CUC Travel Service, 49 Music Sq. W, Nash-
ville, TN 37203, tel. 800/548–1116; $49 annually, single or
family), and **Worldwide Discount Travel Club** (1674 Meridian
Ave., Miami Beach, FL 33139, tel. 305/534–2082; $50 annually
for family, $40 single).

Smoking Since February 1990, smoking has been banned on all domestic
flights of less than six hours duration; the ban also applies to
domestic segments of international flights aboard U.S. and foreign carriers. On U.S. carriers flying to Philadelphia and other
destinations abroad, a seat in a no-smoking section must be
provided for every passenger who requests one, and the section
must be enlarged to accommodate such passengers if necessary
as long as they have complied with the airline's deadline for
check-in and seat assignment. If smoking bothers you, request
a seat far from the smoking section.

From the Airport Allow at least a half hour, more during rush hour, for the 8-mile
to Center City trip between the airport and Center City. By car, the airport is
accessible via I–95 south or I–76 east.

Airport Express trains leave every 30 minutes from 6:10 AM to
12:10 AM. The trip takes about 20 minutes and costs $4.75 if you
purchase the ticket from one of the machines on the train platform
(up to $6.75 if you buy your ticket on the train). Trains serve the
30th Street, Suburban, Market East, and North Broad stations.
For schedules and other information, call the Airport Information
Desk (tel. 215/492–3181) or SEPTA (tel. 215/580–7800).

Taxis at the airport are plentiful but expensive—about $19 plus
tip. "Limos" (vans, not stretch limousines) cost about $10 per per-
son, but service is less frequent and most limos stop only at certain hotels and downtown points. Among them are Deluxe
Transportation (tel. 215/463–8787) and Limelight Limousine (tel.
215/342–5557).

By Car

Getting to and around Philadelphia by car is often difficult and,
at rush hour, can be a nightmare. The main east–west freeway
through the city, the Schuylkill Expressway (I–76), is often
tied up for miles.

The main north–south highway through Philadelphia is the
Delaware Expressway (I–95). To reach Center City heading
southbound on I–95, take the Vine Street exit.

From the west, the Pennsylvania Turnpike begins at the Ohio
border and intersects the Schuylkill Expressway (I–76) at Val-

ley Forge. The Schuylkill Expressway, with recently completed renovations, has several exits in Center City. The Northeast Extension of the turnpike runs from Scranton to Plymouth Meeting, north of Philadelphia. From the east, the New Jersey Turnpike and I-295 access U.S. 30, which enters the city via the Benjamin Franklin Bridge, or New Jersey Route 42 and the Walt Whitman Bridge into South Philadelphia.

Parking in Center City can be tough. A spot at a parking meter, if you're lucky enough to find one, costs 25¢ per 15 minutes. Parking garages charge up to $1.50 per 15 minutes.

For routing information, AAA members can call the Keystone Automobile Club (tel. 215/569-4321).

By Train

Philadelphia is a major stop on **Amtrak's** Northeast Corridor line. Trains stop at the 30th Street Station (30th and Market Sts.). North Philadelphia Station is in a deteriorated neighborhood and should be avoided. Amtrak also serves Philadelphia from points west, including Harrisburg, Pittsburgh, and Chicago. For Amtrak information, phone 215/824-1600 or 800/872-7245.

At 30th Street Station you can connect with Southeastern Pennsylvania Transportation Authority (SEPTA) commuter trains to two downtown stations—Suburban Station at 16th Street and John F. Kennedy Boulevard (near major hotels), and Market East Station at 10th and Market streets (near the historic district)—and to outlying areas.

By Bus

Greyhound Lines (tel. 215/931-4000 or 800/231-2222) operates long-haul service out of a new terminal at 10th and Filbert streets, just north of the Market East commuter rail station. **NJ Transit** (tel. 215/569-3752) stops at the Greyhound terminal and offers service between Philadelphia and Atlantic City, and other New Jersey destinations.

Staying in Philadelphia

Important Addresses and Numbers

Tourist Information The **Philadelphia Visitors Center** (tel. 215/636-1666), located at 16th Street and John F. Kennedy Boulevard, one block from City Hall, is open 9-5 daily, until 6 in summer. The **National Park Service** (tel. 215/597-8974 or 215/627-1776 for a recorded message) operates a Visitor Center at 3rd and Chestnut streets in the heart of the historic district. Open 9-5 daily.

Emergencies **Police, fire,** and **ambulance** (tel. 911).

Hospitals Near the historic area, **Pennsylvania Hospital** (8th and Spruce Sts., tel. 215/829-3358). Near City Hall, **Hahnemann University Hospital** (Broad and Vine Sts., tel. 215/448-7963). Near Rittenhouse Square, **Graduate Hospital** (1800 Lombard St., tel. 215/893-2350).

Late-Night   Downtown, **Corson's Pharmacy** (15th and Spruce Sts., tel. 215/
Pharmacies   735–1386) is open 9 AM to 9:45 PM Monday–Friday, until 5 PM
Saturday, and until 2:30 PM Sunday. **Medical Tower Pharmacy**
(255 S. 17th St., tel. 215/545–3525) is open 8:30 AM to 9 PM weekdays and until 5 PM Saturday. **CVS Pharmacy** (10th and Reed
Sts., tel. 215/465–2130) in South Philadelphia is open till midnight on weekdays. **CVS Pharmacy** (6501 Harbison Ave., tel.
215/333–4300) in the northeast section of the city is open 24
hours, but is about a 25-minute drive from downtown.

Getting Around

"Temporary inconvenience; permanent improvement." That's
been the catchphrase for Philadelphia transportation for decades. By and large, the transportation system has been getting
better. The Center City commuter rail tunnel is operating; an
express train connects the airport and downtown; and the airport has been expanded and improved, including a new $125
million international terminal. The situation on the highways
has also improved: Interstate 95, the superhighway that
stretches from Maine to Florida, now runs unbroken through
Philadelphia, with new ramps to Center City; and you can now
drive crosstown in two minutes via the new Vine Street
Expressway. It took more than 20 years to happen, but I–476,
the infamous "Blue Route," now connects the Northeast Extension of the Pennsylvania Turnpike with I–95.

By Subway,   The Southeastern Pennsylvania Transportation Authority
Trolley, and Bus   (SEPTA) operates an extensive network of buses, subways,
and commuter trains.

The Broad Street Subway runs from Fern Rock Station in the
northern part of the city to Pattison Avenue and the sports
complex in South Philadelphia. The Market–Frankford Line
runs across the city from the western suburb of Upper Darby to
Frankford in the northeast. Both lines shut down from midnight to 5AM, during which time "Night Owl" buses operate along
the same routes.

Buses comprise the bulk of the SEPTA system, with 110 routes
extending throughout the city and into the suburbs. Bus route 76,
called the "Ben FrankLine," connects the zoo in west Fairmount
Park with Penn's Landing at the Delaware River, stopping at major tourist sites along the way including the Pennsylvania Convention Center and the Museum of Art. Route 76 costs 50¢ and
operates daily from around 9 AM to 6 PM.

The "Chestnut Hill Trolley" operates on Saturday and Sunday
along Germantown Avenue in the northwest section of the
city. This final remnant of SEPTA's once extensive trolley network gives nostalgia buffs a chance to ride in some of the few remaining Presidential Conference Committee cars, popular in the
1940s.

The base fare for subways, trolleys, and buses is $1.50 in exact
change or a token. Transfers cost 40¢. Senior citizens (with valid
ID) ride free during off-peak hours and holidays. Tokens sell for
$1.05 and can be purchased in packages of five or 10 from cashiers
along the Broad Street Subway and Market–Frankford lines, and
in many downtown stores (including some Rite Aid pharmacies).
You can purchase tokens and transit passes in the SEPTA Sales
Offices located in the concourse below the northwest corner of

15th and Market streets, in Market East Station at 8th and Market streets, and in 30th Street Station at 30th and Market streets. A "Day Pass" costs $5 and is good for 26 hours of unlimited use on all SEPTA vehicles within the city, plus one trip to or from the airport on the Airport Express train. A weekly transit pass costs $16. Tokens and transit passes are good on buses and subways but not on commuter rail lines.

Maps of the SEPTA system cost $2 at train stations, downtown hotels, and on some buses. For route information, call 215/580–7800. Be prepared for a busy signal and, once you get through, a long time on hold. To have a schedule mailed to you, call 215/580–7777.

Subway cars are crowded and safe during the day. Subway crime has diminished in recent years, but platforms and cars can be relatively empty in the late evening hours—you may be more comfortable taking a cab. After dark, avoid the station at 13th and Market streets; large numbers of homeless people currently settle there every night.

By Commuter Train Philadelphia's fine network of commuter trains serves both the city and the suburbs. The famous Main Line got its start—and its name—from the Pennsylvania Railroad route that ran westward from Center City.

All trains serve 30th Street Station (30th and Market Sts.), where they connect to Amtrak trains, Suburban Station (16th St. and John F. Kennedy Blvd., across from the Visitors Center), and the new Market East Station (10th and Market Sts.) beneath the Gallery at Market East shopping complex. Fares, which vary according to route and time of travel, range from $2 to $6.25 one way. These trains are your best bet for reaching Germantown, Chestnut Hill, Merion (site of the Barnes Foundation), and other suburbs. For information, call 215/574–7800. To have a schedule for any of the commuter lines mailed to you, call 215/580–7777.

PATCO (Port Authority Transit Corporation) High Speed Line trains run underground from 16th and Locust streets to Lindenwold, New Jersey. Trains stop at 13th and Locust, 9th and Locust, and 8th and Market streets, then continue across the Benjamin Franklin Bridge to Camden. Fares run 75¢ to $1.60. Sit in the very front seat for a great view going across the bridge. For information, call 215/922–4600.

By Taxi Cabs cost about $2 for the flag throw and then $1.80–$2.30 per mile. They are plentiful during the day downtown—especially along Broad Street and near hotels and train stations. At night and outside Center City, taxis are scarce. You can call for a cab, but they frequently show up late and occasionally never arrive. Be persistent: Calling back if the cab is late will often yield results. The main cab companies are **Quaker City Cab** (tel. 215/728–8000), **United Cab** (tel. 215/625–2881), and **Yellow Cab** (tel. 215/922–8400).

Guided Tours

Orientation Tours The **Fairmount Park Trolley Bus** (tel. 215/636–1665) has a daily schedule of tours. You can buy your ticket at the Visitors Center (16th St. and Kennedy Blvd.); the cost is $10 for adults, $5 for children. **Gray Line Tours** (tel. 215/569–3666) offers chartered group tours of the historic and cultural areas.

Special-interest Tours ABC Bus and Walking Tours (tel. 215/677–2495) offers tours of historic Philadelphia, the Italian Market, and Valley Forge.

Combine lunch or dinner with a sightseeing cruise on the Delaware River on the *Spirit of Philadelphia* (tel. 215/923–1419). This three-deck ship leaves Pier 3 (Delaware Ave. and Market St.) for lunch, dinner, and "Moonlight Cruises." Dinner cruises include a band and singing waitstaff, while "moonlight" cruises feature a bar, band, and dancing.

The *Liberty Belle II* (tel. 215/629–1131), a 93-foot Great Lakes steamer, offers lunch, dinner, and Sunday brunch cruises with a banjo player, sing-alongs, and a Cajun-style buffet. Moonlight cruises, with music and dancing, depart daily at 11 PM. Occasional private charters affect the daily schedule. Board at Penn's Landing (Delaware Ave. below Market St.).

Walking Tours Several walking tours of historic Philadelphia are available. **Audio Walk and Tour** (tel. 215/925–1234) at the Norman Rockwell Museum, 6th and Sansom streets, offers go-at-your-own-pace tours of historic Philadelphia with cassette players and an accompanying map. **Centipede Tours** (tel. 215/735–3123) offers a candlelight stroll through Society Hill led by guides in Colonial dress. Tours begin at the Thomas Bond House (129 S. 2nd St) Friday and Saturday at 6:30 PM, May–October. Theme and area tours given by the **Foundation for Architecture** (tel. 215/569–3187) focus on architecture but also touch on the history of each destination. Area tours include Chestnut Hill, Manayunk, and Spruce Hill. Theme tours include Art Deco, skyscrapers, the University of Pennsylvania campus, Washington Square, and Judaic architecture and influence. Most tours begin weekends at 2 PM, and occasionally on Wednesday at 6 PM.

Multilingual Tours Some tour companies provide interpreters and foreign-language guides. **Centipede Tours** (tel. 215/735–3123) can supply German-, French-, Spanish-, Russian-, Chinese-, Japanese-, Swedish-, Finnish-, Danish- or Italian-speaking guides for all parts of Philadelphia.

Carriage Rides Numerous horse-drawn carriages wend their way through the narrow streets of the historic area. Tours last anywhere from 15 minutes to an hour and cost from $15 to $60. Carriages line up on Chestnut and 5th streets near Independence Hall and at Head House Square, 2nd Street between Pine and Lombard streets, from about 10 AM to 2 AM. You can reserve a carriage and be picked up anywhere downtown. Carriages operate year-round, except when the temperature is below 20 or above 94 degrees Fahrenheit. Carriage operators include **Ben Franklin Carriages** (tel. 215/923–8516), **Philadelphia Carriage Company** (tel. 215/922–6840), **76 Carriage Company** (tel. 215/923–8516), and **Society Hill Carriage Company** (tel. 215/627–6128).

2 Portraits of Philadelphia

Portrait of an Amish Family

By Carolyn
Meyer

You'll spot Jacob Stoltzfus working his fields with a team of horses as you drive the back roads of Lancaster County. You will certainly encounter his somber black buggy on one of the traffic-choked highways. You might exchange a few words with his wife, Becky, in her plain dark dress and white cap, if you happen to stop by their farmhouse to buy fresh eggs or inspect the homemade quilts she has for sale. If you're on the right road at the right time, you might see their younger children playing in the yard of a one-room schoolhouse. And on certain Sundays, you may pass the farmhouse where the Stoltzfus family and other Amish people gather to worship.

Stoltzfus is the most common of a dozen Amish family names; Jacob and Becky and their children are fictitious but typical of the more than 16,000 Amish (pronounced AH-mish) in this area. Their roots and religious tradition reach back to 16th-century Europe. Every detail of their lives, from their clothing to the way they operate their farms, is an expression of their faith in God and their separateness from "the world"; every detail is dictated by the *Ordnung*, the rules of their church.

Becky Stoltzfus, like Amish women of any age, wears a one-piece dress in a dark color (bright colors and printed patterns are forbidden). The sleeves are long and straight, her full skirt hemmed modestly halfway between knees and ankles. The high, collarless neck is fastened shut in front with straight pins; buttons and safety pins are forbidden although the Ordnung of some church districts allows hooks and eyes. Over her shoulder she wears a shawl the same color as her dress, pinned in front and back to the waistband of an apron also in the same color. Since apron strings tied in a bow are considered frivolous and therefore forbidden, her apron is also pinned. She wears black stockings rolled below the knee, and black low-heeled oxfords. At home in warm weather Becky and her family go barefoot.

Soon after her daughters were born, Becky made sure they wore the white organdy prayer cap. When Katie turned 12, she changed to a black cap for the Sunday preaching; after she marries she will wear the white cap all the time. The head coverings may look identical to outsiders but subtle differences tell the Amish a great deal about one another. The width of the front part, the length of the ties, the style of the seams, the way the pleats are ironed all indicate where the woman lives and how conservative or liberal her church district is.

Becky has never cut or curled her hair nor has she let it hang loose. She pins it in a plain knot at the back of her neck. She parts little Hannah's hair in the middle, plaits it, and fastens the two little braids in the back. When Becky is away from home she wears a black bonnet with a deep scoop brim over her prayer cap.

The clothes Jacob wears are also carefully dictated by the Ordnung of his church district. For Sunday preaching he wears a *Mutze*, a long black frock coat with split tails and hook-and-eye closings but no collar or lapels. His vest is also fastened with hooks and eyes.

Jacob's broadfall or "barn-door" trousers have no fly, just a wide front flap that buttons along the sides; they have no creases and no belt—homemade suspenders hold them up. There are buttons on his shirt, the number specified by the Ordnung. Colored shirts are permitted, but stripes and prints are out. Neckties are forbidden.

When he's not dressed up, Jacob hangs up his Mutze and puts on a *wamus*, a black sack coat with either a high round neck or V neck and nei ther lapels nor outside pockets. Sometimes the wamus has hooks and eyes, but more liberal church districts allow buttons. Buttoned sweaters are sometimes permitted and there are also buttons on the long greatcoats some of the older men wear in cold weather.

In winter Jacob and his sons wear broad-brimmed black felt hats; in summer they switch to straw. Ben and Ezra, Jacob's younger boys, have been wearing hats with three-inch brims since they were little. Sam, the oldest son, wears a hat with a crease around the top of the crown, a sign (along with his sprouting beard) that he is newly married. The hat is a status symbol among the Amish. The grandfather's hat is higher in the crown than the father's and its brim is four inches wide. At the top of the hierarchy, the bishop who preaches at the Sunday service is recognizable by his hat's high rounded crown and its brim, the broadest in the district.

The width of an Amish man's hat brim also signifies his degree of conservatism: The broader the brim, the more conservative the wearer. Young rebels like Jacob's middle son Joe sometimes trim their hat brims to just a little less than the prescribed width.

Jacob's long beard is as much the mark of an Amishman as a broad-brimmed hat. He shaves only his upper lip, since mustaches are against the rules. He cuts his hair straight around well below the ears. Ben and Ezra have theirs parted in the middle with bangs across the forehead. Cutting it short—up to the earlobe, as Joe did—is another form of rebellion.

The style of the Amish buggy is as carefully prescribed as the style of his hat. The Stoltzfus family owns a black carriage with a gray top and big wooden wheels. The battery-powered side lamps, reflectors, and bright orange triangles have been added as required by Pennsylvania state law. The iron-tired wheels are precisely set, toed in slightly, farther apart at the top than at the bottom. A gear assembly at the pivot of the front axle adds stability. The brakes are operated by hand, an iron block pressed hard against the rear tire. This kind of brake is prescribed by the Ordnung; different groups permit different kinds of brakes. The Ordnung tells the buggy owner whether or not he may have roll-up side curtains or sliding glass doors, and if he is allowed a dashboard, a whipsocket, and other variations. The Stoltzfus family also owns a farm wagon and young Joseph was given his own horse and open one-seater when he turned 16.

The waiting list is long for handmade buggies. Carriage-making used to be a non-Amish occupation but the growing Amish population, the toll of wrecked carriages, and the need for approved work in addition to farming have brought some Amish into the trade. The carriage maker is in a more liberal church district that allows power tools.

Incidentally, the Amish can—and do—ride in cars owned by non-Amish people, travel on trains, buses, even airplanes and taxis. But they are not allowed to *own* a car. Teenage Amish boys sometimes manage to buy a car and hide it out of sight of their families. They are not subject to the rules of the Ordnung until they have been baptized, an event that takes place in their late teens or early 20s after they've had time to sow some wild oats.

No electric wires lead from the power lines along the road into the neat, well-kept buildings of the Stoltzfus farm, a difference that distinguishes Amish farms from their non-Amish neighbors'. The farms are small, no more than 50 or 60 acres, which is all that can be handled by a farmer limited to horsepower. Tractors, like electricity, are taboo among most of the Amish.

The Stoltzfuses' house is spacious and uncluttered. There is no wall-to-wall carpeting to vacuum; plain, unpatterned linoleum covers the floor. There are no curtains to wash or draperies to clean; although some church districts allow plain curtains on the lower half of the windows, this district permits only dark green roller shades. There are no slipcovers to launder or upholstery to shampoo, because upholstered furniture is not allowed.

Becky has a large kitchen where the family eats around a big wooden table. Afterward Becky and Katie and Hannah clean up the kitchen, washing the dishes and putting away leftover food in the gasoline-operated refrigerator. A one-cylinder engine in the cellar chugs noisily, powering the water pump, but many Amish families still rely on windmills or water power. A creek that runs through a farm also supplies water. Although labor-saving devices are generally forbidden, Becky does have a washing machine that runs by gasoline. Her refrigerator is also gasoline powered. Her stove burns kerosene; she would prefer bottled gas, but that is forbidden by the Ordnung of her district. She uses a treadle sewing machine and sews by the bright and steady light of a gasoline lamp.

About once a year, it is the Stoltzfuses' turn to host the every-other-Sunday preaching service. As many as 175 people may attend: There are 90 members in the district, and double that number counting unbaptized children. The removable partitions built into the downstairs walls are folded back and furniture moved aside. The district's backless oak benches are brought in and set up in rows. For that one Sunday morning the entire district fills the big house for the long service, staying on for a hearty lunch that Becky has been preparing for days.

Jacob and Becky Stoltzfus are fluent in English but the language they speak among themselves is Pennsylvania Dutch, a German dialect related to the dialects spoken in the part of Germany from which their Amish ancestors came. It is primarily a spoken language and spelling varies with the writer. "Dutch" actually means *Deutsch*, or German, and some scholars call the dialect "Pennsylvania German." Many Pennsylvanians of German descent speak the dialect, but among the Amish it is the "mother tongue," the first language an Amish child learns to speak and another mark of separation from the world.

When Hannah, Becky's youngest child, starts school, she will learn to speak and read and write in the language of "the world." Jacob and Becky want their children to know English, because their survival depends on good business relationships with English-speaking people. Sometimes when the Amish converse in English, they resort to dialect translated literally into English. The results are the quaint expressions that amuse tourists and inspire souvenir manufacturers to decorate switchplates and cocktail napkins with "typical Amish" expressions like "Outen the light" and "Throw Papa down the stairs his hat."

About the same time Hannah Stoltzfus starts to learn English, she will also be taught High German, the language of religion. The family Bible is written in High German and she and her brothers and sisters must learn to read it. By the time they are baptized in their late teens, they will be able to understand most of the Sunday sermon and to join in the prayers and hymns. Most Amish can't carry on a conversation in High German and have no need to unless they are ordained church officials who must preach sermons and pray. But everyone needs to be able to read and to listen.

The outsider may not notice the inconspicuous building on a back road where Ben and Ezra and Annie Stoltzfus attend school, along with eight grades of children in one room taught by a young Amish woman with only an eighth-grade education. Amish children are not sent to public school and Amish schools go only as far as the eighth grade. That's time enough to learn the basics of reading, writing, and arithmetic! The *real* education for their lives takes place at home, on the farm.

At age five, Hannah Stoltzfus would be old enough for kindergarten if the Amish had one. But they believe children should be at home with their parents until they are six. Annie loves school and wishes she could continue, but her brothers can hardly wait until their 14th birthdays, the end of school for them. Schools are built to serve children within a 2-mile radius so that no one has far to walk. Some children go to old one-room schoolhouses once owned by the public-school district. When districts consolidated, the Amish bought the obsolete schools and remodeled them—not modernizing them but ripping out the electric wiring. Since none was available near the Stoltzfus farm, the Amish fathers in that area built a plain cinder-block structure with big windows to take advantage of natural light.

Stepping into an Amish schoolhouse is like entering a time machine and emerging 70 or more years in the past. At 8:30 the teacher pulls the rope to ring the old-fashioned bell on the roof. Ben and Ezra and Annie come early, after they've finished their farm chores, so they have a chance to play before school begins. When the bell rings, the children line up and file through the big front door into the cloakroom. They hang their hats and jackets on pegs, line up their lunch boxes, and go quietly to their carefully refinished old-fashioned desks.

The school day begins with the roll call. During peak periods of farm work, the Amish close down the schools for a few days; they stop earlier in the spring than the public schools. They make up for the time by taking only a short Christmas break and celebrating none of the national holidays. Except in the case of illness, everyone stays home to work or goes to school to learn.

Next, the teacher reads to the pupils from the German Bible and then everyone recites the Lord's Prayer in German. Except for the lessons in reading German Scriptures and prayers, the teacher speaks English exclusively in the classroom.

Beside the teacher's desk is a "recitation bench." There are more than 30 students in the eight grades and each class of three or four or five comes forward by turns to recite its lessons. There is no competition to come up with the answer first and they all respond in a singsong chorus.

Because it is essential to the work of a farmer, arithmetic is considered very important. Picking readers for the pupils was not easy. The parents want the subject matter to be farm children, not city life; they want the stories to teach a moral lesson; fairy tales, myths, and fantasies are taboo. The Amish think most modern readers are too worldly, showing families with clothes, cars, and too many material possessions. Outsiders would consider the books they use hopelessly outdated.

During the 15-minute morning recess, Ezra and Ben and the other boys resume their baseball game. One of the rules of the Amish schoolyard is that children are never allowed to stand around by themselves; everyone must be included in the group. Annie and the older girls play blindman's bluff; the younger ones, joined by their teacher, race around in a game of tag.

During recess and lunchtime, the yard rings with conversation in English, Pennsylvania Dutch, and mixtures of the two. Parents disagree about which language should be used in the schoolyard. More pragmatic parents want their children to become as fluent as possible in English. The more traditional argue that using English when it's not necessary helps to drive a wedge between the Amish child and the Amish community.

The Amish want their children to learn to work together as a group, not to compete as individuals. Preserving tradition is a goal; reasoning abstractly is not. Asking too many questions is not acceptable. Discipline is strict; the only voices heard in the schoolroom are those of the teacher and the pupils who are reciting. The Amish expect pupils to master the material unquestioningly: Memorization replaces reasoning in a culture dominated by oral tradition. Rapid learning is not considered an advantage; thoroughness is valued more. Teachers believe that intellectual talents are a gift from God and that children should be encouraged to use the gift by helping others in the school.

Before the day is over, there is time for singing. Singing is a vital part of the Amish tradition, important in their religious life and in their social life as well. There are no harmonized part-songs for the Amish; unaccompanied unison singing is the universal rule. The Amish have their own style of singing, in which the leader (*Vorsanger*) sings the first word and everybody else joins in for the rest of the line.

When it's time to go home, students put away their books, sweep out the room, line up the desks neatly, wash the old-fashioned slate blackboards, and clap the erasers until they are clean. In cold weather they carry in the wood for the stove and take turns cleaning out the ashes and banking tomorrow's fire.

For years public-school authorities were in conflict with the Amish. Truancy laws were enforced and Amish fathers were often arrested and jailed for refusing to send older children to school. But in 1972 the United States Supreme Court ruled that the Amish are exempt from state compulsory education laws that require a child to attend beyond the eighth grade, claiming that such laws violate the Constitutional right to the freedom of religion.

Today, the Amish accept the idea of sending their children to school for eight years to learn what they need to survive in the 20th-century rural economy. But what an Amish child really needs to know to survive in the Amish culture he learns from his parents and from other adults in the community. Most of the practical knowledge of farmers and housewives is acquired not in books but in a family apprenticeship.

The marriage of Jacob and Becky Stoltzfus is a very practical affair. The Amish are quite realistic about their expectations. They do not marry for "love" or "romance" but out of mutual respect and the need for a partner in the kind of life they expect to live. The farmer needs a wife and they both need children. Marriage is essential to the Amish community; divorce is unknown; separation is rare. Marriage is the climax of the rite of passage that begins with baptism, the signal of the arrival of adulthood and sober responsibility. It signifies that young people have really joined the community.

From the time they reach the age of *Rum Schpringe* ("running around"—about 16 for boys, a little younger for girls) and for the next half-dozen years until each marries, Joe Stoltzfus and his sister Katie do much of their socializing at Sunday night singings usually held at the farm where the preaching service took place in the morning. Singings are functions of the church district, which helps keep dating and eventually marriage within the group. In Lancaster County, young people from several church districts with similar interpretations of the Ordnung may get together for a joint singing. Although the main activity is singing hymns, these occasions are more social than religious.

At the more conservative singings, boys sit on one side of a long table in the barn and the girls sit on the other, and between joking and teasing they take turns in the role of Vorsanger. The hymns they sing are the "fast tunes" (some of them familiar Protestant hymns) rather than the "slow tunes" or chants sung at the preaching service. At around 10 o'clock the singing ends and the girls serve snacks. The couples, now paired off—Joe is with Leah Zook, as usual, and Katie has somehow ended up with Reuben Beiler—start home.

Although outsiders believe that the social life of an Amish teenager begins with a singing and ends with a buggy ride home at a respectably early hour, Amish dating is actually much livelier. Among the more liberal groups, the old-fashioned singings can turn quickly into rowdy, foot-stomping hoedowns. A few bring out harmonicas, guitars, and other forbidden instruments; older boys haul in cases of beer. Few outsiders attend these events.

On the "off Sunday" when there is no preaching service, Joe and Leah and other young unmarried people go courting— but always in secret. Before they marry, they are never seen together in public as a couple except as they leave a singing or a barn dance.

Bundling, the practice of courting in bed fully clothed, is usually attributed to the Amish. Actually it is an English word with no equivalent in Amish dialect and the custom dates back to New England where it had more to do with keeping warm in a cold house than with sex. No one is quite sure whether the Amish do or don't, but the consensus is that the girl's parents, rather than the Ordnung, have the final say. Leah's father and Jacob Stoltzfus have both said "no."

There is a saying that if a boy can persuade his girl to take off her prayer cap, she'll have sex with him. Evidently that doesn't happen often because the rate of premarital pregnancies among the Amish is quite low. Premarital sex is forbidden, birth control is taboo, and sex education is nonexistent. The Amish child growing up on a farm isn't ignorant of the reproductive process, but human "facts of life" usually remain somewhat mysterious until the age of marriage.

When Jacob's son Sam married Sarah Beiler, their wedding was held after the harvest in November; December is the second most popular month for weddings and there are traditionally only two possible days in the week for the ceremony: Tuesday and Thursday. Sarah chose Thursday. There was no honeymoon but every weekend throughout the winter the couple went to visit relatives. Now they're living on the Stoltzfus farm.

The average age at marriage of Amish couples has been rising because of the problems of accumulating enough money to establish a household and to acquire land. Many Amish parents retire while they are still relatively young, especially if they have a son who needs a farm. Sam and Sarah have moved into the "grandfather's house," a section of Jacob's farmhouse built to accommodate a second generation. In a few years, when Sam assumes full responsibility for the farm and has children, he and Sarah will move into the larger part of the house and Jacob and Becky will move into the grandfather's house.

Recently Sam told his parents that a new little "woodchopper" or "dishwasher" is expected, the first grandchild of Jacob and Becky. A new generation of the Stoltzfus family and for the Amish community is on the way.

The roots that nourish Amish beliefs and bring vitality to Amish tradition reach back hundreds of years. Theirs is a complex story of persecution from without and division within. Remembrance of the past is a part of the present for the Amish every day of their lives, not something reserved for Sunday worship and special ceremonies.

To understand the Amish as something more than a quaint anachronism, turn back the calendar to 16th-century Europe. The poor, by far the majority, were exploited by the rich and powerful few. The Roman Catholic Church wielded tremendous influence and many blamed the church for society's ills. When Martin Luther launched the Protestant Reformation in 1517, he had many opponents in addition to the Roman Catholic Church. One was Ulrich Zwingli, a radical Swiss Protestant, who in turn opposed Conrad Grebel. Grebel's followers wanted to establish free congregations of believers baptized as adults who made a confession of faith and committed themselves freely to a Christian life. Backing Zwingli, the Great Council of Zurich announced that babies must be baptized within eight days after their birth or the parents would be exiled.

This marked the beginning of Anabaptism, which means "rebaptized." Regarded as radically left wing, the Anabaptist movement posed a threat to both Roman Catholic and Protestant establishments. Anabaptist leaders were imprisoned, beaten, tortured, and killed until, by the end of the 16th century, nearly all the Anabaptists of Switzerland and Germany had been put to death.

But the movement spread through Central and Western Europe. Menno Simons, a former Roman Catholic priest, became one of those persecuted for Anabaptist preaching. His followers were called Mennonites. (In Switzerland they were known as the Swiss Brethren.) And although they were hounded by Catholics and other Protestants, dissension began to grow among the Mennonites themselves. A principal source of disagreement was the interpretation of the *Meidung*, the practice of shunning church members who had broken a rule. Shunning was based on St. Paul's advice to the Corinthians to avoid keeping company and eating with sinners. The Mennonites interpreted this to mean the member was to be subjected to Meidung only at communion. But Jacob Amman, a young Mennonite bishop, insisted that the Meidung meant that the rule-breaker must be shunned totally; even his wife and family must refuse to have anything whatever to do with him until he repented and had been forgiven.

The controversy grew and in 1697 the stubborn and fiery Jacob Amman broke away from the Mennonites. His followers, known as the Amish, were as stubborn and inflexible as

Amman himself and they became known for their unwillingness to change. Although differences in details of clothing were not a primary issue, they did become symbolic of the split. The Amish became known as the *Haftlers* (Hook-and-eyers) while the more worldly Mennonites were called the *Knopflers* (Buttoners).

Meanwhile, King Charles II of England granted a large province in the American colonies to William Penn. A devout Quaker, Penn believed he could offer refuge, freedom, and equality to the persecuted. Penn arrived in 1682, and the following year Francis Daniel Pastorius of the Frankfort Land Company brought the first group of Mennonites to Pennsylvania. They established themselves in Germantown, northwest of Philadelphia. The first Amish immigrants left Switzerland and the Palatinate of Germany in 1727, settling near Hamburg north of Reading. When Indian raids threatened that community, the Amish moved toward the southwest.

By the start of the Revolutionary War, about half of the 225,000 Pennsylvania colonists were German, but only a small minority were Amish and Mennonite. Although the Germans were excellent farmers, Benjamin Franklin dismissed them as "stupid boors." The English scorned them and tried to Anglicize them. But the Amish and Mennonites were determined to hold on to their religion, which was a way of life that included their language and their plain dress.

The Amish of Pennsylvania were all of one conservative mind until 1850, when a schism divided the Amish into two main factions. The more progressive group built meeting houses which earned them the label "Church Amish," to distinguish them from the stricter "House Amish" who continued to worship in their homes. Since then, innumerable splits have been caused by various interpretations of the Meidung (as happened in the days of Jacob Amman) or by different details of the Ordnung—by Haftlers who want to live more like Knopflers but still remain Amish.

Every society changes to some extent and in every society there are a few people who cannot adjust. The Amish are no exception. Many leave; there is generally a shortage of young men in the Amish community because most of the dissidents who leave are male. But some exert pressure for changes in the Ordnung that result in splits. Today there are 7 Amish, 21 Mennonite, and 9 Brethren groups in the Lancaster area.

The ultimate control exerted by the Amish to keep the members in strict adherence to the Ordnung is the Meidung. No one will speak to the person, eat with him, conduct business with him, or have anything whatever to do with him while he is under the ban. It can last for a lifetime, unless the sinner mends his ways, begs for forgiveness, and is readmitted to fellowship by a unanimous vote of the congregation.

Visitors are sometimes surprised to learn that "Pennsylvania Dutch" and "Amish" are not synonymous. Many of the early settlers of Pennsylvania came from Germany at Penn's invitation; many were farmers, most were Protestant, and they spoke the same dialect. Despite these similarities, the Amish refer to all non-Amish as "English." These English are the Pennsylvania Dutch who permit hex signs on their farms (the Amish do not) and whose ancestors decorated useful items such as furniture and dishes with colorful peasant-style designs. The work of Amish craftsmen is competent but plain.

The Amish are generally friendly and hospitable people. Tape recorders and cameras are not welcome but a visitor sincerely interested in the Amish people who does not act like an interrogator can quietly learn something about their unique way of life.

The Search for Intelligent Life

By Paul Fussell

Paul Fussell is as involved in the culture of Philadelphia today as he was when this essay appeared in Philadelphia Magazine, *in 1988.*

Well, not exactly a newcomer. I've been living here four years now, long enough to regard the scaffolding on City Hall tower as a permanent part of the architecture, long enough not to expect drivers to yield the right of way at pedestrian crossings, long enough to accept the litter, if not the dog ca-ca, as a natural part of the environment.

But even though I've been here awhile, living in Center City, I'm still poking around trying to see whether Philadelphia is culturally more like London, or Calcutta, or Sauk Centre, Minn. Coming to a conclusion isn't easy because no one knows for sure what "culture" is or how you might experience it or why it's a good thing to have. Some people think you can get it at a specific outlet, like Lincoln Center in New York or The Kennedy Center in Washington. Others—Matthew Arnold, for example—think it's not a commodity at all, but a state of mind, not easily come by and acquired by a prolonged immersion in "the classics," whatever they may be. A Nazi storm trooper in a popular German play of the 1930s thought he could detect it easily and was prepared to protect his loved ones from its pernicious influences. "Whenever I hear the word 'culture,'" he said, "I release the safety catch on my pistol." Today the word can cause plenty of confusion, as the *Inquirer* unwittingly reveals each Sunday by titling one of its sections "Entertainment and the Cultural Arts." This awards equal time to symphony and opera and dance and country music and prole movies, thus suggesting that the "Cultural Arts" include anything not edible or portable or obviously utilitarian that readers can be enticed to spend money on.

And the *Inquirer* may be right. For T. S. Eliot, culture included much more than art, music, and beautiful letters. It embraced, he said, "all the characteristics and interests of the people." For the British that included, he maintained, the dart board and (ugh) "boiled cabbage cut into sections." If that's what culture means, I'd have to look into cheesesteaks and soft pretzels with mustard, Frank Rizzo's impressive bod and the pitiable performances of the Iggles. But for me culture still means what it meant before anthropologists began using the term to include everything. For me it still designates things that don't make money, that engage your mind and imagination, that address your aesthetic sense and gratify your curiosity and connect you with the past. Culture invites you to think about time and history. It means things that government is disinclined or embarrassed to subsidize. It means those things that institutions are always begging for funds to house and maintain and exhibit. It is comparable to those things a philistine school board, considering the annual budget, would stigmatize as "frills."

Before moving to Philadelphia I lived in Princeton for many years, and there "my city" was New York, an easy cultural commuting distance away. I'd visited Philadelphia a few times, once for an opera, once for a road-show play, once for some soccer at Veterans Stadium, once for a not-so-hot seafood dinner. But because I knew very little about Philadelphia and its cultural operations, I consulted the estimable *Places Rated Almanac* (1981 edition). This rated American urban areas on the basis of their presumed cultural attractiveness according to various criteria, not all of which were plausible. From the *Almanac* I learned that Philadelphia ranked seventh among metropolitan areas for its number of actors. But the problem is that Philadelphia's are now mostly waiters. ("Hi. My name is Gary. We have a number of specials tonight I'd like to tell you about.") I learned also that Philadelphia's public library system ranked seventh in the United States, beaten not just by New York and Chicago and Boston (no surprise there) but astonishingly enough, by Cleveland and—shock!—Cincinnati. Another of the *Almanac's* measures of cultural adequacy was the number of authors in residence. New York had a reputed 4,382, Philadelphia only 449, just above Detroit (395). There weren't many dancers here, but a lot of painters and sculptors and a vast number of musicians and composers, giving Philadelphia a ranking for music fourth in the nation, just behind New York, Los Angeles, and Chicago. Considering all its criteria of cultural desirability together, the *Almanac* concluded that Philadelphia ranked seventh in the country, a ranking earned in very large part, I'd say, by the efforts of Stokowski, Ormandy, and Muti. Above Philadelphia: New York, Washington, Chicago, Boston, Los Angeles, and San Francisco. Below it: Denver, Minneapolis, Dallas, Buffalo, Baltimore, Houston, and Atlanta, not to mention Fort Smith, Ark., Greeley, Colo., and Laredo, Texas. At the bottom of the list of 277 places ranked is poor Lafayette, La., apparently a locus of bowling alleys, fast-food dispensaries, porno theaters, and dirt auto-racing tracks.

Now, if you need a shot of civic pride, look into the second edition of the *Almanac*, dated 1985. Philadelphia is now ranked sixth in the country as a metropolitan area rich in the arts and—hold your hats—first in the country (out of 328 metropolitan areas) in higher education. Eat your heart out, Boston: You're only 14th.

But as I confronted such statistics and tried to make sense of them, I remembered something more about Philadelphia, and it was mighty encouraging. Long ago, when I was returning to the States after living a year in London and encumbered with a whole lot of household stuff to bring back, friends advised encountering U.S. Customs in Philadelphia rather than New York. "People are nicer there," they said, and they were right. No one at the Philadelphia airport displayed open envy or contempt because of my good fortune in spending a year abroad. No one was rude for the fun of it. The sensitive questioning of the customs officer allowed me to bring in all my stuff without any trouble at all. This was a memorable experience of Philadelphia niceness, and since then I've had many more.

But there's a problem with niceness. It exacts cultural costs. I hadn't lived here very long before I sensed a deadly critical vacuum in Philadelphia. The most awful things—books, plays, restaurants, buildings, public utterances—passed without complaint or satire or abuse. I got the impression that Philadelphians really cared as little about a strenuously earned excellence as about spotless streets, a safe, well-run mass transit system, and an uncorrupt judiciary.

Because no one seems to care enough, literary culture in Philadelphia has suffered a notable erosion. The major book publishers have decamped, and with them the agents and most of the editors and writers. The book trade has been largely taken over by chains, mass-market bookstores where no one has heard of Flaubert or Veblen, let alone Montaigne or Sir Thomas Browne. And books are not authoritatively reviewed here. In one Sunday book-review section of the *Inquirer* recently, there were 10 full reviews. All were either by *Inquirer* staff people, some apparently recruited from the mail room, or by freelance writers. There were no national authorities whatsoever reviewing books, and this left the unhappy impression that the amateur and the parochial were good enough for Philadelphia. Not that the *Inquirer* hasn't some good, sharp critics, such as Carlin Romano on books, William B. Collins on theater, Elaine Tait on restaurants, and pre-eminently Thomas Hine on architecture and urban imagery. But the general critical tone in Philadelphia is soft and nice, rather like the local pretzel, and that's no way to encourage a culture for grown-ups.

If literary culture here seems in decline, theater is, of course, in a worse state. The curse here is the lack of a permanent, stable repertory company with knowledge and taste. By this lack Philadelphia betrays its cultural inferiority not just to New York, but to San Francisco and Washington, not to mention New Haven and Cambridge, Mass. One of my bitter disappointments in moving here was discovering that whatever it does, the immensely expensive Annenberg complex at the University of Pennsylvania does not consider it a duty to stage plays in the historical repertory, which means not only that I can't profit from repeated attendance at *Antony and Cleopatra, Major Barbara, Six*

Characters in Search of an Author and *Krapp's Last Tape*, but that, worse, the local students can't. I think they're being cheated.

Having said that, I must recognize that there's wonderful stuff here, even if it takes some nosing around to find it. That's because Philadelphia culture is decentralized. You don't find it all in one place, or even in one district. If this were New York, the building of The Pennsylvania Academy of the Fine Arts on Broad Street would probably have been torn down years ago and its contents consolidated with those of the Philadelphia Museum of Art. The same with the Rodin Museum. And Philadelphia's culture is unique for another reason. It's rather shy. New York has the pompous Morgan Library, looking like a rich man's palace designed to awe beholders. Philadelphia has The Rosenbach Museum and Library, established in a town house on a quiet domestic street. It seems the same here with the least important cultural things. It took me some time to notice, passing almost daily, that Firstrust Savings Bank on Rittenhouse Square provides a lending library for its clients. But there's little indication in front that there you can borrow books as well as money. That suggests Philadelphia's cultural style at its best: Don't shout, just quietly and modestly deliver something good. And wait for the cultural clients to find it.

A decentralized culture like Philadelphia's has large and subtle advantages. Other cities' "cultural centers" give the impression that culture can be assembled all in one place. That makes it seem a luxury isolated from real life and thus fit to be ignored. But when it's spread all around, you can't help meeting some of it all the time, passing and perhaps dropping in to the Balch Institute or the Atwater Kent or the Afro-American or American Jewish museums, or the Historical Society of Pennsylvania or The University Museum, or noticing the delightful group of "Dutch Renaissance" buildings on Walnut Street between 19th and 20th streets. And the more you walk around, the more you're likely to notice that there's an oboe repair shop on Pine Street.

The Gideon Bibles placed in hotel rooms offer specific "how-to" advice for alleviating common spiritual and psychological maladies. Like, "If you are weary and discouraged, read Matthew 11:28-30," or "When your friends seem to go back on you, read I Corinthians 13." In the same way, here are some nuggets of cultural therapy for Philadelphians, all possible because of a happily decentralized culture.

- When you feel that residence in or around Philadelphia is beginning to blunt your sense of humor, as well as of beauty, go to the Art Museum and contemplate Oldenburg's hypertrophied cherry wood multiple plug, hung up near the ceiling. You will smile.

- While at the museum, if you feel the need of a sexual lift combined with artistic refreshment, seek out Duchamps's *Etant Donnés*. More or less X-rated, it has to be kept from the children and thus is not easy to find. But it's eminently worth the search and inquiries.

- When you are persuaded that these days "young people are no good," devoted only to drink and drugs and dumb movies, go hear a recital by the devoted kids at The Curtis Institute. And when you've convinced yourself that the federal government and its agencies are distinguished by no artistic instincts whatsoever, go hear the Curtis students in a free noontime recital at, of all places, the Federal Reserve Bank on 6th Street, presented in its own civilized, comfortable, small auditorium.

- When you feel that despite your costly education your ability to entertain two conflicting ideas simultaneously is feebler than it should be, go to the corner of 15th and Market streets and study, really study, the *Clothespin*. Or is it lovers embracing? Is it a clothespin becoming lovers or lovers becoming a clothespin? Or both at once?

- When you feel that Philadelphia radio offers little but proletarian call-in shows, turn to WFLN (95.7 FM) for 24 hours of intelligent music, with lots of Baroque from midnight to morning.

- When you're overcome with the depressing conviction that Philadelphia is hopelessly provincial, ruinously out of touch with Europe and Asia and the world's significant history, join the Alliance Française and speak French, and after that drop into the Rosenbach and contemplate the manuscript of Joyce's *Ulysses*. Then look into The University Museum. If you were sent by *The Last Emperor*, try exercising your imagination on the crystal ball, which once delighted the Dowager Empress.

- If your experience of contemporary politics, and especially tax policy, has persuaded you that the rich and famous of all places are necessarily selfish swine and always have been, spend an hour in "The Titanic and Her Era" exhibit at the Maritime Museum on Chestnut Street. There you can reacquaint yourself with the fact that boundlessly rich men within living memory sacrificed themselves, when the chips were down and the odds very bad, so their wives and children could live. It's a mind-expanding experience to wonder if you would do the same, and if not, why not.

- When wearied and bored by the sight of the new business architecture all over town, which gives the impression that plate glass and aluminum are interesting, stroll across the Schuylkill and regale yourself with the facade of the original Drexel Institute Main Building (Chestnut at 32nd). You will enjoy the sexy muse or angel or whatever at the top. They don't make them like that anymore. Contemporary women have breasts that good, but no wings.

3 Exploring Philadelphia

By Rathe Miller and Michael Schwager

Rathe Miller is a writer and editor, and a contributer to many Fodor's publications. His work has appeared in the Philadelphia Inquirer, Philadelphia magazine and the New York Times. Michael Schwager writes articles and books ranging from Philadelphia history to personal finance. Their joint work has appeared in the Philadelphia Inquirer, the Philadelphia Inquirer Magazine and the Boston Globe. They have lived in the Philadelphia area for a total of 85 years.

"On the whole I'd rather be in Philadelphia." W. C. Fields may have been joking when he wrote his epitaph, but if he were here today he could make the statement seriously. They no longer roll up the sidewalks at night in Philadelphia. An entertainment boom, a restaurant renaissance, and a cultural revival have helped transform the city.

The birthplace of the nation has become a city of superlatives. Philadelphia has the world's largest municipal park, the best public collection of art in the United States, the widest variety of urban architecture in America, and the highest concentration of institutions of higher learning in the country.

In addition, Philadelphia is a city of neighborhoods: Shoppers haggle over the price of tomatoes in South Philly's Italian Market; families picnic in the parks of Germantown; street vendors hawk soft pretzels in Logan; and all over town, kids play street games such as stickball, stepball, wireball, and chink.

Philadelphia's compact 2-square-mile downtown (William Penn's original city) is nestled between the Delaware and the Schuylkill rivers. Thanks to Penn's grid system of streets— laid out in 1681—the downtown area is easy to navigate. The traditional heart of the city is Broad and Market streets (Penn's Center Square), where City Hall now stands. Market Street divides the city north and south; 130 S. 15th Street, for example, is in the second block south of Market. North–south streets are numbered, starting with Front (First) Street, at the Delaware River, and increasing to the west. Broad Street is equivalent to 14th Street.

The city extends north, south, and west from downtown into more than 100 neighborhoods covering 130 square miles. The Benjamin Franklin Parkway breaks the rigid grid pattern by leading out of Center City into Fairmount Park, which straddles the Schuylkill River and the Wissahickon Creek for 10 miles. It's a distance of 30 miles from the northeast corner to the southwest tip.

Sections of Philadelphia range from posh old-money enclaves to inner-city slums. The downtown is comparatively safe during the day. After dark, exercise caution, especially in areas like Market Street east of Broad Street; 13th Street; and the neighborhoods ringing the downtown. Ask hotel personnel about the safety of places you're interested in visiting. At night, cabs are safer than walking.

Philadelphia has too many attractions to see in one day. Unless you severely limit your itinerary, figure on spending several days. We have divided the downtown into four walking tours. Tour 3 can be done in a day—if you move fast. Each of the other three takes more than a day of sightseeing.

Tour 1. Historic District

Numbers in the margin correspond to points of interest on the Tours 1 and 2 map.

This tour covers what is called the most historic square mile in America. Most of the sites are part of **Independence National Historical Park,** administered by the National Park Service. Except as noted, all have free admission, the same telephone number (tel. 215/597–8974), and the same hours: daily 9–5.

Admission to Independence Hall, the Bishop White House, and the Todd House is by guided tour only. Tickets for the Bishop White and Todd houses can be obtained at the Visitor Center on the day of your visit. No tickets are required for tours of Independence Hall; admission is first come, first served. From early May to Labor Day, you may wait from 15 minutes to an hour for the Independence Hall tour.

During the summer the Park offers four daily guided walking tours: "Washington Walk" departs from the Liberty Bell at noon and 4 PM; "Crisis in the Capital" departs from the Commodore Barry statue behind Independence Hall at 11 AM and 3 PM; "Franklin Family Tour" departs from Franklin Court at 2 and 5 PM; and "Friends Walking Tour" departs from the front of Independence Hall at 7 PM.

❶ Start the tour at the **Visitor Center** (3rd and Chestnut Sts.). Operated by the National Park Service, the center is staffed by several park rangers who answer questions and distribute maps and brochures on Independence National Historical Park and other sites in the historic area. The main attraction, *Promise of Permanency*, is a video-computer exhibit that gives Constitutional perspectives on contemporary issues such as gun control, drug testing, and sex discrimination. Shown in two 300-seat auditoriums, the 28-minute movie *Independence*, directed by John Huston, dramatizes events surrounding the birth of the nation. The center's bookstore offers an excellent selection of books, videos, brochures, prints, and wall hangings, on historic figures and events. For $2.50 you can buy a reproduction of a 1787 map of Philadelphia; copies of the Declaration and the Constitution on parchment-like paper cost just a buck. The most popular items are the tiny Liberty Bells that sell for $3.55 and $5.55. A city information desk is also inside the center.

❷ Directly across 3rd Street is the **First Bank of the United States,** the oldest bank building in the country and headquarters of the government's bank from 1797 to 1811. Symbolizing the hope of prosperity for the new republic, the pediment carving depicts a cornucopia and an oak branch on either side of an American eagle. Executed in 1797 by Clodius F. Legrand and Sons, it is made of mahogany and is one of the few remaining examples of 18th-century wood carving. No other outdoor wooden sculpture from that period is known to have survived in such excellent condition (it has withstood acid rain better than the bank's marble pillars). The building is not open to the public, but you can walk up the front steps to the windows and get a good look at the columns and the carvings of the rotunda inside.

Next to the bank is a wrought-iron gateway topped by an eagle. Pass through it and you step out of modern-day Philadelphia and into Colonial America.

A red-brick path alongside manicured lawns and ancient oaks and maples leads to the first group of historic buildings, Car-
❸ penter's Court, which includes **Carpenter's Hall.** Built in 1770, this was the headquarters of the Carpenters' Company, a guild founded to teach carpenters architecture and to aid their families. In September 1774 the First Continental Congress convened here and addressed a declaration of rights and grievances to King George III. Re-creations of Colonial set-

tings include original chairs and candle sconces and displays of 18th-century carpentry tools. The building, with features such as a tile floor and marble fireplaces, is still owned and operated by the Carpenters' Company. *320 Chestnut St., tel. 215/597–8974. Open Tues.–Sun. 10–4.*

Next door are two buildings of interest to military history buffs—the **Army-Navy Museum** and the **Marine Corps National Memorial.** Dioramas in the Army-Navy Museum depict highlights of the Revolutionary War. Authentic weapons on display include powderhorns, swords, and a 1763 flintlock musket. The second-floor exhibit puts you behind the cannon of an 18th-century battleship. The Marine Corps National Memorial is a small museum displaying weapons, uniforms, and medals dating from 1775 to 1815. *Chestnut St. east of 4th St., tel. 215/597–8974. Open daily 9–5.*

Leave Carpenter's Court and continue west on the red-brick path across 4th Street to the **Second Bank of the United States.** Built in 1824 and modeled after the Parthenon, the Second Bank is an excellent example of Greek Revival architecture. Housed in the building are portraits of prominent Colonial Americans by noted artists such as Charles Willson Peale, William Rush, and Gilbert Stuart. Peale's portrait of Jefferson is the only one that shows him with red hair. The permanent exhibit, "Portraits of the Capital City," opened in 1988, has a life-size wooden statue of George Washington by William Rush; a mural of Philadelphia in the 1830s by John A. Woodside Jr.; and the only known likeness of William Floyd, a lesser-known signer of the Declaration of Independence. *420 Chestnut St., tel. 215/597–8974. Open daily 9–5.*

As you continue west on the red-brick path, which now runs along cobblestoned Library Street, on your right you'll see **Library Hall,** the library of the American Philosophical Society. A research library for historians, its vaults contain such artifacts as a copy of the Declaration of Independence handwritten by Thomas Jefferson, William Penn's 1701 Charter of Privileges, and Benjamin Franklin's will. Exhibits in the lobby change frequently; recent ones have included "Modern Physics in America" (on four physicist members who were involved in the Manhattan Project); "Scientific Broadsides" (posters from the 19th century); and "Thomas Jefferson Statesman of Science." *105 S. 5th St., tel. 215/440–3400. Open weekdays 9–4:45.*

Crossing 5th Street, you arrive at **Independence Square,** where, on July 8, 1776, the Declaration of Independence was first read in public. Although the square is not as imposing today, you can easily imagine the impact that this setting had on the Colonials.

The first building on your right is **Philosophical Hall** (104 S. 5th St., tel. 215/627–0706), the headquarters of the American Philosophical Society. Founded by Benjamin Franklin in 1743 to promote "useful knowledge," it is the oldest learned society in America. The membership, which is limited to 500 Americans and 100 foreigners, has included Washington, Jefferson, Lafayette, Emerson, Darwin, Edison, Churchill, and Einstein. The building (dating from 1785) is closed to the public except by appointment.

Next is **Independence Hall.** Opened in 1732 as the State House for the Colony of Pennsylvania, this was the scene of many ear-

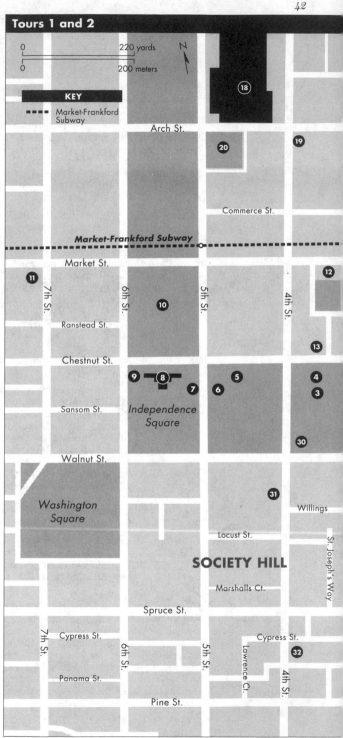

Arch Street Friends Meeting House, **19**

Army-Navy Museum and Marine Corps National Memorial, **4**

Betsy Ross House, **17**

Bishop White House, **29**

Carpenter's Hall, **3**

Christ Church, **14**

Christ Church Burial Ground, **20**

Congress Hall, **9**

Declaration House, **11**

Elfreth's Alley, **15**

Fireman's Hall Museum, **16**

First Bank of the United States, **2**

Franklin Court, **12**

Gazela of Philadelphia, **24**

Head House Square, **34**

Hill-Physick-Keith House, **32**

Independence Hall, **8**

Liberty Bell, **10**

Library Hall, **6**

New Jersey State Aquarium, Riverbus Landing, **25**

Newmarket, **35**

Penn's Landing, **21**

Penn's Landing Trolley Company, **26**

Philadelphia Contributionship for the Insurance of Houses from Loss by Fire, **31**

Philadelphia Maritime Museum, **13**

Philadelphia Merchant's Exchange, **28**

Philosophical Hall, **7**

Powel House, **36**

Second Bank of the United States, **5**

Thaddeus Kosciuszko National Memorial, **33**

Todd House, **30**

United States Mint, **18**

USS *Becuna*, **23**

USS *Olympia*, **22**

Visitor Center, **1**

Welcome Park, **27**

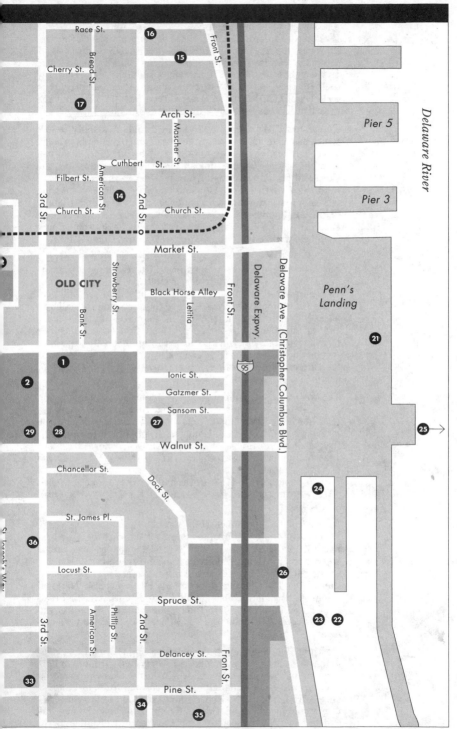

ly events in the nation's history. The Second Continental Congress convened here on May 10, 1775. In June 1775, George Washington accepted appointment as general of the Continental Army. A year later Virginia delegate Richard Henry Lee offered a resolution declaring "that these United Colonies are, and of right ought to be, free and independent States." On July 4, 1776, the Declaration of Independence was adopted. The Articles of Confederation were signed here in 1778 and the Constitution was formally adopted on September 17, 1787.

The site of these events was the first-floor Assembly Room, which has been painstakingly restored and now displays many historic items. Especially notable are the inkstand, designed by Philip Syng and used for signing the Declaration and the Constitution; and the chair from which Washington presided over the Constitutional Convention. After the Constitution was adopted, Franklin said about the sun carving on the chair, "I have the happiness to know that it is a rising and not a setting sun." Also on the first floor is the Pennsylvania Supreme Court chamber, with judge's bench, jury box, and prisoner's dock.

The 100-foot Long Room on the second floor was the site of banquets, receptions, balls, and suppers. The building at the corner of 5th and Chestnut streets is Old City Hall, home of the U.S. Supreme Court from 1791 to 1800 and part of the Independence Hall complex today. Attached to Independence Hall by a short colonnade is the East Wing. Free tours start there every 15 to 20 minutes; admission is first come, first served. The tour lasts 35 minutes, but you may have to wait in line up to an hour during the busy season from early May to Labor Day. *Chestnut St. between 5th and 6th Sts., tel. 215/597–8974. Open daily 9–5; early July–early Sept. 9–9.*

The West Wing of Independence Hall contains a book shop and
❾ gift store. At the corner of 6th and Chestnut streets is **Congress Hall,** formerly the Philadelphia County Courthouse and the meeting place of the U.S. Congress from 1790 to 1800. On the first floor is the House of Representatives, where President John Adams was inaugurated in 1797. On the second floor is the Senate chamber, where George Washington was inaugurated for his second term in 1793. Both chambers have been authentically restored. *6th and Chestnut Sts., tel. 215/597–8974. Open daily 9–5.*

In front of Independence Hall, next to the statue of George Washington, note the plaques marking the spot where Abraham Lincoln stood on February 22, 1861, and a few steps away where John F. Kennedy delivered an address on July 4th, 1962. On July 4th, 1993, President Bill Clinton joined in the presentation of the Philadelphia Liberty Medal to African National Congress President Nelson Mandella and South African President F. W. de Klerk. With Independence Hall in front of you and the Liberty Bell behind you, it's a place to stand for a moment and soak up a sense of history.

North of Independence Hall, one block up the mall, is Phila-
❿ delphia's best-known symbol, the **Liberty Bell.** Ordered in 1751 and originally cast in England, the bell cracked during testing and was recast in Philadelphia by Pass and Stow in 1753. To keep it from falling into British hands during the Revolution— they would have melted it down for ammunition—the bell was spirited away by horse and wagon to Allentown 60 miles north.

The bell is the subject of much legend; one story says that it cracked when tolled at the funeral of Chief Justice John Marshall in 1835. Actually, the bell cracked slowly over a period of years. It was repaired but cracked again in 1846 and was then forever silenced. You can stand within touching distance of the 2,080-pound bell and read its biblical inscription, "Proclaim liberty throughout all the land unto all the inhabitants thereof." It was called the State House Bell until 1839, when a group of Abolitionists adopted it as a symbol of freedom and renamed it the Liberty Bell. After being housed in Independence Hall for more than 200 years, the bell was moved to a glass-enclosed pavilion for the 1976 Bicentennial. The new home is an incongruous setting for such a historic object, but it does display the bell 24 hours a day. While the building is open, rangers and volunteers tell the story. After hours you can press a button on the outside walls to hear a recorded account of the bell's history. *Market St. between 5th and 6th Sts., tel. 215/597–8974. Open daily 9–5; early July–early Sept. 9–9.*

Head west on the walkway between Market and Chestnut streets under the Rohm and Haas Building. You'll pass the sculpture-fountain *Milkweed Pod.* Installed in 1959, it was one of the first examples of Philadelphia's law requiring public buildings to spend 1% of construction costs for art. The walkway will lead you to 7th Street and **Declaration House** (formerly the Graff House), where Thomas Jefferson wrote the rough draft of the Declaration of Independence in June 1776. Jefferson rented rooms from bricklayer Jacob Graff. The bedroom and parlor in which he lived that summer have been re-created with period furnishings. The first floor has a Jefferson exhibit and a seven-minute film, *The Extraordinary Citizen.* The display on the Declaration of Independence shows changes Jefferson made in the writing. The first draft had an antislavery clause, which did not survive debate. *7th and Market Sts., tel. 215/597–8974. Open daily 9–5.*

Time Out On 5th Street across from the Liberty Bell Pavilion is the **Bourse,** Philadelphia's former stock exchange and now a festive complex of shops, offices, and eateries. The ground floor of this magnificently restored 1895 building is now a bustling food court. Inside the east entrance, a window display tells the history of the Bourse.

Now walk east to 316 Market Street, the entrance to **Franklin Court.** First notice the post office, where letters are handstamped with the cancellation "B. Free Franklin." Pass through the archway and you'll see a steel-girder superstructure in the shape of Franklin's last house, which stood on the site. Down the long ramp is an underground museum, which has displays and a 20-minute film on Franklin's life and achievements. Beside the post office are three restored homes once owned by Franklin. No. 318 has architectural and archaeological displays of the houses themselves and artifacts found in the court. No. 320–322 was the print shop and office of the Colonial newspaper, *The Aurora,* published by Franklin's grandson Benjamin Franklin Bache. *314–322 Market St. (or enter from Chestnut St. walkway), tel. 215/597–2760. Open daily 9–5; early July–early Sept. 10–6.*

When you leave the underground museum, you'll be facing the entrance of the **Philadelphia Maritime Museum.** If you like things nautical you'll want to stop here. Four floors hold everything from scrimshaw to battleships, including art, artifacts, navigator's instruments, figureheads, and model ships. "The Sea Around Us" is a continuing exhibit showing the evolution from sail to steam in ship design. In the spring of 1995 the Maritime Museum is scheduled to relocate to a more appropriate location, the Port of History Museum at Penn's Landing on the Delaware River. *321 Chestnut St., tel. 215/925–5439. Admission: $2.50 adults, $1 senior citizens, students, and children under 12. Open Tues.–Sat. 10–5, Sun. 1–5.*

⑭ Walk one block east on Market Street and a half-block north on 2nd Street to **Christ Church,** where noted Colonials, including 15 signers of the Declaration, worshiped. The congregation was organized in 1695 on this site; the present church—a fine example of Georgian architecture—was completed in 1754. The bells and the steeple were financed by lotteries run by Benjamin Franklin. Brass plaques mark the pews of Washington, Robert Morris, Betsy Ross, and others. (The church burial ground, two blocks west, is No. 20 on this tour.) *2nd St. north of Market St., tel. 215/922–1695. Open Mon.–Sat. 9–5, Sun. 1–5. Services Sun. at 9 and 11.*

⑮ Continuing north on 2nd Street for a block and passing Arch Street, you come to a small street on the right. **Elfreth's Alley** is the oldest continuously occupied residential street in America, dating back to 1702. The Elfreth's Alley Association has restored No. 126, a Colonial craftsman's home, with authentic furnishings and a Colonial kitchen. On the first weekend in June, residents celebrate Elfreth's Alley Days by dressing in Colonial garb and opening their houses to the public. In December the houses are open for a one-night Christmas tour. The rest of the year, only No. 126 is open. *Off Front and 2nd Sts. between Arch and Race Sts., tel. 215/574–0560. Open daily 10–4, Mar.–Dec.; weekends 10–4, Jan. and Feb.*

⑯ Walk back to 2nd Street, turn right, and a few footsteps take you to the **Fireman's Hall Museum.** Housed in an authentic 1876 firehouse, the museum traces the history of firefighting, from the volunteer company founded in Philadelphia by Benjamin Franklin in 1736 to the professional departments of the 20th century. The collection includes early hand- and horse-drawn fire engines (such as an 1815 hand pumper and a 1907 three-horse Metropolitan steamer); fire marks; uniforms; and other memorabilia. *147 N. 2nd St., tel. 215/923–1438. Open Tues.–Sat. 9–5.*

⑰ Walk south on 2nd Street and turn right to 239 Arch Street, the **Betsy Ross House.** The ongoing debate over whether or not Betsy Ross sewed the first American flag and whether she ever lived in this three-story brick house only adds to the interest of the site. Owned and maintained by the City of Philadelphia, the eight-room house is crammed with artifacts such as a family Bible and Betsy Ross's wardrobe and yardstick. Alongside the house is brick-paved Atwater Kent Park, with a fountain, benches, and the graves of Betsy Ross and her third husband, John Claypoole. *239 Arch St., tel. 215/627–5343. Open Mon.–Sat. May–Oct. 10–6, Nov.–Apr. 10–5.*

Continuing west on Arch Street, you'll see an eight-foot-high bust of Benjamin Franklin made of 80,000 pennies donated by Philadelphia schoolchildren and children of city firefighters.

⑱ Across 4th Street, the **United States Mint** stands just two blocks from the first U.S. mint, which opened in 1792. Built in 1969, this is the largest mint in the world. A self-guided tour shows how blank discs are turned into U.S. coins. The visitors' gallery has an exhibit of medals from the nation's wars, including the Medal of Honor, the Purple Heart, and the Bronze Star—once made at the mint. Also on display are bullion boxes used to transport gold bars during the days of the Pony Express: The boxes had special locks that counted the number of times they were opened. The David Rittenhouse Room on the mezzanine level has a display of U.S. gold coins. Seven Tiffany glass-tile mosaics depict coin making in ancient Rome. A shop in the lobby sells special coins and medals—in mint condition. *5th and Arch Sts., tel. 215/597-7350. Open daily 9–4:30; closed weekends Sept.–Apr., Sun. May–June. Coinage machinery operates weekdays only.*

⑲ Catercorner is the **Arch Street Meeting House,** built in 1804 for the Philadelphia Yearly Meeting of the Society of Friends. It is still used for that purpose—aside from bi-weekly services, 13,000 Quakers congregate here for five days each March. A small museum in the church presents a series of dioramas and a 14-minute slide show depicting the life and accomplishments of William Penn, and from April 15 to October 30, Quaker guides give tours. *4th and Arch Sts., tel. 215/627-2667. Open Mon.–Sat. 10–4; services Thurs. at 10 and Sun. at 10:30.*

⑳ A block west on Arch Street is the **Christ Church Burial Ground**, resting place of five signers of the Declaration and other Colonial patriots. The best-known graves are those of Benjamin Franklin and his wife, Deborah. According to local legend, throwing a penny on Franklin's grave will bring you good luck. A peaceful, cloistered spot in the center of the city. *5th and Arch Sts. Open daily late spring, summer, and early fall 9:30–4:30, weather permitting.*

Tour 2. Society Hill and the Waterfront

㉑ You start Tour 2 at **Penn's Landing,** the spot where William Penn stepped ashore in 1682. This is the hub of a 37-acre park that stretches from Market Street on the north to Lombard Street on the south. The development of this area—an ambitious effort to reclaim the Delaware River waterfront—began in 1967. Plans include condominiums, offices, more recreation areas, hotels, and restaurants. In warm weather, the Great Plaza at Penn's Landing—an outdoor amphitheater—is the scene of concerts, jamborees, festivals, and other special events; pick up a calendar at the Visitor Center (3rd and Chestnut Sts.) or call the Penn's Landing Info-Line (tel. 215/923-4992). Walk along the waterfront and you'll see scores of pleasure boats moored at the marina, and cargo ships chugging up and down the Delaware. Philadelphia's port, which includes ports in New Jersey and Delaware, is one of the world's largest freshwater ports.

One ship docked at Penn's Landing played a key role in American maritime history. The **USS *Olympia*** was Commodore **㉒** George Dewey's flagship at the Battle of Manila in the Spanish-American War. Dewey entered Manila Harbor after midnight on May 1, 1898. At 5:40 AM, he told his captain, "You may fire when ready, Gridley," and the battle began. By 12:30 the Americans had destroyed the entire Spanish fleet. The *Olympia* was the last ship of the "New Navy" of the 1880s and 1890s, the beginning of the era of steel ships, and it is the only remaining ship from the Spanish-American War. You can tour the entire restored ship, including the officers' staterooms, engine room, galley, gun batteries, pilothouse, and conning tower. *Penn's Landing at Spruce St., tel. 215/922–1898. Admission: $5 adults, $3 senior citizens, $2 children under 12 (includes USS Becuna). Open daily 10–5, summer weekends 10–6.*

㉓ Opportunities to board a submarine come infrequently, but you can follow the *Olympia* with a tour of ᵗhe adjacent **USS *Becuna*.** This "guppy class" sub is 318 feet long and had a crew of 88. It was commissioned in 1944 and conducted search-and-destroy missions in the South Pacific. After World War II it became a training vessel; by the time it was decommissioned in 1969, it had made 10,000 dives. Note the crew's cramped quarters as you step through the narrow walkways, climb the ladders, and glimpse the torpedoes in the torpedo room. Especially appealing to kids. All guides are World War II submarine vets. *Penn's Landing at Spruce St., tel. 215/922–1898. Admission: $5 adults, $3 senior citizens, $2 children under 12 (includes USS Olympia). Open daily 10–5, summer weekends 10–6.*

㉔ Docked a block north is the ***Gazela of Philadelphia,*** formerly *Gazela Primeiro.* Built in 1883, this 177-foot square-rigger is the last of a Portuguese fleet of cod-fishing ships. Still fishing as late as 1969, it is the oldest and largest wooden square-rigger still sailing. As the Port of Philadelphia's ambassador of goodwill, the *Gazela* sails up and down the Atlantic Coast to harbor festivals and celebrations. It is also a sail-training ship and a museum. The all-volunteer crew of 35 works all winter to maintain it and sails it in summer. Climb aboard to view the crew's living quarters, the hold where fish were kept, the galley, spars and rigging, and captain's and officers' quarters. *Penn's Landing at Market St., tel. 215/923–9030. Suggested donation: $2.50. Open Memorial Day–Labor Day, daily 10–6; rest of year, weekends noon–5.*

From Penn's Landing at Walnut Street you can catch the "ferry to the fishies:" The **Riverbus** crosses the Delaware River to Camden in less than 10 minutes and you arrive a few steps away ㉕ from the **New Jersey State Aquarium.** It opened in 1992, and now 3,000 fish call it home. A diver inside the 760,000-gallon tank (the second largest in the United States) can answer your questions via a "scubaphone." There's a petting tank filled with sharks and rays. No kidding. *Riverbus: Penn's Landing near Walnut St., tel. 609/365–1400. Cost: $4 round-trip, $2 children and senior citizens. Departs every 30 min. on the ¼ hour, from approximately 9 AM to 6 PM, later on weekends and in summer. Aquarium: S. Riverside Dr., Camden, New Jersey, tel. 609/365–3300. Admission: $8.50 adults, $7 students and senior citizens, $5.50 children under 12. Open daily 9:30 AM–5:30 PM.*

In the middle of Delaware Avenue (also called Christopher Columbus Boulevard) are the tracks of the **Penn's Landing Trolley** ㉖ **Company.** You can board an authentic turn-of-the-century trolley at Dock Street or Spruce Street for a 20-minute round-trip along the Delaware River waterfront. The conductor provides a guided tour as you ride. *Delaware Ave. at Spruce St., tel. 215/627–0807. Fare: $1.50 adults, 75¢ children under 12, for an all-*

day pass. Runs 11–dusk weekends and holidays from mid-Apr. to late Nov.; also Thurs. and Fri. in July and Aug.

㉗ Watch out for traffic as you leave the trolley, and head back to Front Street at Sansom Street. As you walk west on Sansom Street, you'll spot **Welcome Park,** site of the slate-roof house where William Penn lived briefly and where he granted the Charter of Privileges in 1701. (The *Welcome* was the ship that transported Penn to America.) On a 60-foot-long map of Penn's Philadelphia carved in the pavement in the park sits a scale model of the Penn statue from atop City Hall. The wall surrounding the park displays a time line of his life, with information about his philosophy and quotations from his writings.

Time Out Walk north one block to the corner of 2nd and Chestnut streets for a wide selection of bars and restaurants, including Rib-It, Serrano, Los Amigos, the Middle East, and Philadelphia Fish and Company.

㉘ A half-block west on Walnut Street, the **Philadelphia Merchant's Exchange** (3rd and Walnut Sts., tel. 215/597–8974) stands behind Dock Street, a cobblestone thoroughfare that is closed to traffic. Designed by the well-known Philadelphia architect William Strickland and built in 1832, the Greek Revival structure served as the city's commercial center for 50 years. It was both the stock exchange and a place where merchants met to trade goods. In the tower, a watchman scanned the Delaware and notified merchants of arriving ships. Now it's the regional offices of the National Park Service and the interior is not open to the public.

㉙ On the corner of 3rd and Walnut streets a small, lovingly maintained garden leads to the **Bishop White House,** home of Bishop William White, rector of Christ Church, first Episcopal bishop of Pennsylvania, and spiritual leader of Philadelphia for 60 years. Built in 1786, this upper-class house has been restored to Colonial elegance. White, who was chaplain to the Continental Congress, entertained many members of the first families of the country, including Washington, Franklin, and Robert Morris (the bishop's brother-in-law). The second-floor study contains much of the bishop's own library. Unlike most houses of the period, the bishop's house had an early form of flush toilet. The house tour is not recommended for children (they get bored). *309 Walnut St., tel. 215/597–8974. Open daily 9:30–4:30; obtain tickets at the Visitor Center for a free 1-hr tour that includes the Bishop White House and the Todd House.*

㉚ On the same block, the simply furnished **Todd House** stands in direct contrast to the lavish Bishop White House. Built in 1775, it has been restored to its appearance in the 1790s, when its best-known resident lived here. Dolley Payne Todd lost her husband, the lawyer John Todd, to the yellow-fever epidemic of 1793. She later married James Madison, who became the fourth president. *4th and Walnut Sts., tel. 215/597–8974. Open daily 9:30–4:30; obtain tickets at the Visitor Center for a free 1-hr tour that includes the Todd House and the Bishop White House.*

㉛ A few steps south on 4th Street is the nation's oldest fire-insurance company, the **Philadelphia Contributionship for the Insurance of Houses from Loss by Fire.** The contributionship was founded by Benjamin Franklin in 1752; the present building dates from 1836. This is still an active business, but a small museum is open to the public; supervised visits to the upstairs room and garden are available by appointment. *212 S. 4th St., tel. 215/627–1752. Open weekdays 10–3.*

32 A block south on 4th Street is the 22-room **Hill-Physick-Keith House,** built in 1786. Philip Syng Physick, a leading physician in the days before anesthesia, is known as the "Father of American Surgery." He developed techniques and instruments that helped place American surgery at the forefront of the profession. While caring for victims of the yellow-fever epidemic of 1793, he contracted the disease himself. His most famous patient was Chief Justice John Marshall, who came from Washington and was successfully treated for bladder stones. This is the only free-standing house left in Society Hill. On three sides is a garden filled with plants common in the 19th century. *321 S. 4th St., tel. 215/925–7866. Admission: $2 adults, 50¢ children. Open Tues.–Sat. 10–4; Sun. 1–4. Tours Tues.–Sat. 11, 1:30, and 3; Sun. 1:30 and 3.*

Take a pleasant walk east on Delancey Street and then turn right on 3rd Street to Pine Street. At the northwest corner is **33** the **Thaddeus Kosciuszko National Memorial.** A Polish general who later became a national hero in his homeland, Kosciuszko came to the United States in 1776 to help fight the Revolution. The first floor has a portrait gallery and a chronology of his life. The second floor displays many of the general's possessions. A six-minute film in English and Polish portrays his activities during the Revolution. *301 Pine St., tel. 215/597–8974. Open daily 9–5, July and Aug. 10–5.*

34 A block east is **Head House Square** (2nd and Pine Sts.), an open-air Colonial marketplace that extends from Pine Street to Lombard Street. It was established as New Market in 1745. George Washington shopped here. Built in 1804, the Head House was both the home of the market master and a firehouse. Today, on summer weekends, the square is used for craft fairs, food festivals, and other activities. A host of street performers, including jugglers, magicians, and mimes, draws crowds.

35 East of Head House Square is **Newmarket,** a once-thriving but currently vacant complex of boutiques and restaurants. It's still worth a walk-through, from the 18th-century homes on 2nd Street to the contemporary glass facade on Front Street. And soon, new life may be stirring here—a $15 million performing arts and entertainment complex is on the drawing board.

Time Out You can find food and drink on both sides of 2nd Street between Pine and South streets.

Heading north on 2nd Street to Locust Street, note Society Hill Towers, three high-rise apartment buildings dating from 1964; and the Society Hill Townhouses at 3rd and Locust streets, designed in 1962 by I. M. Pei, who also designed the towers.

36 Cross Locust Street and turn right on 3rd Street to the **Powel House,** a brick Georgian house built in 1765 and purchased by Samuel Powel in 1769. Powel was the last mayor of Philadelphia under the Crown and the first in the new republic. The lavish house is furnished with 18th-century antiques and has such appointments as a mahogany staircase from Santo Domingo, a 1765 mahogany secretary, and a signed Gilbert Stuart portrait. Here the "Patriot Mayor" and his wife, Elizabeth, entertained such dignitaries as Washington, Lafayette, and foreign ministers. Next door lived John Penn, governor of Pennsylvania. The house, which has a ballroom on the second floor, can be rented for parties and other events ($1,000 a night). *244 S. 3rd St., tel. 215/627–0364. Admission: $3 adults; $2 students with ID and senior citizens; 50¢ children under 12. Open Tues.–Sat. 10–4, Sun. 1–4. Call ahead as hours can vary.*

Tour 3. City Hall and Environs

Numbers in the margin correspond to points of interest on the Tours 3 and 4 map.

For a visual introduction to the downtown, climb the few steps to the plaza in front of the **Municipal Services Building** at 15th Street and John F. Kennedy Boulevard. No spot on the ground provides a better up-close overview of the city. You'll feel surrounded by Philadelphia—City Hall; the PSFS Building; the Art Museum; the new skyscrapers at Liberty Place; the Clothespin statue; and other places we'll cover.

One block west of the Municipal Services Building plaza is the
❶ **Philadelphia Visitors Center.** Here you can get brochures about the city and surroundings, lists of restaurants and hotels, and information about current events. Volunteers and staff members are on hand to answer your questions. What are the most common questions they hear? Where's the Liberty Bell? Where's Independence Hall? Where's the nearest bathroom? In the gift shop—where the staff wears Colonial garb—you can buy a Philadelphia T-shirt, a necktie with a pattern of Liberty Bells, and a sticker showing a tombstone inscribed, "I would rather be in Philadelphia." *16th St. and John F. Kennedy Blvd., tel. 215/636–1666. Open daily 9–5, until 6 in summer.*

Walk east on Kennedy Boulevard to 15th Street for an incom-
❷ parable, unobstructed view of **City Hall.** Topped by a 37-foot bronze statue of William Penn, the city's founder, City Hall stands 548 feet high and until 1987 was Philadelphia's tallest building. With 642 rooms, it is the largest city hall in the country and the tallest masonry-bearing building in the world: No steel structure supports it. It took 30 years to build (1871 to 1900) and cost the taxpayers more than $23 million. Scattered about the exterior are hundreds of statues by Alexander Milne Calder, who also designed the Penn statue at the top. You now see all the statues and the tower—scaffolding used in restoration work which shrouded it since 1985 was removed in 1990. The observation deck affords a 30-mile view of the city and surroundings. Even the clock, 16 feet in diameter, is visible for miles.

Not only the geographic center of Penn's original city, City Hall is also the governmental center. Start at the northeast corner and ascend one flight to the mayor's ornate reception room (Room 202), and the recently restored Conversation Hall (Room 201). Take a look, too, at the City Council Chambers (Room 400) and the Supreme Court of Pennsylvania. Municipal court sessions are open to the public. *Broad and Market Sts., tel. 215/686–1776; Mayor's Office of Information, Room*

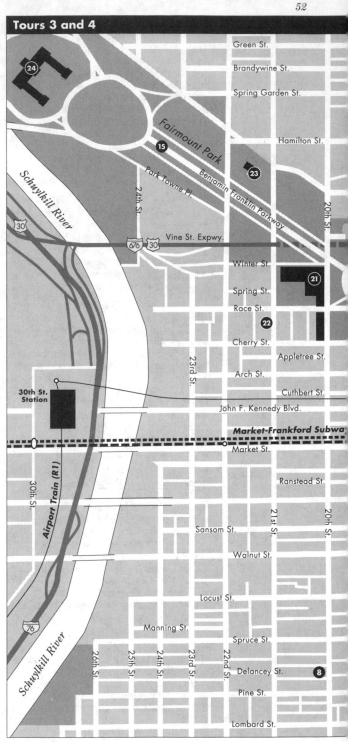

Tours 3 and 4

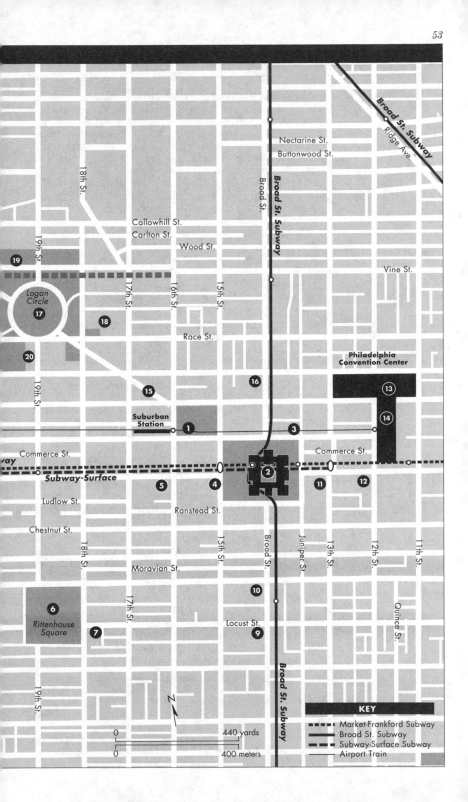

121, tel. 215/686–2250; 1-hr tours of City Hall weekdays at 12:30, tel. 215/568–3351.

Leave City Hall by the northern exit and cross Kennedy Boulevard to the **Masonic Temple.** Philadelphia is the mother city of American Masonry, and the temple is home to the Grand Lodge of Free and Accepted Masons of Pennsylvania. The gavel used at the laying of the cornerstone in 1868 was the one that Brother George Washington used to lay the cornerstone of the U.S. Capitol. Designed by Brother James H. Windrim and built by Masons, the ornate interior consists of seven Lodge Halls built to represent seven styles of architecture: Corinthian, Ionic, Italian Renaissance, Norman, Gothic, Oriental, and Egyptian. The collection of Masonry items includes handwritten letters from Washington to brothers of the Grand Lodge and Benjamin Franklin's printing of the first book on Freemasonry published in America. *1 N. Broad St., tel. 215/988–1917. Free 45-min tours weekdays 10, 11, 1, 2, and 3; Sat. 10 and 11. Closed Sat. July and Aug.*

Walk to 15th and Market streets and you'll see Claes Oldenburg's 45-foot-high, 10-ton steel *Clothespin* in front of the Center Square Building. Lauded by some and scorned by others, this pop art piece contrasts with the traditional statuary so common in Philadelphia.

Time Out There's alfresco snacking at the **Politico Cafe** on the northwest corner of the City Hall apron. Enjoy a sprout sandwich with tahini dressing for $3.25. Open from May to October.

Two blocks west is **Liberty Place. One Liberty Place** (1650 Market St.) is the 945-foot, 63-story office building that propelled Philadelphia into the "ultra-high" skyscraper era. Built in 1987 at a cost of $225 million, it became the tallest structure in Philadelphia, breaking an unwritten law against buildings higher than the William Penn statue atop City Hall. The Art Deco structure, reminiscent of New York's Chrysler Building, is visible from almost everywhere in the city. In 1990, the adjacent 58-story tower, **Two Liberty Place,** opened with a shopping complex, food court, and The Ritz-Carlton Hotel.

Walk to 18th Street, head south, and you soon come upon **Rittenhouse Square** (between 18th and 19th Sts. at Walnut St.). Once grazing ground for cows and sheep, this is now Philadelphia's classiest park. At lunchtime, workers from surrounding office buildings picnic on the grass and feed the squirrels. Until 1950 town houses bordered the square, but they have now been replaced on three sides by swank apartment buildings and hotels. The square is also the scene of annual events such as the Rittenhouse Square Flower Market, the Easter Parade, the Fine Arts Annual, the Clothesline Art Exhibit, and the Mozart on the Square Festival.

East of the square are the Barclay Hotel; the Philadelphia Art Alliance, a gay-'90s mansion with galleries open to the public; and the **Curtis Institute of Music** (1726 Locust St., tel. 215/893–5261), a tuition-free school for outstanding students whose graduates include Leonard Bernstein, Samuel Barber, Ned Rorem, and Anna Moffo. You may recognize the exterior of the Curtis Institute from the Eddie Murphy film *Trading Places.* Free student and faculty concerts are given from October through May at 8 PM, almost every Monday, Wednesday, and Friday.

West of the square are Holy Trinity Episcopal Church, a branch of the Free Library of Philadelphia, and the Rittenhouse Hotel.

Leave the square on the southern side, continue south on 19th Street to Delancey Place, and turn right. A block west is the ❽ **Rosenbach Museum and Library,** which has more than 130,000 manuscripts and 30,000 rare books. This 1863 three-floor town house is furnished with Persian rugs and 18th-century British, French, and American antiques such as Chippendale, Adam, and Hepplewhite furniture. Amassed by Philadelphia collectors Philip H. and A.S.W. Rosenbach, the collection includes paintings by Canaletto, Sully, and Lawrence; drawings by Daumier, Fragonard, and Blake; book illustrations ranging from medieval illumination to Maurice Sendak; the first edition of Benjamin Franklin's *Poor Richard's Almanac;* and manuscripts of Chaucer's *Canterbury Tales* and James Joyce's *Ulysses. 2010 Delancey Pl., tel. 215/732–1600. Admission: $3.50 adults, $2.50 senior citizens and students. Open Tues.–Sun. 11–4. Guided 1-hr tour (come no later than 2:45). Closed Aug. and national holidays.*

On your way back to Rittenhouse Square, you may want to wander through the neighborhood west of the square. Cypress Street just north of Delancey Place, and Panama Street just south, are two of the many intimate streets lined with trees and town houses characteristic of the area.

From Rittenhouse Square, walk east on Locust Street four ❾ blocks to the **Academy of Music** (Broad and Locust Sts., tel. 215/893–1900 or 215/893–1930 for the box office). Modeled after Milan's La Scala opera house, it opened with a lavish ball in 1857. Home of the Philadelphia Orchestra, the academy attracts not only music lovers and students but also many members of Philadelphia's elite. Friday afternoon concerts are legendary for their audience of "Main Line matrons." Tickets are available at the box office; if you're willing to wait in line and sit in the cramped amphitheater four levels above the stage, you can take advantage of one of the cultural world's great bargains, the $4 "nosebleed" seats. The academy is also home to the Opera Company of Philadelphia and the Luciano Pavarotti International Voice Competition, and the site of the Pennsylvania Ballet's annual Christmas production of *The Nutcracker.*

As you walk along the west side of Broad Street, between Spruce and Walnut streets, notice the more than 30 plaques in the sidewalk honoring some of those who contributed to Philadelphia culture. Where else could Frankie Avalon and Dizzy Gillespie rub shoulders with Anna Moffo and Eugene Ormandy?

A block north of the academy is the second "Grande Dame of ❿ South Broad Street," the former **Bellevue Stratford Hotel** (Broad and Walnut Sts., tel. 215/893–1776). The epitome of the thirst for opulence characteristic of the early 1900s, it was the city's leading hotel for decades. It closed after the 1976 outbreak of Legionnaire's disease, which spread through the building's air-conditioning system during an American Legion convention. Reopened as the Fairmont several years later, it failed to regain its luster and closed again in 1986. When renovations were completed in 1989, this magnificent building re-opened as home to a number of shops and offices, as well as the luxurious Hotel Atop the Bellevue (*see* Chapter 7).

As you continue up Broad Street, you pass a French Renaissance–style building, the **Union League of Philadelphia** (140 S. Broad St.). A bastion of Philadelphia conservatism, the Union League is a social club founded during the Civil War to preserve the Union.

⑪ Just east of City Hall is the **John Wanamaker Store,** the grandest of Philadelphia's department stores. Wanamaker began with a clothing store in 1861 and became one of America's most innovative and prominent retailers. From 1889 to 1893 he was U.S. Postmaster General under President Benjamin Harrison. Designed by the Chicago firm of D. H. Burnham and Company, the building has a nine-story grand court with a 30,000-pipe organ—the largest ever built—and a 2,500-pound statue of an eagle, both remnants of the 1904 Louisiana Purchase Exposition in St. Louis. "Meet me at the Eagle" is a popular way for Philadelphians to arrange get-togethers. Organ performances are held at 11:15 and 5:15. The store is famous for its Christmas sound-and-light show. *13th and Market Sts., tel. 215/422–2000. Open Mon.–Sat. 10–7, Wed. 10–8, Sun. noon–5.*

⑫ Leave Wanamaker's at the Market Street exit, turn right, and go one block to 12th Street. Here is the **Philadelphia Saving Fund Society (PSFS) Building,** one of the city's first skyscrapers. The 1930 structure still looks modern and was influential in the design of other American skyscrapers. Pay special attention to the enormous escalators and the main banking floor, two striking contrasts to the utilitarian approaches of architecture today. This is now part of Mellon Bank; if you have any banking needs, here's a place to handle them and see an interesting sight at the same time. *12th and Market Sts., tel. 215/636–6000. Open Mon.–Fri. 8–4.*

⑬ Across Market Street at 12th Street is the old Reading Railroad Headhouse, purchased by the city to become the grand entrance to the new **Pennsylvania Convention Center.** Opened in June 1993 with galas, parties, and Vice President Al Gore cutting the ribbon, the $522 million center is being counted on to help rejuvenate Philadelphia's struggling economy. After visitors enter the headhouse, escalators will take them through the Reading Train Shed (scheduled to open in March 1994), then across another bridge over Arch Street to the main exhibition hall (with 313,000 square feet, equal to the size of seven football fields). The final part of the complex will be the 1,200-room Marriott hotel, connected to the center by a bridge over 12th Street, due to open in December 1994.

⑭ A half-block north on 12th Street is the **Reading Terminal Market.** One floor beneath the former Reading Railroad's 1891 train shed, the sprawling market has 79 stores, stalls, and other places of business. Some 70 are food-related; the remainder include a flower shop, bookstores (one just for cookbooks), and a wine shop. Some stalls change daily, offering items from hooked rugs and handmade jewelry to Mexican and African crafts. No other place in the city offers a wider variety of eating places—a vegetarian restaurant, a gourmet ice cream store, a cookie shop, and a Philadelphia cheesesteak store. Many stalls have their own counters with seating; there's also a central eating area, where at lunchtime on the second Friday of each month a group of amateur musicians (a politician, a doctor, and a lawyer) called the Reading Terminals play jazz. You can also buy a large variety of fresh food to cook from vegetable and fruit stands, butchers, fish stores, and Pennsylvania Dutch markets. The entire building is a National Historic Landmark and the train shed is a National Engineering Landmark. The city's new convention center is being built above and behind the market, but pledges and legal guarantees are in place to preserve this Philadelphia treasure. *12th and Filbert Sts., tel. 215/ 922-2317. Open Mon.-Sat. 8-6 PM.*

Tour 4. Museum Area

⓯ The spine of this tour is the **Benjamin Franklin Parkway,** which angles across the city grid system from City Hall to Fairmount Park. It was not part of William Penn's original plan for Philadelphia. Lined with a distinguished assemblage of museums, institutions, hotels, and apartment buildings, this 250-foot-wide boulevard inspired by the Champs Élysées was designed by French architect Jacques Greber and built in the 1920s. Adorned by fountains, statues, trees, and flags of every country, the parkway is the route of most of the city's parades and the site of many festivals, including the Thanksgiving and Easter parades, "Super Sunday," the Big Apple Circus, and the CoreStates Pro Cycling championship.

⓰ Before heading out the parkway, we'll take a short detour to the **Pennsylvania Academy of the Fine Arts.** Starting at the Visitors Center (16th St. and Kennedy Blvd.), walk east on Kennedy Boulevard and turn left on Broad Street; go two blocks to Cherry Street and you'll see a High Victorian Gothic building (1876) that's a work of art in itself. Designed by the noted, sometimes eccentric, Philadelphia architects Frank Furness and George Hewitt, the multicolored stone-and-brick exterior is an extravagant blend of columns, friezes, Art Deco, and Moorish flourishes. Inside, the oldest art institution in the United States (founded 1804) boasts a collection that ranges from Winslow Homer and Benjamin West to Andrew Wyeth and Red Grooms. The academy faculty has included Thomas Sully, Thomas Eakins, and Charles Willson Peale. The permanent collection is supplemented by constantly changing exhibits of sculpture, paintings, and mixed-media artwork. *Broad and Cherry Sts., tel. 215/972-7600. Admission: $5 adults, $3 senior citizens, $2 students; free Sat. 10-1. Open Tues.-Sat. 10-5, Sun. 11-5.*

Head west on Cherry Street past the American Friends Service Committee and the Race Street Friends Meeting House. At 17th Street, you'll find yourself on the Benjamin Franklin Parkway.

⓱ Walk northwest on the parkway one block to **Logan Circle.** Originally this was one of four squares Penn had built at the corners of a rectangle around Center Square, where City Hall now stands. (The others are Franklin Square to the northeast, Washington Square to the southeast, and Rittenhouse Square to the southwest.) The focal point of Logan Circle is the Swann Fountain of 1920, designed by Alexander Stirling Calder, son of Alexander Milne Calder, who did the William Penn statue atop City Hall. The main figures in the fountain symbolize Phil-

adelphia's three leading waterways: the Delaware and Schuylkill rivers and Wissahickon Creek. Around Logan Circle are
some examples of Philadelphia's magnificent collection of outdoor art, including *General Galusha Pennypacker*, the *Shakespeare Memorial*, and *Jesus Breaking Bread*.

⑱ The **Cathedral of Saints Peter and Paul** at 18th Street and the
parkway is the basilica of the Archdiocese of Philadelphia and
the spiritual center for the Philadelphia area's 1.4 million Roman Catholics. Topped by a huge copper dome, it was built between 1846 and 1864 in the Italian Renaissance style. Many
interior decorations were done by Constantino Brumidi, who
painted the dome of the United States Capitol. Six Philadelphia
bishops and archbishops are buried beneath the altar. *18th and
Race Sts., tel. 215/561–1313. Open 9–3:30.*

Walking counterclockwise around Logan Circle, you'll see twin
marble Greek Revival buildings off to your right. The nearer is
⑲ the city's Family Court; the other is the **Free Library of Philadelphia.** Along with a collection of more than 2 million volumes
(*see* Libraries and Museums, *below*), the central unit of the
public-library system presents concerts, movies, lectures, and
historical displays. *19th St. and Benjamin Franklin Pkwy.,
tel. 215/686–5322. Open Mon.–Wed. 9–9, Thurs. and Fri. 9–6,
Sat. 9–5, Sun. (Sept.–May) 1–5. Closed Sun. in summer.*

Time Out The rooftop cafeteria of the **Free Library** (19th St. and Benjamin Franklin Pkwy.) provides inexpensive meals at umbrellaed
tables.

⑳ Cross Logan Circle to the **Academy of Natural Sciences,** America's first museum of natural history. Founded in 1812, the
present building dates from 1868. The collection is famous for
stuffed animals from around the world, displayed in 35 natural
settings. The third-floor "Outside In" exhibit is a mini-museum
where children handle fossils, dinosaur teeth, even live animals
such as snakes and lizards. Since 1986 the main attraction has
been "Discovering Dinosaurs": reconstructed skeletons of a ty-
rannosaurus and others, movies, computer videos, and a Creta-
ceous landscape complete with animals and plants. Step on a
scale to compare your weight with a dinosaur's. *19th St. and
Benjamin Franklin Pkwy., tel. 215/299–1020. Admission: $6
adults, $5 children. Open weekdays 10–4:30, weekends and
holidays 10–5.*

From the Academy, walk west on Race Street to 20th Street
㉑ and the **Franklin Institute.** Founded to honor Benjamin Franklin, the institute is a science museum with an abundance of
hands-on exhibits. You can sit in the cockpit of a T-33 jet train-
er, trace the route of a corpuscle through the world's largest
artificial heart (15,000 times life-size), and ride to nowhere on a
350-ton Baldwin steam locomotive. The many exhibits cover energy, motion, sound, physics, astronomy, aviation, ships, me-
chanics, electricity, time, and other scientific subjects. You'll
also find a working weather station, computers to operate, and
the world's largest pinball machine. The Fels Planetarium features shows about the stars, space exploration, comets, and
other phenomena. Opened in May 1990, the $72 million Futures
Center has eight permanent exhibits, exploring such issues as
space, computers, careers, energy, and health. The 300-seat
Omniverse Theater, with a 79-foot domed screen and a 56-

speaker high-tech sound system, transports you down ski slopes and up mountains. *20th St. and Benjamin Franklin Pkwy., tel. 215/448–1200. Admission: ticket packages range from $7 to $12.50. Open daily 9:30–5.*

Winter Street bounds the Franklin Institute to the north. Take it west one block to 21st Street; cross it and turn left to the **㉒ Please Touch Museum,** the only U.S. museum designed specifically for children seven and younger. (It also appeals to adults.) The premise here is hands-on, feet-on, try-on: Perform in a circus ring; pet small animals in the "Animals as Pets" exhibit; dress up in costumes, wigs, and masks. The museum also has two special exhibits a year, theater programs, workshops, and a resource center with computers, games, books, and other educational activities. *210 N. 21st St., tel. 215/963–0667. Admission: $6. Open daily 9–4:30, in summer till 6.*

Cross to the north side of the parkway and walk northwest. On your right is the Youth Study Center (a detention center for juvenile offenders) with two striking tableaux depicting families.

At the next corner, guarded by the statue of *The Thinker*, is **㉓ the Rodin Museum,** the best collection of Auguste Rodin's works outside France. Before entering, marvel at the *Gates of Hell*, a 21-foot-high sculpture with more than 100 human and animal figures. Inside are 124 sculptures by the French master, including *The Kiss, The Burghers of Calais, Eternal Springtime*, and hands and busts of his friends. One small room is devoted to the French novelist Balzac. Photographs by Edward Steichen show Rodin at work. *22nd St. and Benjamin Franklin Pkwy., tel. 215/787–5431. Donation requested. Open Tues.–Sun. 10–5.*

Atop Faire Mount, the plateau at the end of Franklin Parkway, **㉔ stands the Philadelphia Museum of Art.** This mammoth building of Minnesota dolomite is modeled after ancient Greek temples but on a grander scale. Covering 10 acres, it has 200 galleries and a collection of over 300,000 works. You can enter the museum from the front or the rear; we recommend the front, where you can run up the 99 steps made famous in the movie *Rocky* (Rocky ran up only 72). From the expansive terrace, look up to the pediment on your right at a group of 13 glazed, multicolored statues of classical gods. After passing Jacques Lipchitz's statue *Prometheus Strangling the Vulture*, climb the last flight of steps, and, before entering the museum, turn around to savor the view down the parkway.

Once inside, you'll see the grand staircase and Saint-Gaudens's statue of *Diana*, which formerly graced New York's old Madison Square Garden. The John G. Johnson Collection covers Western art from the Renaissance to the 19th century. The Arensberg and A. E. Gallatin collections contain modern and contemporary works by artists such as Brancusi, Braque, Matisse, and Picasso. Famous paintings from among these collections include Van Eyck's *St. Francis Receiving the Stigmata*, Rubens's *Prometheus Bound*, Benjamin West's *Benjamin Franklin Drawing Electricity from the Sky*, Van Gogh's *Sunflowers*, Renoir's *The Bathers*, and Picasso's *Three Musicians*.

Marcel Duchamps is a specialty of the house; the museum has the world's most extensive collection of his works. Another specialty is reconstructions of entire buildings: a 12th-century French cloister, a 16th-century Indian temple hall, a 16th-century Japanese Buddhist temple, a 17th-century Chinese palace hall, and a Japanese ceremonial teahouse. Among the other collections: costumes, early American furniture, and Amish and Shaker crafts. An unusual touch—and one that children especially like—is the Kienbusch Collection of Arms and Armor. Special exhibitions scheduled for 1994 include the Barnes Collection of Impressionist and Post-Impressionist Art. Pick up a map of the museum at either of the two entrances and wander on your own; or choose from a variety of guided tours. *26th St. and Benjamin Franklin Pkwy., tel. 215/763–8100, 215/787–5488 for 24-hr taped message. Admission: $6 adults, $3 senior citizens, students, and children; free Sun. 10–1. Open Tues.–Sun. 10–5; closed on legal holidays. Special programs on some Wednesday evenings.*

Although the bulk of Philadelphia tourist attractions are located in and around Center City, other areas also merit your attention. Here we'll present a tour of one area and briefly describe two others.

Fairmount Park Tour

Numbers in the margin correspond to points of interest on the Fairmount Park map.

Stretching from the edge of downtown to the city's northwest corner, Fairmount Park is the largest city park in the world. The total park system, including other parks under the Fairmount Park Commissioner's jurisdiction, contains 8,900 acres. Fairmount Park itself covers about 4,500 acres.

The park encompasses beautiful natural areas—woodlands, meadows, rolling hills, two scenic waterways, and a forested 5½-mile gorge. It also contains tennis courts, ball fields, playgrounds, trails, exercise courses, several celebrated cultural institutions, and some fine early American country houses.

Philadelphia has more works of outdoor art than any other city in North America. More than 200 of these works—including statues by Frederic Remington, Jacques Lipchitz, and Auguste Rodin—are scattered throughout Fairmount Park.

The park was established in 1812 when the city purchased 5 acres behind Faire Mount, the hill upon which the Philadelphia Museum of Art now stands, for waterworks and public gardens. Through private bequests and public purchases (which continue today), it grew to its present size and stature.

The following tour highlights many of the park's treasures. Do it by car, starting near the art museum, or take a narrated tour on the Fairmount Park Trolley Bus. The trolley bus visits many of these sites, and you can get on and off all day (*see* Chapter 1).

Although some of the directions may sound complicated, signs help point the way. An excellent map of the park is available at Memorial Hall and most park mansions and sites for 25¢.

1 The park tour starts where the park began, at **Faire Mount,** now the site of the Philadelphia Museum of Art (*see* Tour 4, *above*). In 1812 a reservoir was built here to distribute water throughout the city.

2 Park behind the art museum and walk down to the **Waterworks.** Designed by Frederick Graff, this National Historic Engineer-

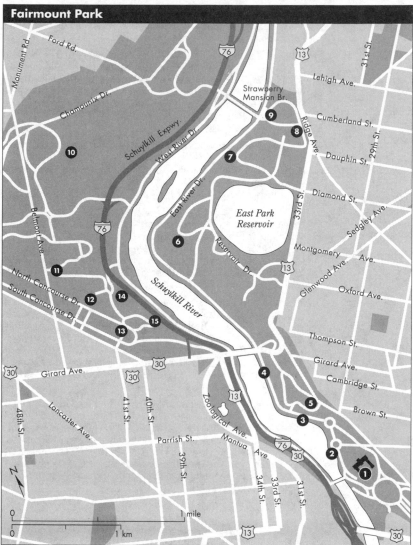

Belmont Plateau, **10**
Boathouse Row, **3**
Cedar Grove, **14**
Ellen Phillips Samuel Memorial Sculpture Garden, **4**
Faire Mount, **1**
Japanese House, **11**
Laurel Hill, **7**
Lemon Hill, **5**

Memorial Hall, **12**
Mt. Pleasant, **6**
Smith Civil War Memorial, **13**
Strawberry Mansion, **9**
Sweetbriar, **15**
Waterworks, **2**
Woodford, **8**

ing Landmark was the first steam pumping station of its kind in the country. The notable assemblage of Greek Revival buildings is undergoing extensive renovation.

3 A few steps north of the Waterworks, **Boathouse Row** begins. These 11 architecturally varied 19th-century buildings are home to the 13 rowing clubs that make up the "Schuylkill Navy." The view of the houses from the west side of the river is splendid—especially at night, when they're outlined with hundreds of small lights.

4 Continuing north along Kelly Drive, you soon reach the **Ellen Phillips Samuel Memorial Sculpture Garden.** Bronze and granite statues by 16 artists stand in a series of tableaux and groupings on riverside terraces. Portraying American themes and traits, they include *The Quaker* by Harry Rosen, *Birth of a Nation* by Henry Kreis, and *Spirit of Enterprise* by Jacques Lipchitz.

5 Drive north on Kelly Drive for about 200 yards. Take the second right (at the end of Boathouse Row) and go up to **Lemon Hill.** Built in 1800 on a 350-acre farm, this is a beautiful example of a Federal country house. *Poplar Dr., East Fairmount Park, tel. 215/232–4337. Admission: $1.50. Open Wed.–Sun. 10–4:30. Closed Jan.–Feb. Call ahead as hours may vary.*

6 Head back to Kelly Drive, turn right, and then right again at the equestrian statue of Ulysses S. Grant. The first left takes you to **Mt. Pleasant.** Built in 1761 by Captain John Macpherson, a pirate, the house was later purchased by the Revolutionary War traitor Benedict Arnold. John Adams called the Georgian mansion "the most elegant seat in Pennsylvania." *Mt. Pleasant Dr., East Fairmount Park, tel. 215/763–8100, ext. 333. Admission: $1.50. Open Tues.–Sun. 10–4:15.*

7 Double back to Reservoir Drive, pass Rockland and Ormiston (two other park mansions), and take the next left, Randolph Drive, to **Laurel Hill.** Built around 1767 on a laurel-covered hill overlooking the Schuylkill, the Georgian house was once owned by Dr. Philip Syng Physick (*see* Tour 2, *above*). On some Sunday evenings during the summer, Women for Greater Philadelphia sponsors candlelight chamber-music concerts here. *E. Edgely Dr., East Fairmount Park, tel. 215/235–1776. Admission: $1.50. Open Wed.–Sun. 10–4.*

8 Edgely Drive turns into Dauphin Street. Just before reaching 33rd Street, turn left on Strawberry Mansion Drive and you're at **Woodford,** a fine Georgian mansion built about 1756. Inside is the Naomi Wood collection of household goods, including furniture, unusual clocks, and English Delftware. *Near 33rd and Dauphin Sts., East Fairmount Park, tel. 215/229–6115. Admission: $1.50. Open Tues.–Sun. 10–4.*

9 A few steps northwest of Woodford stands the house that gave its name to the nearby section of Philadelphia, **Strawberry Mansion.** The largest mansion in Fairmount Park, it has furniture from the three main phases of its history: Federal, Regency, and Empire. In the parlor is a collection of rare Tucker porcelain; in the attic is a fine assortment of antique dolls. *Near 33rd and Dauphin Sts., East Fairmount Park, tel. 215/228–8364. Admission: $1.50. Open Tues.–Sun. 10–4.*

Go back to Strawberry Mansion Drive, turn left, and cross the Strawberry Mansion Bridge to West Fairmount Park. Looping through the park, you'll reach Chamounix Drive, a long straightaway. Turn left on Belmont Mansion Drive to **Belmont Plateau.** Here are Playhouse in the Park and Belmont Mansion, but the main attraction is the view, from 243 feet above river level. In front of you lie the park, the Schuylkill River winding down to the Philadelphia Museum of Art, and—4 miles away—the Philadelphia skyline.

Follow Belmont Mansion Drive down the hill. Where it forks, stay to the left, cross Montgomery Drive, and turn left to reach the Horticulture Center (*see* Parks, Zoos, and Gardens, *below*). Loop all the way around the Horticulture Center to the **Japanese House,** a reconstructed 16th-century house and garden built in Japan, exhibited temporarily at the Museum of Modern Art in New York, and reassembled here in 1958. Enjoy the serenity of the architecture and the waterfall, gardens, Japanese trees, and the pond. The house is called Shofu-So, which means "pine breeze villa." *Lansdowne Dr. east of Belmont Ave., West Fairmount Park, tel. 215/878–5097. Admission: $2.50. Open June–Aug., Wed.–Sun. 11–4; May, Sept., and Oct. weekends.*

Go back around the Horticulture Center and continue through the gates straight to Belmont Avenue. Turn left and then left again at the first light (North Concourse Drive). On your left is **Memorial Hall,** the only major building remaining from the Philadelphia Centennial Exposition of 1876. This grand stone building with a glass dome and Palladian windows was the Centennial art museum. Sometimes open for viewing is a 20-by-40-foot model of the exposition. *N. Concourse Dr., West Fairmount Park, tel. 215/686–1776. Admission free. Open daily 8:30–5.*

The two towers to your left as you leave Memorial Hall are part of the **Smith Civil War Memorial** (N. Concourse Dr., West Fairmount Park). Built from 1897 to 1912 with funds donated by wealthy foundry owner Richard Smith, the memorial honors Pennsylvania heroes of the Civil War. Among those immortalized in bronze are Generals Meade and Hancock—and Smith himself. At the base of each tower is a curved wall with a bench. If you sit at one end and listen to a person whispering at the other end, you'll understand why they're called the Whispering Benches. Unfortunately, the litter around the site reflects its location near a declining neighborhood.

To the east stands **Cedar Grove,** where five styles of furniture—Jacobean, William and Mary, Queen Anne, Chippendale, and Federal—reflect the accumulations of five generations of the Paschall-Morris family. The house stood in Frankford for 180 years before being moved to this location in 1927. *Lansdowne Dr. off N. Concourse Dr., West Fairmount Park, tel. 215/763–8100, ext. 4013. Admission: $1.50. Open Tues.–Sun. 10–4:15.*

Just south of Cedar Grove atop a hill sloping gently down to the Schuylkill is **Sweetbriar.** Built in 1797, it was the park's first year-round residence. *Lansdowne Dr. off N. Concourse Dr., West Fairmount Park, tel. 215/222–1333. Admission: $1.50. Open daily except Tues. 10–4. Call ahead.*

A trip farther down Lansdowne Drive takes you to the Philadelphia Zoological Gardens (*see* Parks, Zoos, and Gardens, *below*).

The northwest section of Fairmount Park is **the Wissahickon.** A gorge carved out by the Wissahickon Creek, it is 5½ miles of towering trees, cliffs, trails, and animals, and retains many traces of history.

Of the Philadelphia areas that William Penn encountered, the Wissahickon has changed the least. You can easily visualize the Lenni-Lenape Indians who lived there, beat its trails, and gave the creek its name. "Wissahickon" is an Anglicized version of the Lenni-Lenape words for yellow creek and catfish creek.

Forbidden Drive, a dirt-and-gravel pathway along the west side of the creek, is a haunt of joggers, bikers, horseback riders, fishermen, and nature lovers. For the more adventurous there are foot trails along both sides of the creek.

Many inns once stood along the banks of the Wissahickon; only two remain. One is a police station; the other is the **Valley Green Inn,** built in 1850 on the site of an earlier inn. It is today a restaurant filled with restored antiques and is the focal point of the Wissahickon.

The inn is nestled in one of the loveliest parts of the Wissahickon gorge. Sit on a bench alongside the creek, feed bread crumbs to the ducks, look at the stone bridge reflected in the water, and savor the beauty and the tranquillity. It's an experience you'll long remember.

Valley Green Inn is an excellent departure point for exploring the Wissahickon. You can saunter along one of the trails, enjoy the stream, lose yourself in the wilderness, and investigate some of the sights. To find the sights listed here, ask a mounted policeman or inquire at the inn; a map of the Wissahickon showing all the trails and sites is available ($4) at the inn's snack-booth window.

To reach Valley Green Inn, take the Schuylkill Expressway west to the Lincoln Drive–Wissahickon Park exit (Exit 32). Follow Lincoln Drive to Allen's Lane, then turn right. At Germantown Avenue turn left, go about a mile, turn left at Springfield Avenue, and follow it to the end.

South of Valley Green Inn About a quarter mile south of Valley Green Inn on the east side of the creek, near where Cresheim Creek joins the Wissahickon, is a picturesque spot with an intriguing name—**Devil's Pool.** Neighborhood kids dive off the rocks into the pool, which local legend says is bottomless. (It's really about 10 feet deep.) Along the path near the pool, look for **Shakespeare Rock,** with a quotation, appropriate to the setting, carved on its face:

The current that with gentle murmur glides
. . . makes sweet music with th' enamell'd stones,
Giving a gentle kiss to every sedge . . .
And so by many winding nooks he strays
With willing sport, to the wild ocean.

Fingerspan, the newest addition to the Wissahickon, is a steel sculpture of a bridge spanning a ravine. It was done by local artist Jody Pinto.

Toleration, a granite statue of William Penn erected in 1883, stands on Mom Rinker's Rock. This dramatic spot affords a magnificent view of the Wissahickon Valley.

Rittenhousetown, near where Forbidden Drive runs into Lincoln Drive, is a cluster of six small historic whitewashed Colonial buildings. One house, built in 1707, is the birthplace of David Rittenhouse, the clockmaker, astronomer, and patriot after whom Rittenhouse Square is named (*see* Tour 3, *above*). Built around 1683, the mill is the sole survivor of the 60 mills that once lined the Wissahickon. It was the first paper mill in America.

Hermit's Cave was a favorite hangout of the Wissahickon's most famous inhabitant, the German mystic Johannes Kelpius. In 1694, Kelpius and his followers, the Society of the Woman in the Wilderness, moved to the Wissahickon to await the millennium. Kelpius is buried in an unmarked grave near his cave. Look up and you'll see the graceful arch of the Henry Avenue Bridge and, nearby, the broad rock outcropping called **Lover's Leap**—for obvious reasons.

North of Valley Green Inn On the east side of the Rex Avenue Bridge (1 mile north of Valley Green Inn), a path through a stone arch leads up, up, up to **Indian Rock,** where the Lenni-Lenape held council until their disappearance from the valley around 1750. Atop the rock is a stone statue of a kneeling warrior, called Tedyuscung, after a local chief.

The red wooden **Covered Bridge** at the foot of Thomas Mill Road is 97 feet long and 14 feet wide. Built in 1855, it's the last covered bridge still standing within the boundaries of a major American city.

At the north end of Forbidden Drive (2½ miles north of Valley Green Inn) is the **Andorra Natural Area.** Its Tree House Visitors Center has exhibits, a reference library, self-guiding materials including trail maps, and a changing collection of local fauna—toads, rabbits, turtles, and snakes. Tree House hours vary, but the information center is always open (tel. 215/685–9285). The center's director, Sioux Baldwin, is probably the world's foremost authority on the Wissahickon.

To explore the Wissahickon in more detail, see *Rediscovering the Wissahickon*, by Sarah West. Published in 1993, the book gives mapped geology and history walks, plus information on the ecology, flora, and fauna of the valley.

Selected Neighborhoods Worth a Visit

Chinatown Philadelphia's numerous ethnic groups lend their distinctive qualities to the fabric of the city. One prominent group, the Chinese, has been here since the 19th century.

Centered on 10th and Race streets just two blocks north of Market Street, Chinatown serves as the residential and the commercial hub of the Chinese community. Along with more than 50 restaurants (*see* Chapter 6), Chinatown attractions include grocery stores, souvenir and gift shops, martial-arts studios, a fortune-cookie store, bilingual street signs, and red-and-green pagoda-style telephone booths.

One striking Chinatown site is the **Chinese Friendship Gate** straddling 10th Street at Arch Street. This intricate and colorful 40-foot-tall arch—the largest authentic Chinese gate outside China—was created by Chinese artisans, who brought their own tools and construction materials. The citizens of

Tianjin, Philadelphia's sister city in the People's Republic of China, donated the building materials, including the ornamental tile.

From February to May, you can celebrate Chinese New Year with a 10-course banquet at the **Chinese Cultural Center** (125 N. 10th St., tel. 215/923–6767). The center occupies an 1831 example of the Peking Mandarin palace style.

University City University City, in West Philadelphia directly west of Center City across the Schuylkill River, has three college campuses— the University of Pennsylvania, Drexel University, and the Philadelphia College of Pharmacy and Science. It also has the University City Science Center (a leading think tank), a large and impressive collection of houses, and a variety of restaurants, movie theaters, stores, and bars catering to students and other residents.

Prominent on your itinerary here should be the **University of Pennsylvania.** For a good look at the Ivy League campus stop at the **Information Center** at 34th and Walnut streets (tel. 215/ 898–1000), then follow **Locust Walk** between 33rd Street and 40th Street.

Starting at 33rd Street, you see **Franklin Field,** the university football stadium and home of the Penn Relays (*see* Festivals and Seasonal Events in Chapter 1; and Spectator Sports in Chapter 5). At 33rd and Spruce streets is the **University Museum** (*see* Libraries and Museums, *below*). And just north of Locust Walk along 33rd Street is the Moore School of Engineering, home of **ENIAC,** the world's first all-electronic general-purpose digital computer (*see* Off the Beaten Track, *below*).

At 34th Street and Locust Walk is the **Furness Building.** Formerly the university's main library and now the graduate-school fine-arts library, it is an architectural gem by the innovative Frank Furness. A $16½ million restoration by the architectural firm of Robert Venturi was completed in February 1991 to celebrate the building's centennial.

You're now at the edge of **College Green** (Blanche Levy Park), the crossroads of the campus. In the middle stands a statue of Benjamin Franklin, who founded the university in 1740. To your right, the huge **Van Pelt Library** stretches from 34th Street to 36th Street. In front is Claes Oldenburg's *Broken Button* statue. To your left is **College Hall,** an administration building said to be the inspiration for the scary Addams House of the cartoonist Charles Addams.

Just west of 36th Street, the **Annenberg School of Communication** and the **Annenberg Center** (*see* Chapter 8) are to the right, and the famed **Wharton School of Economics** is to the left. As you pass the intersection of 37th Street, say hello to Ben Franklin sitting on a bench.

At 38th Street is the well-stocked **University Bookstore** (*see* Chapter 4). A footbridge takes you over 38th Street (turn around for a good view of Center City) to **Superblock,** three high-rise student dormitories. Locust Walk ends at 40th Street with the Dental School, a row of stores, restaurants, and two movie theaters.

Two other notable university sights a short distance from Locust Walk are the **Hospital of the University of Pennsylvania** at

34th and Spruce streets and the **Quad** near 37th and Spruce streets. The university's first dorm buildings, the Quad was designed by Cope and Stewardson in 1895 and became the prototype of the Collegiate Gothic style prevalent in campuses coast to coast.

Germantown and Chestnut Hill In the late 1600s, Francis Pastorius led 13 families out of Germany to seek religious freedom in the New World. They settled 6 miles northwest of Philadelphia in what is now Germantown.

The Germantown area is rich in history. It was the site of Philadelphia's first gristmill (1683) and America's first paper mill (1690). The American Colonies' first English-language Bible was printed here (1743). By the time of the Revolution, Germantown had become a bustling industrial town. In 1777, Colonial troops under George Washington attacked part of the British force here and fought the Battle of Germantown in various skirmishes.

Germantown was incorporated into the City of Philadelphia when the city was consolidated in 1854. Today, Germantown is a successfully integrated neighborhood with a wealth of still-occupied and exceptionally well-preserved architectural masterpieces.

You can reach Germantown from Center City via the no. 23 trolley, by the two Chestnut Hill SEPTA commuter trains, or by car. The best way to tour the area is by car. From City Hall, drive north on Broad Street for about 3½ miles to Pike Street (two blocks north of Erie Ave.). Turn left, go one block to Germantown Avenue, and turn right.

About a mile up Germantown Avenue on the left side is **Loudon,** an 1801 Greek Revival house filled with antique furniture, household goods, and paintings. A fire in 1993 destroyed some of the home's contents. *4650 Germantown Ave., tel. 215/685-2067. Open Tues., Thurs., and Sat. 1-4. Call ahead as renovations may affect hours through 1994.*

Six blocks farther north is **Grumblethorpe.** Built by John Wister in 1744, this Georgian house is one of Germantown's leading examples of early 18th-century architecture. *5267 Germantown Ave., tel. 215/843-4820. Open Tues. and Thurs. 10-4.*

Two blocks north is the **Deshler-Morris House,** where President Washington lived in 1793-94 while the yellow-fever epidemic plagued Philadelphia. It was known as the Germantown White House. *5442 Germantown Ave., tel. 215/596-1748. Admission: $1 adults, 50¢ students. Open Tues.-Sun. 1-4. Closed Dec.-Mar.*

Across the street is the **Germantown Historical Society,** with a historical and genealogical library and collections of industrial and decorative arts. It also serves as an orientation point for visiting all the Germantown houses. *5501 Germantown Ave., tel. 215/844-0514. Open Tues. and Thurs. 10-4, Sun. 1-5.*

Both the house and the garden of **Wyck,** are notable examples of early-American lifestyle. The house remained in the ownership of the same Quaker family from 1736 to 1973. *6026 Germantown Ave., tel. 215/848-1690. Open Tues., Thurs., Sat. 1-4, and by appointment. Closed mid-Dec.-Mar.*

To see fabulous Germantown architecture, wander the area west of Wyck, between Walnut Lane and Tulpehocken Street.

Included here is the **Ebenezer Maxwell House.** Built in 1859, this Gothic extravaganza of elongated windows, arches, and a three-story tower is the incarnation of an old haunted house and Philadelphia's only mid-19th-century house-museum. *200 W. Tulpehocken St., tel. 215/438–1861. Admission: $4 adults, $3 senior citizens, $2 students. Open Thurs.–Sun. 1–4*

If you have time for only one site in Germantown, make it **Cliveden.** Built in 1763 by Benjamin Chew, Germantown's most elaborate country house was occupied by the British during the Revolution. On October 4, 1777, Washington's unsuccessful attempt to dislodge the British resulted in his defeat at the Battle of Germantown. You can still see bullet marks on the outside walls. Today a museum, the house occupies a 6-acre plot with outbuildings and a barn converted into offices and a gift shop. It remained in the Chew family until 1972, when it was donated to the National Trust for Historic Preservation. *6401 Germantown Ave., tel. 215/848–1777. Admission: $4 adults, $3 students. Open Tues.–Sat. 10–4, Sun. 1–4.*

Across the street from Cliveden is **Upsala,** built about 1755 and one of Germantown's best examples of Federal-style architecture. Continental troops set up their cannons on Upsala's front lawn and shelled the British at Cliveden. *6430 Germantown Ave., tel. 215/842–1798. Open Tues. and Thurs. 1–4. Closed Jan.–Mar.*

North of Germantown is the residential community of Mount Airy, and north of that is Chestnut Hill. One of Philadelphia's poshest neighborhoods, Chestnut Hill has numerous impressive mansions, more than 120 shops and restaurants, several art galleries, two train stations, and an arboretum.

Chestnut Hill sights include **Pastorius Park** at Lincoln Drive and Abington Avenue (one block west of the 8100 block of Germantown Ave.) and **Morris Arboretum** (*see* Parks, Zoos, and Gardens, *below*). The **Woodmere Art Museum** (9201 Germantown Ave., tel. 215/247–0476) displays paintings, tapestries, sculpture, porcelains, ivories, Japanese rugs, and works by contemporary local artists.

Historical Buildings and Sites

Many of Philadelphia's historic sites have been described in the Exploring section. Here are some that are not on the tours.

Andalusia. In the early 1800s, Philadelphia banker Nicholas Biddle toured Greece and returned determined to re-create its architecture in his backyard. He commissioned the prominent architect Thomas U. Walter to add a Doric colonnade and other alterations to his 18th-century farmhouse, Andalusia, which transformed it into one of the nation's first examples of Greek Revival architecture. Wander throughout the 220-acre estate to see the boxwood and rose gardens, various outbuildings, and the grotto. The house remains in the Biddle family; it is administered by the National Trust for Historic Preservation. *State Rd., Andalusia, Bucks County, tel. 215/848–1777. Cost: $9 per person, 7-person minimum. Open for guided tours Tues.–Sat. 10–2, by appointment only; 10 days' notice requested.*

Gloria Dei. One of the few remnants of the Swedes who settled Pennsylvania before William Penn is Gloria Dei (Old Swedes') Church. Organized in 1642, Gloria Dei is the oldest church in

Pennsylvania. Built in 1698, the church has numerous religious artifacts, such as a 1608 Bible owned by the Swedish Queen Christiana, and carvings on the lectern and the balcony salvaged from the congregation's first church, which was destroyed by fire. Models of two of the ships that transported the first Swedish settlers hang from the ceiling—right in the center of the church. Grouped around the church are the parish hall, caretaker's house, rectory, guild house, and graveyard. *916 Swanson St., near Christian and Delaware Aves., tel. 215/ 389–1513. Usually open daily 9–5, but it's best to call first.*

Mikveh Israel Synagogue and Cemetery. Nathan Levy, a Colonial merchant whose ship, *The Myrtilla*, brought the Liberty Bell to America, organized the synagogue in 1740. It is the oldest synagogue in Philadelphia and the second-oldest in the United States. Originally located at 3rd and Cherry streets, it now occupies the same building as the National Museum of American Jewish History (*see* Libraries and Museums, *below*). The cemetery was organized in 1738. Levy acquired the land from William Penn as a family burial ground, and it was later expanded to accommodate the Jewish community. Buried there are Haym Salomon, financier of the American Revolution, and Rebecca Gratz, the inspiration for Rebecca in Sir Walter Scott's novel *Ivanhoe*. *Synagogue: 44 N. 4th St., tel. 215/ 922–5446. Open Mon.–Thurs. 10–5, Fri. 10–3, Sun. noon–5. Services Sat. 9 AM and Fri. evenings. Cemetery: Spruce St. between 8th and 9th Sts., tel. 215/922–5446. A guide is present in summer, weekdays 10–4. From Sept. to June, visiting arrangements can be made through the Park Service or the synagogue.*

Fort Mifflin. Because of its Quaker origins, Philadelphia had no defenses until 1772, when the British began building Fort Mifflin. It was completed in 1776 by Revolutionary forces under General Washington. In a 40-day battle in 1777, 300 Continental defenders held off British forces long enough for Washington's troops to flee to Valley Forge. The fort was almost totally destroyed and was rebuilt in 1798 from plans by Pierre Charles L'Enfant, who designed the plan for Washington, D.C. In use until 1962, the fort has served as a prisoner-of-war camp, an artillery battalion, and a munitions dump. On the 49-acre National Historic Landmark, you can see its cannons and carriages, officers' quarters, soldiers' barracks (which contain an exhibit called "Defense of the Delaware"), an artillery shed, a blacksmith shop, a bomb shelter, and a museum. *Island Rd. and Hog Island Rd. on the Delaware River near Philadelphia International Airport, tel. 215/365–9781. Admission: $2 adults, $1 children under 12. Open Wed.–Sun. 10–4. Tours at 11, 1, and 3. Closed mid-Dec.–early Mar.*

Pennsylvania Hospital. Another in the long list of "firsts" and institutions founded by Benjamin Franklin is Pennsylvania Hospital, the oldest hospital in the United States. Inside the fine 18th-century original buildings are the nation's first medical library and first surgical amphitheater, an 1804 innovation with a skylight, and the only one still in existence. It also has a portrait gallery, early medical instruments, art objects, and a rare-book library with items that date from 1762. The artwork includes the Benjamin West painting *Christ Healing the Sick in the Temple*. Today Pennsylvania Hospital is a full-service modern medical center. Pick up a copy of *Pennsylvania Hospital: A Walking Tour* in the marketing department on the second floor of the Pine Building. *8th and Spruce Sts., tel. 215/829–3971. Admission free. Open weekdays 8:30–5. Call to arrange a guided group tour.*

Libraries and Museums

Libraries If you want to read or do research, Philadelphia is the place to be. In addition to the Free Library—the vast public-library system—the city also has some of the oldest, largest, and most comprehensive private collections in the country. All five libraries described below are located within the boundaries of our downtown Exploring tours, and all are open to the public.

Housed in a national landmark Italianate brownstone dating from the mid-1800s, the **Athenaeum of Philadelphia** is a research library specializing in 19th-century social and cultural history. Founded in 1814, the library contains significant materials on the French in America and early American travel, exploration, and transportation. Its American Architecture Collection has close to a million items. Besides books, the Athenaeum houses notable paintings and period furniture. *219 S. 6th St., tel. 215/925–2688. Admission free; tours by appointment. Open weekdays 9–5.*

Free Library of Philadelphia. Philadelphia calls its public-library system the Fabulous Freebie. Founded in 1891, the central library has more than 1 million volumes. With its grand entrance hall, sweeping marble staircase, 30-foot ceilings, enormous reading rooms with long tables and spiral staircases leading to balconies, this Greek Revival building looks the way libraries ought to look. With more than 12,000 musical scores, the Edwin S. Fleisher Collection is the largest of its kind in the world. Tormented by a tune whose name you can't recall? Hum it to one of the Music Room's librarians and he'll track it down. The Social Science and History Department has nearly 100,000 charts, maps, and guidebooks. The Newspaper Room stocks papers from all major U.S. and foreign cities and back issues on microfilm, some going all the way back to Colonial times. The Rare Book Room is a beautiful suite that has first editions of Dickens, ancient Sumerian clay tablets, illuminated medieval manuscripts, and more-modern manuscripts, including Poe's *Murders in the Rue Morgue* and "The Raven." *19th St. and Benjamin Franklin Pkwy., tel. 215/686–5322. Open Mon.– Wed. 9–9, Thurs. and Fri. 9–6, Sat. 9–5, Sun. 1–5. Closed Sun. June–Aug. Tours of Rare Book Room Mon.–Fri. at 11.*

The **Historical Society of Pennsylvania** contains more than a half-million books and 14 million manuscripts—the largest privately owned manuscript collection in the United States. Founded in 1824 for the purpose of "elucidating the history of the state," the society has expanded its scope to cover the original 13 colonies. Notable items from the collection include Penn family archives, President Buchanan's papers, a printer's proof of the Declaration of Independence, and the first draft of the Constitution. The staff in the genealogical library will help you trace your roots. The first floor has changing exhibits from the permanent collection of portraits and artifacts. Paintings include the earliest portrait of Washington (1772) and the last of Franklin (1789), both by Charles Willson Peale. *1300 Locust St., tel. 215/732–6200. Use of library $5; museum and exhibits $2.50. Open Tues.–Sat. 10–5, Wed. 1–9.*

The **Library of the American Philosophical Society** is one of the country's leading institutions for the study of science. Its collection includes first editions of Newton's *Principia Mathematica*, Franklin's *Experiments and Observations*, and Darwin's *On the Origin of Species*. The collection also covers American natural history, medical science, and American Indians. Here you'll find many of Franklin's original books and papers as well as journals from the Lewis and Clark expedition of 1803–1806. Non-research visitors can view the lobby exhibit, recently "Thomas Jefferson Statesman of Science." *105 S. 5th St., tel. 215/440–3400. Admission free. Open weekdays 9–4:45.*

Founded in 1731, the **Library Company of Philadelphia** is one of the oldest cultural institutions in the United States and the only major Colonial American library that has survived virtually intact. From 1774 to 1800, it functioned as the de facto Library of Congress, and until the late 19th century it was the city library. Its membership has included 10 signers of the Declaration of Independence, among them Robert Morris, Benjamin Rush, and Thomas McKean. The 400,000-volume collection includes 200,000 rare books. First editions—many of which were acquired when they were first published—include Melville's *Moby Dick* and Whitman's *Leaves of Grass*. The library is particularly rich in Americana up to 1880, black history to 1915, the history of science, and women's history. *1314 Locust St., tel. 215/546–3181. Admission free. Open weekdays 9–4:45.*

Museums Some of Philadelphia's most interesting museums fall outside the confines of our walking tours but are most certainly worth a visit. Here are a few:

Afro-American Historical and Cultural Museum. Opened in the Bicentennial year of 1976, this is the first museum of its kind funded and built by a city. Exhibits are dedicated to the history, arts, crafts, and culture of blacks in the United States—with a focus on blacks of Philadelphia and Pennsylvania. Recent exhibits included "The Great Migration" from the South to the North between the 1880s and World War I and "Black Photographers Bear Witness." Every year the museum presents a "Jazz and Music" series and a literary series with appearances by major black writers. Its bookshop offers the area's widest selection on black culture, history, fiction, poetry, and drama. The gift shop features carvings from Togo, Senegal, and Ghana, and hand-cut jewelry from Zaire. *7th and Arch Sts., tel. 215/574–0380. Admission: $3.50 adults, $1.75 senior citizens and children. Open Tues.–Sat. 10–5, Sun. noon–6.*

American-Swedish Historical Museum. The Swedes settled the Delaware Valley in the mid-1600s before William Penn but few traces remain other than Old Swedes' Church (Gloria Dei) (*see* Historical Buildings and Sites, *above*) and the American-Swedish Historical Museum. Modeled after a 17th-century Swedish manor house and located on land settled by the Swedes, the museum's 14 galleries trace the history of Swedes in the United States. The newest exhibit is "Before Penn," the nation's only permanent exhibit on the New Sweden colony. The John Ericsson room honors the designer of the Civil War ironclad ship, the *Monitor;* the Jenny Lind room contains memorabilia from the Swedish Nightingale's American tour of 1848 to 1851; other rooms display handmade, costumed Swedish peasant dolls; crafts; paintings; and drawings. *1900 Pattison Ave., tel.*

215/389-1776. Admission: $2 adults, $1 students and senior citizens, children under 12 free. Open Tues.-Fri. 10-4, Sat. and Sun. noon-4.

Atwater Kent Museum. Founded in 1938 and housed in an elegant 1826 Greek Revival building, the museum portrays Philadelphia history from the beginning to the present day. It includes exhibits on municipal services such as police, fire, water, and gas; shipbuilding; model streets and railroads; and maps showing the city's development. One gallery, "The City Beneath Our Feet," has changing exhibits culled from the thousands of artifacts uncovered during 20th-century excavations. Recent temporary exhibits have included "Tune In—Philadelphia Radio, 1820–1950." *15 S. 7th St., tel. 215/922-3031. Admission free. Open Tues.-Sat. 9:30-4:45.*

Balch Institute for Ethnic Studies. More a research center than a museum, the Balch Institute has a 60,000-volume library on immigration history and ethnicity. The institute's permanent exhibit, "Freedom's Doors—Immigrant Points of Entry to the U.S.," focuses on immigration in port cities such as Philadelphia, Boston, and Baltimore. Recent temporary exhibits have included "The Korean Community in the Delaware Valley" and "Ethnic Images in Toys and Games." *18 S. 7th St., tel. 215/925-8090. Suggested donation: $2 adults; $1 students, senior citizens, and children. Exhibits open Mon.-Sat. 10-4, library 9-5.*

Barnes Foundation. Located just over the city line in Merion (Montgomery County) is one of the Philadelphia area's best attractions, and one of the great collections of paintings in the world. The Barnes Foundation contains more than 1,000 works—mostly French Impressionists—hung one on top of another just as Dr. Albert C. Barnes left them. Barnes made millions from the invention of Argyrol, an eye disinfectant, and he spent it on art. The collection includes 175 Renoirs, 66 Cézannes, 65 Matisses, and numerous works by van Gogh, Rousseau, Degas, El Greco, and Tintoretto, among many others. The museum, which was Barnes's home, also has Pennsylvania Dutch bric-a-brac, Mayan ornaments, and 16th-century Chinese art. Interested in art for teaching's sake, Barnes wanted no part of the art establishment, critics, or the general public: Until a 1961 court order, the collection was open only to students. Barnes's public-be-damned attitude has been more or less perpetuated: Hours are limited; no catalogue of the works has even been published; there's no gift shop and no postcards for sale. The board is proposing numerous changes, including selling some of the paintings. *300 Latches La., Merion, tel. 215/667-0290. Closed for renovations till 1995. Call for new schedule and admission prices.*

Mummers Museum. Even if you aren't in Philadelphia on New Year's Day, here's a chance to see a unique local institution and a phenomenon. Famous for extravagant sequined-and-feathered costumes and string bands, the Mummers spend the entire year preparing for an all-day parade up Broad Street every January 1. The museum has costumes, photos of parades from as far back as the turn of the century, and audiovisual displays of Mummerabilia. You can push buttons to compose your own Mummers medley with banjos, saxophones, and xylophones, and dance the Mummers strut to the strains of "Oh, 'Dem Golden Slippers." A 45-inch screen shows filmed highlights of past parades. On most Tuesday evenings from May to September, the museum presents free outdoor concerts (weather permitting). *2nd St. and Washington Ave., tel. 215/336–3050. Admission: $2.50 adults, $2 children under 12 and senior citizens. Open Tues.–Sat. 9:30–5, Sun. noon–5.*

Mutter Museum. Skulls, antique microscopes, and a cancerous tumor removed from President Grover Cleveland's mouth in 1893 form just part of the medical collection in the Mutter Museum. The museum has hundreds of anatomical and pathological specimens, medical instruments, and organs removed from patients, including John Marshall's bladder stones and a piece of John Wilkes Booth's neck tissue. The collection contains 139 skulls plus items belonging to Madame Curie, Louis Pasteur, and Joseph Lister. Also included is a 7-foot-6-inch skeleton, the tallest on public exhibition in the United States. The autopsy of Chang and Eng (the original Siamese twins) was done here, and the museum displays their joined livers and a plaster cast of their torsos. *19 S. 22nd St., tel. 215/563–3737 ext. 241. Admission free; donations accepted. Open Tues.–Fri. 10–4.*

National Museum of American Jewish History. This is the only museum in the country devoted to Jewish participation in the growth and development of America. It opened on July 4, 1976. Its permanent exhibit, the "American Jewish Experience," documents American Jewish history from 1654 to the present. It also has changing exhibits, lectures, workshops, films, and theater; and a collection of art, artifacts, and archival material. *55 N. 5th St., tel. 215/923–3811. Admission: $2.50 adults, $1.75 senior citizens and students, $1.25 children under 12. Open Mon.–Thurs. 10–5, Fri. 10–3, Sun. noon–5.*

Poe House. Edgar Allan Poe lived here, the only one of his Philadelphia residences still standing, from 1843 to 1844. During that time, some of his best-known short stories were published: "The Telltale Heart," "The Black Cat," and "The Gold Bug." You can tour the 19th-century three-story brick house; to evoke the spirit of Poe, the National Park Service deliberately keeps the house empty. The adjoining house has exhibits on Poe and his family, his work habits, his literary contemporaries, and his "statement of taste," an eight-minute slide show and a small Poe library; and a reading room. At night, a statue in the garden casts the eerie shadow of a raven across the side of the house. *532 N. 7th St., tel. 215/597–8780. Admission free. Open daily 9–5.*

Norman Rockwell Museum. The Curtis Publishing Company Building, where Rockwell delivered his paintings to the editors of the *Saturday Evening Post*, now has the world's largest collection of the artist's works. Displays include all 324 Rockwell *Post* cover illustrations; lithographs, prints, collotypes, and sketches; and a replica of his studio in Stockbridge, Massachusetts. A 10-minute video illustrates Rockwell's life. *6th and Sansom Sts. (lower level), tel. 215/922–4345. Admission: $2 adults, $1.50 senior citizens, children under 12 free when accompanied by an adult. Open Mon.–Sat. 10–4, Sun. 11–4.*

Shoe Collection. Housed on the sixth floor of the Pennsylvania College of Podiatric Medicine, this unusual museum displays 500 pairs of "Footwear Through the Ages." The collection includes burial sandals from ancient Egypt, Eskimo snowshoes, Moroccan two-heeled shoes, and shoes used in the footbinding of Chinese women. Celebrity items include basketball-player Julius Erving's huge sneakers, Joe Frazier's boxing shoes, Billie Jean King's tennis shoes, and Bernie Parent's hockey skates. *8th and Race Sts., tel. 215/629-0300 ext. 185. Open weekdays 9-4. Call to arrange a tour.*

University Museum. Indiana Jones, look out! Rare treasures from the deepest jungles and most ancient tombs make this one of the finest archaeological/anthropological museums in the world. The collection of more than a million objects, gathered largely during worldwide expeditions by University of Pennsylvania scholars, includes a 12-ton giant sphinx from Egypt, a crystal ball owned by China's dowager empress, the world's oldest writing—Sumerian cuneiform clay tablets—and the 4,500-year-old golden jewels from the royal tombs of Ur. Kids run to "The Egyptian Mummy: Secrets and Science" exhibit. Exhibits in 1992 will include "River of Gold: Precolumbian Treasures." *33rd and Spruce Sts., tel. 215/898-4000. Suggested donation: $5 adults, $2.50 children and senior citizens. Open Tues.-Sat. 10-4:30, Sun. 1-5. Closed Sun. Memorial Day to Labor Day.*

The War Library and Museum. This is one of the premier collections of Civil War memorabilia in the Union. Artifacts include two life masks of Abraham Lincoln, dress uniforms and swords of Generals Grant and Meade, plus many other weapons, uniforms, and personal effects of Civil War officers and enlisted men. The library has more than 12,000 volumes on the war. *1805 Pine St., tel. 215/735-8196. Admission: $3. Open Mon.-Sat. 10-4, Sun. 11-4.*

Wagner Free Institute of Science. Well worth the trip to one of Philadelphia's poorest inner-city neighborhoods, this museum consists of an 1865 building with one huge exhibition hall. It's like a museum of a museum—hardly anything has changed in 125 years. The 21,000-specimen collection includes mollusks, minerals, birds, fish, and dinosaur bones. The building and museum are a National Historic Landmark. *17th St. and Montgomery Ave., tel. 215/763-6529. Admission free. Open Tues.-Fri. 9-4. Call ahead for groups.*

Parks, Zoos, and Gardens

In addition to Fairmount Park (*see* Fairmount Park Tour, *above*), Philadelphia boasts recreational areas that range from peaceful landscaped grounds to wilderness preserves.

Bartram's Garden is a 44-acre oasis tucked into a heavily industrialized and depressed corner of southwest Philadelphia. Begun in 1728 by John Bartram, America's oldest surviving botanic garden has remained relatively unchanged while the surrounding areas have altered dramatically. With stone columns and carvings by Bartram himself, the 18th-century farmhouse on the grounds reflects his peculiar vision of classical and Colonial architecture. The self-trained Bartram became botanist to King George III, traveling throughout the Colonies and returning with many unusual species. The house is a National Historic Landmark, and the trails extending to the Schuylkill River are part of the National Recreation Trails System. *54th St. and Lindbergh Blvd., tel. 215/729-5281. Garden open daily, admission free. House open noon-4 Wed.-Sun. May-Oct.; Wed.-Fri. Nov.-Apr. Admission: House and garden tour*

$4.50 adults, $3 children 6–18; house tour only $2 adults, $1 children. No. 36 trolley from City Hall stops at the entrance.

Horticulture Center. Standing on the site of the 1876 Centennial Exposition's Horticultural Hall, the Horticulture Center consists of 22 wooded acres, a display house, and a greenhouse where plants and flowers used on city property are grown. Don't miss the whimsical *Seaweed Girl* fountain in the display house. *N. Horticultural Dr., West Fairmount Park, tel. 215/ 879–4062. Donation ($1) requested. Open daily 9–3. Fairmount Park Trolley Bus stops at door.*

Morris Arboretum. In the very northwest corner of the city, you'll find 166 acres of romantic landscaped seclusion. Morris Arboretum of the University of Pennsylvania is an eclectic retreat with a formal rose garden, English garden, Japanese garden, meadows, and woodlands. Begun in 1887 by siblings John and Lydia Morris and bequeathed to the University of Pennsylvania in 1932, the arboretum typifies Victorian-era garden design, with winding paths, a hidden grotto, tropical ferns, and natural woodland. It has 3,500 trees and shrubs from around the world, including one of the finest collections of Asian plants outside Asia. *Hillcrest Ave. between Germantown and Stenton Aves., Chestnut Hill, tel. 215/247–5777. Admission: $3 adults, $1.50 children and senior citizens. Open daily 10–5 Apr.–Oct.; 10–4 Nov.–Mar. Guided tours weekends at 2. Chestnut Hill East or West commuter trains stop a half-mile away; L bus stops at corner of Hillcrest and Germantown Aves.*

Schuylkill Center for Environmental Education consists of more than 500 acres of wildflowers, ferns, and thickets; ponds, streams, and woodlands; 6 miles of winding trails; and the 8-acre Pine Plantation. You may spot deer, hawks, Canada geese, red fox, and other animals. Hands-on exhibits in the Discovery Museum explain the flora and fauna you see outside. Nature programs on Saturday and Sunday. The bookstore and gift shop follow the nature theme. *8480 Hagy's Mill Rd., Roxborough, tel. 215/482–7300. Admission: $5 adults, $3 children. Open Mon.–Sat. 8:30–5, Sun. 1–5. Closed Sun. in Aug. No. 27 bus stops at Ridge Pike and Port Royal Ave. 1 mi away.*

Tinicum National Environmental Center hosts more than 280 species of ducks, herons, egrets, geese, gallinules, and other birds. Resident earthbound animals include turtles, foxes, muskrats, deer, raccoons, weasels, and snakes. Facilities in this 900-acre wetland, the largest remaining in Pennsylvania (it used to be 6,000 acres), include 8 miles of foot trails, an observation blind, an observation deck, boardwalks through the wet areas, and a canoe launch into the 4½-mile stretch of Darby Creek that runs through the preserve (the best way to see it). Bird-watchers can prepare for their visit by calling 215/567-BIRD for recent sightings. *86th St. and Lindbergh Blvd., tel. 215/365–3118 or 215/521–0662. Admission free. Open daily 8 AM–sunset; visitor center open daily 9–4. The U and no. 37 buses stop nearby.*

Philadelphia Zoological Gardens. Opened in 1874, America's first zoo displays 1,600 animals on 42 acres. Orangutans, gorillas, gibbons, mandrills, and lemurs romp in the World of Primates, a 1-acre outdoor jungle. The African Plain is the stomping ground of giraffes, zebras, and rhinoceroses. Bear Country offers up-close views of sloths, spectacled bears, and polar bears diving off 12-foot cliffs. The George D. Widener Memorial Treehouse provides an animal's-eye view of a four-story tropical tree. The Children's Zoo has pony rides, a petting area, and a sea lion show. In 1993, two rare white lions were added to the zoo. *34th St. and Girard Ave., tel. 215/243–1100. Admission: $7 adults, $5.50 children 2–11 and senior citizens, children under 2 free. Additional charge for Treehouse. Open Mon.–Fri. 9:30–5, Sat. and Sun. 9:30–6.*

Philadelphia for Free

Philadelphia has myriad free events and attractions. Those listed elsewhere in this book include all sites mentioned in **Off the Beaten Track,** below, and all libraries cited in **Libraries and Museums,** above.

In Exploring:

All sites in Independence National Historical Park
Many of the sites in Fairmount Park
Betsy Ross House
Christ Church Burial Ground
City Hall
Curtis Institute of Music recitals
Fireman's Hall
Masonic Temple
Pennsylvania Academy of the Fine Arts (Sat. 10–1)
Philadelphia Museum of Art (Sun. 10–1)
Rodin Museum
U.S. Mint

In Seasonal Events:

All parades and many of the other events listed

In The Arts and Nightlife:

Philadelphia Orchestra Concerts at Mann Music Center

In What to See and Do with Children:

Smith Playground

In Parks, Zoos, and Gardens:

Tinicum Wildlife Preserve

In Museums:

Wagner Free Institute of Science

Others not covered elsewhere:

University of the Arts (320 S. Broad St., tel. 215/875–2200). You can attend student and faculty piano recitals, dance concerts, orchestra performances, and choral programs.

Fleisher Art Memorial (709 Catherine St., tel. 215/922–3456). This art school in a former house has a gallery of changing exhibits and the Sanctuary, a 19th-century Romanesque chapel.

Philadelphia Navy Base and Naval Shipyard (foot of Broad St., tel. 215/897–8775). Take a guided bus tour past the shipyard's battleships, destroyers, a 300-ton shipbuilding crane, submarines, cruisers, and the quarters of officers and enlisted men. Tours are given Friday mornings at 10 and are very popular; call weeks ahead for reservations.

What to See and Do with Children

W. C. Fields may have disliked children, but children love his hometown. In addition to places and events that appeal to children and adults alike, Philadelphia has many special attractions just for kids. This section describes some of the best; others are covered in other sections.

Annenberg Center Theater for Children (37th and Walnut Sts., tel. 215/898–6791). Part of a distinguished full-scale theater program, the Annenberg Center Theater for Children schedules productions in October, February, and April. The annual Philadelphia International Theater Festival for Children, held for five days at the end of May, features professional theater companies from around the world specializing in music, magic, dance, and circus performances.

Free Library Children's Department. With 100,000 books for preschoolers to eighth-graders, the Children's Department houses the city's largest collection of children's books in a made-for-kids setting (the infant-toddler corner, for instance, has infant-toddler-size furniture). Historical collections include such series as the Hardy Boys and Nancy Drew over which adults wax nostalgic. The foreign-language collection has children's books in more than 50 languages. The department holds story hours and film festivals; the annual Spring Book Review features reading lists, displays, and reviews of the previous year's best children's books. *19th St. and Benjamin Franklin Pkwy., tel. 215/686–5372. Open weekdays 9–6, Sat. 9–5, Sun. 1–5.*

Philadelphia Marionette Theater schedules hour-long performances featuring puppets, music, and magic introduced by a lecture-demonstration. Scheduled shows include *Jack and the Beanstalk, Pinocchio,* and *Peter and the Wolf.* Reservations a must. *Playhouse in the Park, Belmont Mansion Dr., West Fairmount Park, tel. 215/879–1213. Admission: $4.50. Performances weekdays at 10:30, some Sun. at 2.*

Sesame Place. A one-hour drive from Center City, Sesame Place is an amusement park based on the popular public-television show. Children play and learn, just as they are encouraged to on the show. It has Muppet characters, animal shows, computer games, climbing tunnels, playgrounds, a water park (bring a bathing suit), and healthful food. It's geared to children ages 3 to 13. *100 Sesame Rd., Langhorne, tel. 215/757–1100. Admission: $19.95. Open May–mid-Sept., daily; mid-Sept.–mid-Oct., weekends only. Call for hours.*

Smith Playground. This mansion, built just for kids, was donated to the city in 1899 by Richard and Sarah Smith in memory of their son Stanfield. For kids five and under the mansion has playrooms, a nature den, and a minivillage with metal kiddie cars from the 1950s. The playground has picnic tables, grills, Jungle Gyms, swings, and an enclosed wooden slide wide enough for 10 children. It also has a wading pool, swimming pool, and equipment for disabled children. Although located at the edge of a disadvantaged inner-city neighborhood, it's a wonderful place to take the children. *33rd and Oxford Sts., East Fairmount Park, tel. 215/765–4325. House open Mon.–Sat. 10–3:30; playground 9–4:45.*

The following children's activities are discussed in other sections, as noted.

Academy of Natural Sciences (*see* Tour 4, *above*).

Franklin Institute Science Museum and Fels Planetarium (*see* Tour 4, *above*).

Penn's Landing: sailing ships, battleships, submarine, pleasure boats (*see* Tour 2, *above*).

Philadelphia Zoological Gardens—especially the Children's Zoo, treehouse, jungle bird walk, and wolf woods (*see* Parks, Zoos, and Gardens, *above*).

Please Touch Museum (*see* Tour 4, *above*).

University Museum of the University of Pennsylvania (*see* Libraries and Museums, *above*).

Off the Beaten Track

Benjamin Franklin Bridge. Cars, trucks, and trains zoom past, and brisk winds make your face tingle as you cross the Delaware River (150 feet below) and get the best view of riverfront Philadelphia. Walking across the Benjamin Franklin Bridge is an adventure few people undertake. When it opened in 1926, its 1,750-foot main span made it the longest suspension bridge in the world. It was designed by Paul Cret, architect of the Rodin Museum. After a new blue paint job and a lighting system specially designed to show off its contours, the bridge is more beautiful than ever. Start the 1.8-mile walk from either the Philadelphia or the Camden side. Only the south walkway is open, but that's the best view anyway. *5th and Vine Sts., tel. 215/925-8780. Admission free. Open daily (except a few days in winter when it gets too icy) 6 AM until around 7 PM (closes earlier in winter).*

Bryn Athyn Cathedral. Located at one of the most beautiful spots in the Philadelphia area is a spectacular cathedral built in 12th-century Romanesque and 14th-century Gothic styles. Atop a hill overlooking the Pennypack Valley, the cathedral is the episcopal seat of the Church of the New Jerusalem, a sect based on the writings of the Swedish scientist and mystic Emanuel Swedenborg. The main patrons of the church are descendants of John Pitcairn, an industrialist who made his fortune in paint and plate glass. Construction of the cathedral began in 1914 and went on for decades. It was built according to the medieval guild system: All materials—wood, metal, glass, stone—were brought to craftsmen at the site, and everything was fashioned by hand. The stained glass includes two colors, striated ruby and cobalt blue, found nowhere else in the Americas. Also on the hill is the former home of Raymond and Mildred Pitcairn, Glencairn, a neo-Romanesque building that's now a museum. *Rte. 232 (Huntingdon Pike) and Paper Mill Rd., Bryn Athyn 19009, 15 mi north of Center City, tel. 215/947-0266. Admission free. Open weekdays 10-5. Visitors are welcome at services Sun. 9:30 and 11. Tours Sat. and Sun. 1-4:30 PM. Visiting hours sometimes pre-empted by special church events. Directions: Go north on Broad St. to Rte. 611, right on County Line Rd., south on Rte. 232 to the 2nd traffic light. It's the cathedral on your right.*

Philadelphia City Council. For drama, comedy, and adventure, nothing rivals the Philadelphia city government. Some of the 17-member legislative branch of municipal government are capable and dedicated, but lawmaking often takes a back seat to righteous indignation, playing to the crowd, outrage, and profanity. Fistfights between council members occasionally break out. In the past 20 years, a half-dozen council members (including one former council president) have been convicted of crimes. Under the leadership of John Street, who became Council President in 1992, the council is becoming less "theater of the absurd" and more "political process." Bad news for theater-goers, good news for Philadelphians. *City Hall, Broad and Market Sts., Council Chamber, Room 400, tel. 215/686-3432. Admission free. Meets Thurs. 10 AM.*

ENIAC. Here's a chance for computer aficionados to see the place where the computer age dawned. During World War II, engineers at the Moore School of Engineering at the University of Pennsylvania undertook a secret project to develop the world's first all-electronic, large-scale, general-purpose digital computer. They called it ENIAC, an acronym for electronic numerical integrator and calculator. The largest electronic machine in the world, it weighed 30 tons and contained 18,000 vacuum tubes—one of which, in the beginning, burned out every few seconds. While most of ENIAC is now in the Smithsonian Institution, a small portion is still on view at the Moore School. Photos and informative signs tell ENIAC's story. *Moore School of Electrical Engineering, University of Pennsylvania, 200 S. 33rd St., tel. 215/898-8294. Enter on 33rd St. just below Walnut St. The room containing ENIAC, at the top of the steps on the right, is usually locked, but you can always see the exhibit through the glass wall. Admission free. Open weekdays 9-5.*

Laurel Hill Cemetery is beautiful and a great place for a stroll. John Notman, architect of the Athenaeum (*see* Libraries and Museums, *above*) and many other noted local buildings, designed Laurel Hill in 1836. It is an important example of an early rural burial ground and the first cemetery in America designed by an architect. Its rolling hills that overlook the Schuylkill River, its rare trees, and monuments and mausoleums sculpted by greats such as Notman, Alexander Milne Calder, Alexander Stirling Calder, William Strickland, and Thomas U. Walter made it a popular picnic spot in the 19th century. Those buried in this 99-acre necropolis include prominent Philadelphians and Declaration of Independence signers. Burials still take place. *3822 Ridge Ave., East Fairmount Park, tel. 215/228-8200. Open weekdays 8-4, Sat. 9-1, closed Sun. Friends of Laurel Hill Cemetery arranges tours (tel. 215/648-0824). Directions: Go north on East River Dr., turn right on Ferry Rd. (the 1st street after the 1st traffic light), go 1 block to Ridge Ave., turn right. The cemetery entrance is about a half-mile on your right.*

The Insectarium. Here you'll find a horrible, ugly, beautiful, diverse collection of 1,500 different creepy crawlers—tarantulas, giant centipedes, scorpions, assassin bugs, butterflies, and metallic beetles that look like gold pieces of jewelry. Even if you hate bugs, you'll love this place. Best bug gift shop in town! *8046 Frankfurt Ave., Northeast Philadelphia, tel. 215/338-3000. Admission: $3.00. Open Mon.-Sat. 10-4.*

4 Shopping

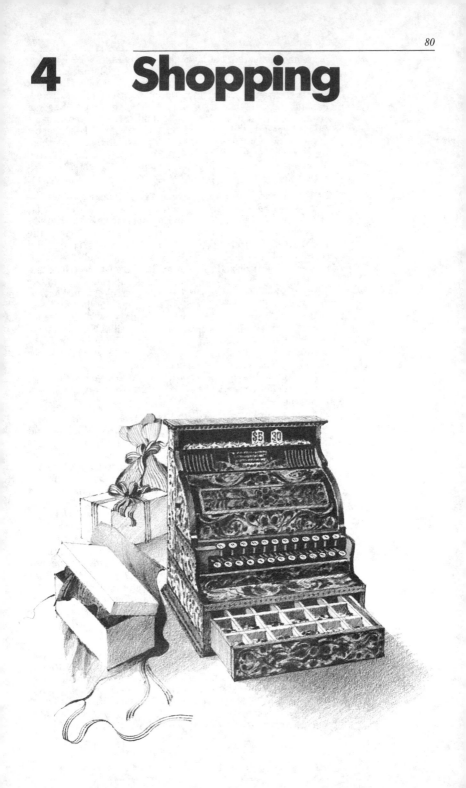

*By Rathe Miller
and Michael
Schwager*

Philadelphia is a shopper's paradise. It has an upscale shopping district centered on 17th and Walnut streets, a jewelers' row, an antiques row, the first downtown indoor shopping mall in the United States, an outdoor food market that covers five city blocks, and numerous department stores including one of the oldest and most elegant in the country.

Bargains are available, too—from discount stores, street vendors, and factory outlets.

You can also buy mementos of Philadelphia: from $1 parchment-like copies of the Declaration of Independence to $500 reproductions of the inkwell used in the signing of the Declaration. One T-shirt store, Destination Philadelphia, sells more than 40 designs featuring Philadelphia. Other stores sell posters of the art museum, Boathouse Row, and Independence Hall.

The leading shopping area is **Walnut Street** between Broad Street and Rittenhouse Square, and the intersecting streets just north and south. These blocks are filled with boutiques, art galleries, jewelers, fine clothing stores, and many other unusual shops. On 18th Street in the block north of Rittenhouse Square, for example, you'll find entrepreneurs both indoors and out: the youthful and trendy department store Urban Outfitters, street-vendor Mary Grace Gardner who sells handmade Peruvian shawls, street-artist Joe Barker who paints watercolors of Philadelphia cityscapes, and a shop that sells more than 40 flavors of frozen yogurt (Scoop De Ville).

The **Chestnut Street Transitway** has rare-book sellers, custom tailors, sporting-goods stores, pinball arcades, and discount drugstores. At 17th and Chestnut streets you'll find **The Shops at Liberty Place.** The city's newest shopping complex includes more than 60 stores and restaurants arranged in two circular levels under a striking 90-foot glass atrium.

A block north of Chestnut Street is Philadelphia's landmark effort at urban renewal cum shopping, the **Gallery at Market East** (tel. 215/925–7162), America's first enclosed downtown shopping mall. The four-level glass-roofed structure on Market Street from 8th Street to 11th Street contains 220 retailers, including 50 food outlets and two department stores—Strawbridge and Clothier (tel. 215/629–6000) and J. C. Penney (tel. 215/238–9100).

Next to the Gallery at Market Street between 7th Street and 8th Street is a pricier urban mall, **Market Place East** (tel. 215/592–8905). Saved from the wrecker's ball at the eleventh hour, the former Lit Brothers Department Store went through a $75 million renovation to emerge in 1987 as an office building featuring a five-level atrium with 20 stores and restaurants.

Jewelers' Row, centered on Sansom Street between 7th Street and 8th Street, is one of the world's oldest and largest markets of precious stones: More than 350 retailers, wholesalers, and craftsmen operate here. The 700 block of Sansom Street is a brick-paved enclave occupied almost exclusively by jewelers.

Pine Street from 9th Street to 12th Street is Philadelphia's **Antiques Row.** The three-block area has dozens of antiques stores and curio shops, many specializing in period furniture and Colonial heirlooms.

Shopping

Cherry St.

Arch St.

20th St.
19th St.
18th St.

Airport Train (R1)

Suburban Station

J. F. Kennedy Blvd.

Broad St.

Philo Read

③

Market-Frankford Subway

Market St. *Subway-Surface*

④

Ludlow St.

City Hall

Chestnut St.

SEE DETAIL MAP

Sansom St.

②

⑤

⑥

12th St.

11th St.

Walnut St.

⑦ **⑨** **⑩** **⑪**

⑫

Locust St.

Rittenhouse Square

Locust St.

Broad St. Subway

Juniper St.

13th St.

Camac St.

Quince St.

⑬

21st St.
20th St.
19th St.
18th St.
17th St.
16th St.
15th St.

Spruce St.

Pine St.

①

Lombard St.

⑧

Broad St.

Watts St.

South St.

Bainbridge St.

N

Fitzwater St.

0 ————— 440 yards

0 ————— 400 meters

Rte. 611

Catherine St.

Barnes & Noble, **2**
Bauman Rare Books, **13**
Best of Philadelphia, **40**
Book Trader, **33**
Bourse Building, **30**
Chef's Market, **41**
Destination Philadelphia, **27**

Food Hall at Strawbridge and Clothier, **21**
G.B. Schaffer Antiques, **18**
Gallery at Market East, **20**
Gargoyles, **39**
Gilbert Luber Gallery, **12**
Harry Sable, **24**
Hats In The Belfry, **31**

Hibberd's, **10**
Howard Heartsfield, **26**
I. Goldberg, **16**
J.E. Caldwell, **5**
Jack Kelmer, **23**
Jansen Antiques, **17**
John Wanamaker, **4**
Kamikaze Kids, **36**
Kosmin's Camera

Exchange, **15**
M. Finkel and Daughter, **19**
Market Place East, **22**
Mid-City Camera Exchange, **9**
Neo Deco, **34**
Le Parfumier, **29**
Popi, **35**
Robin's Bookstore, **6**
Robinson Luggage

Shopping (Sansom and Walnut Streets)

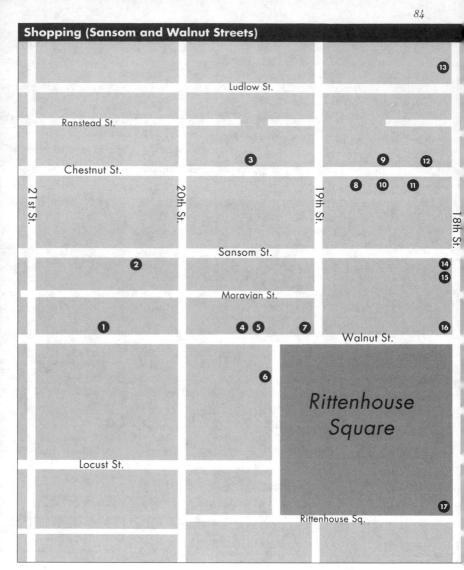

Ludlow St.

Ranstead St.

Chestnut St.

21st St.

20th St.

19th St.

18th St.

Sansom St.

Moravian St.

Walnut St.

Rittenhouse Square

Locust St.

Rittenhouse Sq.

AIA Bookstore, **47**
Allure, **64**
Ambitions, **39**
Bailey, Banks, and Biddle, **57**
Banana Republic, **34**
Beige, **31**
Bernie Robbins, **48**
Borders, **27**
Born Yesterday, **7**
Bottino, **14**

Boyd's, **9**
Brooks Brothers, **58**
Burberry's Ltd., **32**
Calderwood Gallery, **56**
Cambridge Clothing Factory Outlet, **60**
Children's Boutique, **30**
Crabtree and Evelyn, **18**

Country Floors, **40**
Dandelion, **24**
David David Gallery, **17**
Deacon's Luggage, **51**
Edward G. Wilson, **11**
Einstein Books & Toys, **45**
Elder Craftsmen, **53**
Encore, **35**

Everyone's Racquet, **12**
Fat Jack's Comicrypt, **2**
Finish Line Sports, **4**
Freeman Fine Arts, **8**
Gross-McCleaf Gallery, **61**
Godiva Chocolatier, **44**
Hats In the Belfry, **15**

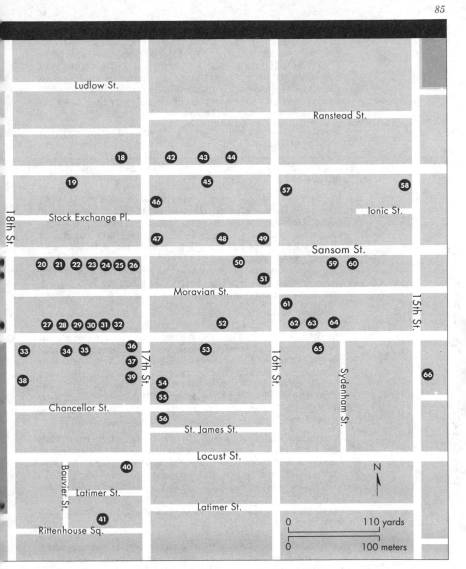

Ludlow St.

Ranstead St.

18th St.

Stock Exchange Pl.

Ionic St.

Sansom St.

Moravian St.

15th St.

17th St.

16th St.

Sydenham St.

Chancellor St.

St. James St.

Locust St.

Bouvier St.

Latimer St.

Latimer St.

Rittenhouse Sq.

N

| 0 | 110 yards |
| 0 | 100 meters |

Helen Drutt, **28**
Holt's Tobacconist, **49**
How-to-Do-It Bookshop, **50**
I. Brewster, **20**
Intima, **23**
Jaeger International Sportswear, **29**
Janet Fleisher, **54**
Joseph Fox, **22**
Kitchen Kapers, **55**

Knit Wit, **37**
Locks Gallery, **65**
Market at the Commissary, **25**
Mendelsohn, **38**
Muse Gallery, **5**
Nan Duskin, **6**
Newman Galleries, **52**
Past, Present, Future, **13**
Plage Tahiti, **26**

Richard Kenneth, **36**
Rittenhouse Bookstore, **41**
Sherman Brothers Shoes, **59**
Strega, **62**
Schwarz Gallery, **10**
Structure, **43**
Theodor Presser, **19**
Toby Lerner, **46**
Touches, **66**

Ultimate Sock, **42**
Urban Objects, **21**
Urban Outfitters, **16**
Wayne Edwards Men's Loft, **63**
What's Your Game, **42**
Whodunit, **3**
William H. Allen, **1**
Wine Reserve, **33**

Across the street from the Liberty Bell is the **Bourse** (5th St. between Market St. and Chestnut St., tel. 215/625–0300), an elegantly restored 1895 commodities-exchange building. The Bourse failed as an upscale mini-mall, but while the designer boutiques are gone, the six-story skylit atrium still contains fun shops such as Destination Philadelphia (Philly-related T-shirts) and Best of Philadelphia (Philly-related gifts), as well as a festive international food court.

South Street, one of Philadelphia's few entertainment strips, is also one of its major shopping areas. From Front Street to 9th Street you'll find more than 300 unusual stores—high-fashion clothing, New Age books and health food, avant-garde art galleries—and 100 restaurants.

If you want local color, nothing compares with South Philadelphia's **Italian Market.** On both sides of 9th Street from Christian Street to Washington Street and spilling onto the surrounding streets, hundreds of outdoor stalls and indoor stores sell such food items as spices, cheese, pasta, fruits, vegetables, freshly slaughtered poultry and beef; household items; clothing; shoes; and other goods. It's crowded and smelly, and the vendors can be less than hospitable—but the food is fresh and the prices are reasonable.

Department stores are the cornerstone of Philadelphia shopping. The king of local department stores is **John Wanamaker** (tel. 215/422–2000), a landmark store (*see* Tour 3 in Chapter 3) that occupies the entire city block from 13th Street to Juniper Street and from Market Street to Chestnut Street. Although only five of the building's 12 floors are now part of the store, the list of departments still fills up more than a column in the local White Pages. The store has fashion boutiques, designer shops for men, the Baker furniture gallery, a travel agency, a ticket office, a watch-repair desk, a beauty salon, and a post office.

Strawbridge and Clothier (tel. 215/629–6000), whose main store is at 8th Street and Market Street in the Gallery, is the other leading department store. It was founded in 1868 and is still owned by the Clothier and Strawbridge families. Once a month, Strawbridge's has Clover Day, with special sale prices on items throughout the store.

Shopping Notes

Local stores have sales throughout the year. If you're looking for a particular item, check the daily newspapers. Most stores accept traveler's checks and Visa, MasterCard, and American Express. Diners Club, Carte Blanche, and Discover are less widely accepted. Policies on personal checks vary. As in many big cities, it's unwise to carry much cash.

Pennsylvania has a 6% sales tax, and the city adds another 1%. These do not apply to clothing, medicine, and food bought in stores.

Downtown shopping hours are generally 9:30 or 10 AM to 5 or 6 PM. Many stores close at 9 PM on Wednesday. Most downtown stores are closed on Sunday, but the Bourse and the Gallery are open from 12 to 5.

Specialty Stores

Antiques Many dealers cluster on Antiques Row—Pine Street between 9th and 12th streets.

W. Graham Arader (1308 Walnut St., tel. 215/735–8811). This dealer claims to stock the world's largest selection of 16th- to 19th-century prints and maps, specializing in botanicals, birds, and the American West.

Architectural Antiques Exchange (715 N. 2nd St., tel. 215/922–3669). Victorian embellishments from saloons and apothecary shops, to stained and beveled glass, gargoyles, and advertising memorabilia.

Calderwood Gallery (221 S. 17th St., tel. 215/732–9444). Art Nouveau and Art Deco furniture, glass, bronzes, and rugs.

M. Finkel and Daughter (936 Pine St., tel. 215/627–7797). Late 18th- and early 19th-century American furniture, quilts, needlework, and folk art.

Freeman Fine Arts (1808 Chestnut St., tel. 215/563–9275). One of the city's leading auction houses. Examine furniture, china, prints, and paintings on Monday and Tuesday; bid for them on Wednesday. Freeman's auctioned one of the original flyers on which the Declaration of Independence was printed and posted throughout the city. It went for $400,000.

Gargoyles (512 S. 3rd St., tel. 215/629–1700) has 11,000 square feet of antiques and reproduction decorative and architectural pieces—archways, mantels, entranceways, carousel horses, stained-glass windows, and ornate mirrors.

G. B. Schaffer Antiques (1014 Pine St., tel. 215/923–2263). Eighteenth-, 19th-, and early 20th-century American furnishings, stained glass, silver, porcelain, paintings, and prints.

Vintage Instruments (1529 Pine St., tel. 215/545–1100). Antique strings and woodwinds. Specializes in violins and also carries American fretted instruments—banjos, guitars, and mandolins.

Edward G. Wilson (1802 Chestnut St., tel. 215/563–7369). Small items such as antique coins, lamps, jewelry, silver, china, glass, and other collectibles. Founded in 1929.

Art For current shows in Philadelphia's numerous galleries, see listings in *Philadelphia* magazine or the Weekend section of the Friday *Philadelphia Inquirer*. Many galleries are located near Rittenhouse Square; others are on South Street or scattered about downtown. Over the past few years, Olde City has become the hottest gallery area. One evening a month on the "First Friday" you can wander 2nd and 3rd streets above Market Street going from gallery to gallery. It's like a refined block-party, with refreshments and performance artists.

I. Brewster (1628 Walnut St., tel. 215/864–9222). Contemporary posters and paintings by Louis Icart, Erté, Andy Warhol, and Red Grooms.

David David Gallery (260 S. 18th St., tel. 215/735–2922). American and European paintings, drawings, and watercolors from the 16th to the 20th centuries.

Helen Drutt (1721 Walnut St., tel. 215/735–1625). Contemporary American and European artists, with a focus on ceramics and jewelry.

Janet Fleisher (211 S. 17th St., tel. 215/545–7562). Pre-Columbian, and 20th-century self-taught American artists.

Gross-McCleaf Gallery (127 S. 16th St., tel. 215/665–8138).

Works by prominent and emerging artists, with emphasis on Philadelphia painters.

Locks Gallery (600 Washington Sq. South, tel. 215/629–1000). Contemporary regional, national, and international painters, sculptors, and mixed-media artists.

Gilbert Luber Gallery (1220 Walnut St., tel. 215/732–2996). Japanese and Chinese antique and contemporary prints and Thai artifacts.

Muse Gallery (60 N. 2nd St., tel. 215/627–5310). Established in 1978 by the Muse Foundation for the Visual Arts, Muse Gallery is a women's cooperative committed to increasing the visibility of women's artwork and presenting experimental work in a variety of media.

Newman Galleries (1625 Walnut St., tel. 215/563–1779). A range of works, from 19th-century paintings to contemporary lithographs and sculpture. Strong on early 20th-century painters from the Bucks County area.

School Gallery of the Pennsylvania Academy of the Fine Arts (1301 Cherry St., tel. 215/972–7600). Rotating exhibits of works by faculty, alumni, and students.

University of the Arts' Rosenwald-Wolf Gallery (333 S. Broad St., tel. 215/875–1116). Works by faculty and students, and local, national, and international artists.

Schwarz Gallery (1806 Chestnut St., tel. 215/563–4887). Eighteenth- to 20th-century American and European paintings, concentrating on Philadelphia artists of the past.

Snyderman Gallery (303 Cherry St., tel. 215/238–9576). One-of-a-kind handmade furniture and glass.

The Works (319 South St., tel. 215/922–7775). Contemporary decorative and applied American crafts in wood, fiber, ceramics, metals, and glass.

Books   **AIA Bookstore** (17th and Sansom Sts., tel. 215/569–3188). Run by the Philadelphia chapter of the American Institute of Architects, this shop specializes in architectural theory, building construction, interior design, furnishings, blueprint posters, international magazines, and unusual gifts.

William H. Allen (2031 Walnut St., tel. 215/563–3398). One of the city's best collections of used and scholarly books. Specializes in history, literature, and philosophy. Extensive collection of books on ancient Greece and Rome, in English and original languages.

Barnes and Noble (1424 Chestnut St., tel. 215/972–8275). A full-scale bookstore, more than 50,000 volumes, in an elegant commercial space. Classical music in the background and strategically placed benches make browsing comfortable.

Bauman Rare Books (1215 Locust St., tel. 215/546–6466). An antiquarian bookstore with volumes from the 19th century and earlier on law, science, English literature, travel, and exploration; print and map collection.

Book Trader (501 South St., tel. 215/925–0219). You'll find great browsing on the two floors of this eclectic used-book store. Prices on the high side. Open daily 10 AM–midnight.

Borders (1727 Walnut St., tel. 215/568–7400). The biggest, the friendliest, the best bookstore in Philadelphia. You can sit on a couch, listening to live guitar music, and read for hours. The 110,000 titles and more than half-million books are spread over a two-level, 17,000-foot selling floor. Each of the 50 staffers had to pass a literature test to be hired. Book lovers get to know each other at the second-floor espresso bar. Frequent lectures and readings; Saturday-morning children's programs at 11:30.

Encore (609 Chestnut St., tel. 215/627–4557). A discount chain with more than 20 locations, Encore offers 35% off *New York Times* best-sellers and up to 80% off closeouts and remainders.

Joseph Fox (1724 Sansom St., tel. 215/563–4184). A small bookstore specializing in art, architecture, and design.

Hibberd's (1310 Walnut St., tel. 215/546–8811). Rare and used books, including a large selection of unusual art books.

How-to-Do-It Bookshop (1608 Sansom St., tel. 215/563–1516). Want to build a computer, grow rutabagas, groom your poodle? If there's a book telling you how to do something, chances are this unique place (with over 20,000 titles) will have it.

Rittenhouse Bookstore (1706 Rittenhouse Sq., tel. 215/545–6072). The best medical bookstore in Philadelphia. If you can't find the book you want, they may be able to get it for you overnight.

Robin's Bookstore (108 S. 13th St., tel. 215/735–9600). Not the biggest bookstore in town, and maybe not the best, but definitely the sentimental favorite. Owner Larry Robin has been promoting literature and fighting literary censorship for more than 30 years. Robin's has an exceptional variety of hard-to-find intellectual titles. Specializes in literature, poetry, and minority studies. A good children's section. Frequent poetry readings and book signings by local authors.

University of Pennsylvania Bookstore (3729 Locust Walk, tel. 215/898–7595). Over 60,000 titles of both popular and scholarly volumes. Especially strong in linguistics, anthropology, psychology, and sociology. The Middle East section may be the only place in town to buy a book of Kurdish grammar.

Whodunit (1931 Chestnut St., tel. 215/567–1478). The city's only store specializing in mysteries, spy stories, and adventure books. It also stocks out-of-print mysteries. Over 25,000 titles. Owner Art Bourgeau has published six mystery books and a nonfiction book on mystery writing.

Women's Clothing   **Ambitions** (212 S. 17th St., tel. 215/546–1133). Specializes in clothes for full-figured women sizes 14 to 24.

Howard Heartsfield (Bourse Bldg., 21 S. 5th St., tel. 215/925–2070). Handmade sweaters, camisoles, and sequined evening wear—woven, knit, or crocheted by fiber artists.

Intima (1718 Sansom St., tel. 215/568–6644; 707 Walnut St., tel. 215/238–7727). Philadelphia's best selection of imported cotton and silk designer lingerie.

Jaeger International Sportswear (1719 Walnut St., tel. 215/751–9285). European collection of distinctive clothing, from classics to the latest silhouettes and proportions.

Knit Wit (1721 Walnut St., tel. 215/564–4760). Trendy fashions and accessories from sportswear to cocktail clothes. Shoes and jewelry, too.

Mendelsohn (229 S. 18th St., tel. 215/546–6333). Classic European and specialty clothing.

Plage Tahiti (128 S. 17th St., tel. 215/569–9139). Showcases promising young high-fashion designers. You'll also find swimwear.

Toby Lerner (117 S. 17th St., tel. 215/568–5760). European high-fashion apparel with strong classic lines. Full line of shoes.

Men's Clothing   **Allure** (1509 Walnut St., tel. 215/561–4242). Classic and stylish Italian clothing and furnishings.

Boyd's (1818 Chestnut St., tel. 215/564–9000). The largest single-store men's clothier in the country. Its nine shops feature the traditional English look, avant-garde Italian imports, and dozens of other styles and designers. Shops for extra tall, large, and short men; more than 60 tailors on the premises. Valet parking.

Brooks Brothers (1500 Chestnut St., tel. 215/564–4100). The oldest men's clothing store in America (founded in New York in 1818). Synonymous with Ivy League business clothing: conservative suits, button-down shirts, and striped ties.

Structure (Shops at Liberty Place, 1625 Chestnut St., tel. 215/851–0835) is hip and stylish, with relatively decent prices. They sell casual clothes, such as silk shirts and baggy pleated pants, in bold colors. Sales can yield real bargains.

Wayne Edwards Men's Loft (1521 Walnut St., tel. 215/563–6801). Exclusive lines of classic contemporary designer clothing from Italy, Japan, France, and the United States.

Women's and Men's Clothing

Banana Republic (1716 Walnut St., tel. 215/735–2247). This store is part of the national chain that helped make famous—and still sells—the photojournalist vest (with a plethora of pockets) and the Kenya convertible pants (with the hidden zippers that convert them into shorts).

Burberrys Ltd. (1705 Walnut St., tel. 215/557–7400). Named after Thomas Burberry, who designed the trench coat in the mid-1850s, this British-owned establishment features British raincoats, overcoats, sportcoats, and cashmere sweaters. High quality, high prices.

Destination Philadelphia (Bourse Bldg., 21 S. 5th St., tel. 215/440–0233). A clothing store where every item bears some form of Philadelphia logo or design—from a soft pretzel to a line drawing of Billy Penn. Sweatpants, sweatshirts, and more than 40 styles of T-shirts.

Hats In The Belfry (525 S. 3rd St., tel. 215/922–6770, and 125 S. 18th St., tel. 215/567–0037). Designer hats, practical hats, formal hats, silly hats, Panamas, baseball caps, and more.

Nan Duskin (210 W. Rittenhouse Sq., in the Rittenhouse Hotel, tel. 215/735–6400). European and American designer clothes, sportswear, gold and costume jewelry, lingerie, and shoes. Boutiques include Hermès, Armani, Chanel, and Valentino.

Neo Deco (414 South St., tel. 215/928–0627). European-style contemporary clothing: sportswear, shoes, and jewelry.

Ultimate Sock (The Shops at Liberty Place, 1625 Chestnut St., tel. 215/567–0801). Designer socks and hosiery by Hue, DKNY, and Hot Sox, plus hundreds of novelty socks—some even play music. Prices range from $8 to $18.

Urban Outfitters (1801 Walnut St., tel. 215/569–3131). This trend-setting store in a Beaux Arts mansion is a favorite of the collegiate crowd. Children's department, books, unusual toys, and apartment accessories.

Children's Clothing

Born Yesterday (1901 Walnut St., tel. 215/568–6556). Unusual selection of clothing and toys for tots. Handmade goods, imported fashions, and styles you won't find elsewhere.

Children's Boutique (717 Walnut St., tel. 215/563–3881). A look between conservative and classic in infant to preteen clothes; complete wardrobes, specialty gifts, and handmade items.

Kamikaze Kids (527 S. 4th St., tel. 215/574–9800). Handmade fashions by local designers for infants to preteens.

Food **Chef's Market** (231 South St., tel. 215/925–8360). Philly's ultimate gourmet supermarket prepares 60 to 70 different entrées
every day; also a fish market, meat market, several hundred
kinds of cheeses, and goods from its own bakery. Packaged
items include 150 varieties of imported jams, 40 olive oils, and
60 flavored vinegars.

Fante's (1006 S. 9th St., tel. 215/922–5557). One of the oldest
gourmet supply stores in the country, it has the largest selection of coffee makers and equipment in the United States. It is
located in the Italian Market. Family-owned since 1906, it is famous for oddball kitchen gadgets such as truffle shavers, pineapple peelers, and croquembouche molds. Supplies restaurants
and bakeries all over the country and overseas.

Food Hall at Strawbridge and Clothier (8th and Market Sts., tel.
215/629–6000). You can eat in, or take out breads, cheeses, salads, and ice cream. Daily cooking demonstrations with free
samples. Also a large candy department and a charcuterie.

Godiva Chocolatier (Shops at Liberty Place, 1625 Chestnut St.,
tel. 215/963–0810). At $2.75 for a single piece of hand-dipped
fruit, to $27 for a one-pound box, it doesn't get any sweeter
than this.

Kitchen Kapers (213 S. 17th St., tel. 215/546–8059). Fine cookware, cutlery, and special foods. Lots of French copper and
porcelain.

Market at the Commissary (1712 Sansom St., tel. 215/568–
8055). Ready-to-eat, ready-to-go gourmet food. Cheeses, pastas, and coffees. Food from the kitchen of the Commissary
—Philadelphia's premier cafeteria—but a greater selection.
Salad bar and dessert case. Opens 7:30 AM; sells food for breakfast, lunch, and dinner.

Gifts and Novelties **Country Floors** (1706 Locust St., tel. 215/545–1040). Ceramic
and terra-cotta hand-painted tiles from the U.S. and all over
Europe, for floors or walls.

Dandelion (1718 Sansom St., tel. 215/972–0999). Almost everything sold in this store is handmade: jewelry; ceramics; porcelains; and glass imported from Indonesia, India, and Africa.
They also have Native American handwoven batik pieces.

Best of Philadelphia (Bourse Bldg., 21 S. 5th St., tel. 215/440–
7016). Lots of cheap Philly schlock: over 100 different items, including jigsaw puzzles, coloring books, Ben Franklin key
chains, T-shirts, and, of course, Liberty Bells.

Holt's Tobacconist (114 S. 16th St., tel. 215/563–0763). The
city's oldest (1898) and largest purveyor of pipes, tobacco, cigars, and lighters. Also the city's largest selection of writing
instruments.

Popi (526 S. 4th St., tel. 215/922–4119). The most extensive selection of foreign, domestic, and exotic magazines in town—
over 5,000 titles and expanding—and more than 100 brands of
imported cigarettes. One entire room is dedicated to back-is-
sue magazines sold at half price.

Touches (225 S. 15th St., tel. 215/546–1221). Attractive shop
with wall-to-wall upscale gifts: handmade shawls, handbags,
belts, unusual jewelry, and children's gifts.

Urban Objects (1724 Sansom St., tel. 215/557–9474). Eclectic
collection of contemporary gifts, home accessories, and antiques (both authentic and reproductions), lamps, and pictures.
Many objects are imported from Europe and Asia but are reasonably priced.

Wine **Wine and Spirits Shoppe** (Bourse Bldg., 21 S. 5th St., tel. 215/560–5504). One of the best selections of fine wines and liquors in a city where liquor stores are state run. For a better selection you have to go to New Jersey.
Wine Reserve (205 S. 18th St., tel. 215/560–4529). Exclusively fine wines and cognacs. It's got wines you won't find in any other state store in Pennsylvania; you can pick up an extra bottle of Louis XIII Cognac for about $900.

Jewelry **J. E. Caldwell** (Juniper and Chestnut Sts., tel. 215/864–8829). A local landmark since 1839, the store is adorned with antique, handblown crystal chandeliers by Baccarat, making it as elegant as the jewels it sells. Along with traditional and modern jewelry, Caldwell's has one of the city's largest selections of giftware and stationery, and a bridal registry.
Bailey, Banks, and Biddle (16th and Chestnut Sts., tel. 215/564–6200). Since 1832 known for diamond and gold jewelry, objets d'art, silver, crystal, and gift-wrap department.
Bernie Robbins (1625 Sansom St., tel. 215/563–2380). Fine jewelry at discount prices.
Jack Kelmer (717 Chestnut St., tel. 215/627–8350). Diamonds, gold jewelry, and gifts at below retail price.
Harry Sable (8th and Sansom Sts., tel. 215/627–4014). The "king of the wedding bands" carries the largest selection in the Delaware Valley; it also sells engagement rings, diamond rings, gold jewelry, and watches.
Richard Kenneth (202 S. 17th St., tel. 215/545–3355). Jewelry from the late Georgian, Victorian, Art Nouveau, Art Deco, and '40s-retro periods. Specializes in antique and estate pieces, repairs, and appraisals.

Luggage and **Deacon's Luggage** (124 S. 16th St., tel. 215/567–5584). Lug-
Leather Goods gage, briefcases, and accessories at discount prices.
Robinson Luggage Company (Broad and Walnut Sts., tel. 215/735–9859). Popular brands of luggage, leather, and travel accessories. The selection of briefcases and attaché cases is the largest in the Delaware Valley.

Records and Music **Theodor Presser** (1718 Chestnut St., tel. 215/568–0964). The best selection of sheet music in Center City. Specializes in classical, but also carries pop and will special-order anything.
Third Street Jazz and Rock (20 N. 3rd St., tel. 215/627–3366). The last major retailer of vinyl records in the area, specializing in hard-to-find jazz and soul records. Also rock, New Wave, reggae, Caribbean, and African music. Salespeople are particularly knowledgeable. Good prices.
Tower Records (610 South St., tel. 215/574–9888). Open 9 AM to midnight 365 days a year. Stocks more than 250,000 CDs and tapes—the largest selection in the city. You can watch music videos on the 30 screens on three floors. Classical-music annex across the street.

Perfumes **Crabtree and Evelyn** (Bourse Bldg., 21 S. 5th St., tel. 215/625–9256). This British firm sells its own line of toiletries and soaps as well as specialty foods.
The Body Shop de le Parfumier (Bourse Bldg., 21 S. 5th St., tel. 215/922–7660). This "scent boutique" for men and women imports new fragrances, some not yet available elsewhere in the United States. Also carries cosmetics, perfume bottles, discontinued scents, and accessories.

Photography   **Kosmin's Camera Exchange** (927 Arch St., tel. 215/627–8231). Film, motion picture equipment, slide projectors, screens, darkroom supplies, and a half-dozen brands of camera.
Mid-City Camera Exchange (1316 Walnut St., tel. 215/735–2522). Sales, service, rentals. This major "stockhouse" has a large line of darkroom equipment and all major camera brands in all formats. It also buys and trades used cameras.
Roth Camera Repairs (1015 Chestnut St., Room 102, tel. 215/922–2498). If you have camera trouble, here's the place to have it fixed. Extra-quick service for tourists.

Sporting Goods   **Everyone's Racquet** (132 S. 17th St., tel. 215/665–1221). Everything related to racket sports: tennis, racquetball, squash. Next-day racket-stringing service.
Finish Line Sports (1915 Walnut St., tel. 215/569–9957). Specialists in shoes and gear for triathlon sports: running, swimming, and cycling. Also aerobic and workout shoes and gear.
I. Goldberg (902 Chestnut St., tel. 215/925–9393). An army-navy-and-everything store. Not stylish but practical, with emphasis on sporting apparel and camping gear. Crammed with government-surplus, military-style clothing, jeans and workclothes, and exclusive foreign imports. Huge stock of sizes. Rummaging here is a sport in itself.

Toys   **Einstein Books and Toys** (1624 Chestnut St., tel. 215/844–0772 or 215/923–3622). This place has everything from a large selection of nonfiction children's books to Gorbachev and KGB dolls to mechanical toys for executives—you name it—and they're all unique.
Fat Jack's Comicrypt (2006 Sansom St., tel. 215/963–0788). Old and new comics at catalogue prices. Over 500,000 available, the largest selection in the Delaware Valley.
Past, Present, Future (24 S. 18th St., tel. 215/854–0444). Distinctive toys, handcrafted jewelry and ceramics, kaleidoscopes, and children's books.
What's Your Game (The Shops at Liberty Place, 1625 Chestnut St., tel. 215/567–0772). Thousands of puzzles and games. French "Arjew" wooden puzzles; metal blacksmith "Tavern" puzzles.

Shoes   **Beige** (1715 Walnut St., tel. 215/564–2395). Women's Italian leather shoes in sizes 4–12, priced toward the high end.
Bottino (121 S. 18th St., tel. 215/854–0907). Men's shoes and accessories, all handmade and imported from Italy. Sylvester Stallone dropped in and bought 13 pairs.
Sherman Brothers Shoes (1520 Sansom St., tel. 215/561–4550). An "off-price" retailer of men's shoes with name-brand merchandise, excellent service, and low prices. Extra-wide and extra-narrow widths, sizes to 14 and 15; 28 lines of shoes.
Strega (1521 Walnut St., tel. 215/564–5932). A wide range of looks for men; exclusive footwear, the Edward Green line from England, and many top Italian designers.

Bargain Shopping   **Cambridge Clothing Factory Outlet** (1520 Sansom St., second floor, tel. 215/568–8248). A manufacturers' outlet for men with 10 national brands starting at 40% off retail. Immediate alterations for out-of-town buyers.
Night Dressing (2100 Walnut St., tel. 215/627–5244). Offers 50% off list prices on designer lingerie, 15% off hosiery.
Thos. David Factory Store (401 Race St., tel. 215/922–4659). Upstairs they make it. Downstairs they sell it—at almost

wholesale prices. High-quality men's and women's business and sportswear.

5 Sports and the Outdoors

Participant Sports and Fitness

Bicycling   A treat for bikers is to ride out on the east side of the Schuylkill River, cross Falls Bridge, and return on the west side of the river. The 8.2-mile loop takes about an hour of casually paced biking. Another great ride is Forbidden Drive in the Wissahickon (*see* Chapter 3), a 5.5-mile dirt and gravel bridle path along a stream. The **Bicycle Club of Philadelphia** (tel. 215/440–9983) organizes bike tours, from afternoon outings to week-long events. Fairmount Park (tel. 215/685–0052) will tell you where to rent bikes.

Boating and Canoeing   Paddle or row through Fairmount Park along the scenic Schuylkill River, but yield the right of way to Olympic-caliber scullers speeding by. Rent canoes or rowboats at the **Public Canoe House.** *Kelly Dr., just south of Strawberry Mansion Bridge, tel. 215/225–3560. Cost for canoes or rowboats: $10/hr with $10 deposit. Photo ID required. Open Mar.–Oct., daily 11 AM–7 PM.*

Bowling   Bowling in Philadelphia seems to have lost some of its popularity. Alleys are no longer located downtown, but you can still bowl in other parts of the city. Two alleys worth trying are **Adams Lanes** (Adams Ave. and Foulkrod St., tel. 215/533–1221, hours vary) and **Oregon Bowling Lanes** (24th St. and Oregon Ave., tel. 215/389–2200, open daily 9 AM–11:30 PM).

Fishing and Hunting   On the banks of Wissahickon Creek and Pennypack Creek, the catch varies but fishing is always good. Both creeks are stocked for the mid-April through December season. You'll need a license ($12.50–$25.50): You can get one at certain local sporting-goods stores and at K-Mart (424 Oregon Ave., tel. 215/336–1778).

Hunting is a popular activity in Pennsylvania, but not in Philadelphia proper. You have to go at least as far out as the suburban counties. For information about hunting regulations, contact the **Pennsylvania Game Commission** (RD 2, Box 2584, Reading, PA 19605, tel. 800/228–0791).

Golf   **Cobbs Creek and Karakung,** two 18-hole courses. Cobbs Creek is the most difficult course listed. *7200 Lansdowne Ave., tel. 215/877–8707. Greens fees: $15–$19 weekdays, $17–$21 weekends and holidays.*
Franklin D. Roosevelt, 18-hole course. *20th St. and Pattison Ave., tel. 215/462–8997. Greens fees: $16 weekdays, $18 weekends.*
J. F. Byrne, 18-hole course. *9500 Leon St., tel. 215/632–8666. Greens fees: $15 weekdays, $17 weekends.*
Juniata, 18-hole course. *L and Cayuga Sts., tel. 215/743–4060. Greens fees: $15 weekdays, $17 weekends.*
Walnut Lane, 18-hole course. *Walnut La. and Henry Ave., tel. 215/482–3370. Greens fees: $14 weekdays, $16 weekends.*

Health Clubs   Some of the downtown clubs allow non-member day guests, for around $10. Three good ones are: **Gold's Gym** (834 Chestnut St., tel. 215/592–9644); **12th Street Gym** (204 S. 12th St., tel. 215/985–4092); and **Rittenhouse Square Fitness Club** (2002 Rittenhouse Sq., tel. 215/985–4095).

Hiking and Jogging   Fairmount Park—especially along the river drives and Wissahickon Creek—is a natural for hikers and joggers. Starting in front of the Philadelphia Museum of Art, an 8.2-mile loop runs up one side of the Schuylkill, across Falls Bridge, and down the other side of the river back to the museum. Forbidden Drive along the Wissahickon offers more than 5 miles of scenic hiking or jogging on a dirt and gravel surface with no automobile traffic.

For organized hiking, check with the following organizations:

American Youth Hostels (tel. 215/925–6004).

Batona Hiking Club (tel. 215/659–3921). These organized hikes tend to be a little more strenuous than those of the other clubs.

The Department of Recreation **Wanderlust Hiking Club** (tel. 215/685–0151 or 215/580–4847).

Horseback Riding Of the numerous bridle paths coursing through Philadelphia, the most popular are the trails of the Wissahickon in the northwest, in Pennypack Park in the northeast, and in Cobbs Creek Park in the southwest. Riding academies that offer instruction and rentals include **Circle K Stables** (4220 Holmesburg Ave., tel. 215/335–9975; $15/hr.) and **Ashford Farms** (River Rd., Miquon, tel. 215/825–9838; cost: trail rides $20/hr, lessons $20–$30).

Tennis Fairmount Park has more than 100 free public courts, but at many players must bring their own nets. Call the **Department of Recreation** (tel. 215/686–3600) for information.

Many indoor courts are located in the surrounding areas. The only one close to Center City, the **Robert P. Levy Tennis Pavilion,** has eight courts open weekdays 7 AM–11 PM, weekends 8 AM–10 PM (closed weekends July and Aug.). *3130 Walnut St., tel. 215/898–4741. Yearly membership fee $60, plus $22–$26/hr.*

Spectator Sports

Philadelphians are avid sports fans who support both professional and collegiate teams. The major-league sports teams play their home games in the sports complex at Broad Street and Pattison Avenue—the Phillies (baseball) and the Eagles (football) at Veterans Stadium, the 76ers (basketball) and the Flyers (hockey) at the Spectrum. Some collegiate games are played there too; others are played on the campuses of the various colleges and universities.

Tickets to professional baseball, basketball, football, and hockey games are available at Veterans Stadium or the Spectrum, at Ticketron outlets, at ticket agencies, and by mail and phone from the respective teams.

Baseball **Philadelphia Phillies,** Box 7575, 19101, tel. 215/463–1000. Apr.–Oct.

Basketball **Philadelphia 76ers,** Box 25050, 19147, tel. 215/339–7676. Nov.–Apr.

Collegiate, "Big Five" basketball features the teams from LaSalle, St. Joseph's, Temple, University of Pennsylvania, and Villanova. *Big Five Office, Hutchinson Gym, 220 S. 32nd St., 19104, tel. 215/898–4747. Dec.–Mar.*

Bicycling One of the world's top four bicycling events, the **CoreStates Pro Cycling Championship,** is held each June. The 156-mile race starts and finishes at Benjamin Franklin Parkway, with 10 loops including the infamous Manayunk "Wall." *Tel. 215/636–1666.*

Football Philadelphia Eagles, Veterans Stadium, 19148, tel. 215/463–5500. Sept.–Dec.

Hockey Philadelphia Flyers, The Spectrum, Broad St. and Pattison Ave., 19148, tel. 215/755–9700. Oct.–Apr.

Horse Racing Thoroughbred racing takes place at **Philadelphia Park,** Street Rd., Bensalem 19020, tel. 215/639–9000. Post time: 1 PM daily except Tues. and Wed. year-round, and **Garden State Park,** Rte. 70, Cherry Hill, NJ 08034, tel. 609/488–8400. Post time: 7:30 PM daily except Sat. and Sun. Thoroughbred racing Feb.–June, harness racing Wed.–Sat., Sept.–Dec.

Rowing The **Dad Vail Regatta** is the largest collegiate rowing event in the country. Held on the Schuylkill River in Fairmount Park in May. Free shuttle buses from remote parking areas. *Tel. 215/ 248–2600.*

Track and Field The **Penn Relays,** the world's largest and oldest amateur track meet, held the last week of April at the University of Pennsylvania's Franklin Field, features world-class performers in track and field. The **Philadelphia Distance Run,** the nation's top half marathon, takes place in September. The **Fairmount Park Marathon** is held in November (tentative for 1994). For more information on these events, call 215/685–0052. The **Broad Street Run** (tel. 215/686–3614), a 10-miler down Broad Street, is held in May.

Tennis The **U.S. Pro Indoor Tennis Championships** are held at the Spectrum (tel. 215/947–2530), usually in February. More than 60 of the world's top pros compete.

6 Dining

Selected and edited by Rathe Miller and Michael Schwager

Though once a hash-and-mash gastronomic desert, since the "restaurant renaissance" of the 1970s Philadelphia has become a first-class restaurant city. You can choose from great steak houses, hotel gourmet dining, and French haute cuisine. The list of national cuisines reads like a roll-call at the United Nations. Chinatown alone has over 50 restaurants. If you want Italian, South Philadelphia is an entire section of the city where the "red gravy" flows. Philly dining has always been reasonably priced (strikingly so by New York standards) and in the past few years of recession, has dropped even further. You can dine at an excellent French restaurant such as Alouette for under $35.

And then there is "Philadelphia Cuisine,"—cheesesteaks, hoagies, soft pretzels with mustard, water ice—"We are the junk food capital of the world," says mayor Ed Rendell. Visitors should not leave town before adequately sampling from the more than 100 varieties of Tastykakes (Butterscotch Krimpets are the number-one seller). Goldenberg's Peanut Chews, available at candy stands everywhere, can be habit forming.

Meal times vary widely but, as a rule, breakfast is served from 7 to 11 AM; lunch from 11:30 AM to 2:30 PM; dinner from 5 to 10:30 PM. Reservations are always advised, especially in the spring and fall, when Philadelphia has many conventions.

Only the fanciest restaurants require a jacket and tie for men. Most places have a liberal dress policy: Anything dressier than jeans and T-shirts is acceptable.

From the hundreds of restaurants in the city, we have provided a representative selection of the better ones. They are listed alphabetically according to cuisine.

To help you find restaurants downtown, we've identified their locations as within the following geographic areas: **Center City, Old City, Society Hill,** and **Chinatown.** Center City is bounded roughly by the Schuylkill River to the west, 6th Street to the east, Lombard Street to the south, and Race Street to the north. Old City is bounded by 6th Street, the Delaware River, and Race and Sansom streets. Society Hill is bounded by 6th Street, the Delaware River, Bainbridge Street, and Walnut Street. Chinatown lies between 9th and 11th streets, and Vine and Arch streets.

We also include several restaurants in **West Philadelphia** (the part of the city west of the Schuylkill River), **South Philadelphia** (south of Bainbridge Street), and **Chestnut Hill** (in the northwest part of the city).

The most highly recommended restaurants in each price category are indicated by a star ★ .

Category	Cost*
Very Expensive	over $35
Expensive	$25–$35
Moderate	$15–$25
Inexpensive	under $15

*per person excluding drinks, service, and sales tax (7%)

The following credit card abbreviations are used: AE, American Express; DC, Diners Club; MC, MasterCard; V, Visa.

American-International

Very Expensive **The Fountain Restaurant.** Nestled in the lavish yet dignified
★ lobby of the Four Seasons, the Fountain has the city's freshest, most varied selection of meals. Cream of celery soup, seafood ravioli, and sautéed foie gras over asparagus are three enticing appetizers. Entrées are predominantly local and American dishes such as sautéed salmon fillet and roasted Pennsylvania pheasant with bacon-flavored cabbage. A special health menu offers foods low in cholesterol, calories, and sodium. The recently improved dessert menu includes a white chocolate mousse dubbed the "Artist's Palette" and Lemon Verbena Ice Cream with poppy-seed cake. Service is attentive and efficient yet relaxing. *1 Logan Sq., Center City, tel. 215/963–1500. Reservations necessary. Dress: informal. AE, DC, MC, V.*

Expensive **Bogart's.** Not your typical hotel restaurant, Bogart's is an excellent eatery that happens to be in a hotel (the Latham). Renovations in 1993 changed much of the Casablanca motif, though ceiling fans and slatted wood ceiling remain to enhance the new minimalist-modern look. The menu is still American and Continental, now somewhat lighter and a bit less expensive. Appetizers include seared sea scallops with baby green beans. Recommended entrées are hanger steak on potato pancakes with onion sauce and the tomato-eggplant-zucchini terrine. For dessert, try the chocolate truffle cake. Specials change every day and there is an à la carte menu. *1700 Walnut St., Center City, tel. 215/563–9444. Reservations recommended. Dress: informal. AE, DC, MC, V.*

The Chart House. People come here less for the food than the atmosphere: dramatic views of the Delaware River; a nautical theme combining ultramodern paintings, sculpture, and striking architecture; and a waterfall descending from the lobby to the lounge. The spacious dining area and lounge seats 250, yet affords a measure of intimacy lacking in many other large restaurants. For appetizers, try the oysters Rockefeller. All fish, including salmon, swordfish, and mahi mahi, is flown in fresh daily and served grilled or baked. Mud pie, the house dessert, is coffee ice cream in a chocolate wafer crust topped with fudge, fresh whipped cream, and diced almonds. *555 S. Delaware Ave., Society Hill, tel. 215/625–8383. Reservations accepted. Dress: informal. AE, DC, MC, V.*

The Garden. A classic Philadelphia dining experience, this town house–turned–restaurant has dining inside and out—on a canopied deck and at umbrella-covered tables in the garden (hence the name). It's Mayor Ed Rendell's all-around favorite Philadelphia restaurant. The specialty of the house is grilled Dover sole. Desserts are all homemade, including ice cream, sorbet, and the house favorite, white chocolate mousse. Two cruvinets (devices for keeping opened bottles of wine fresh) dispense glasses of various red and white wines. *1617 Spruce St., Center City, tel. 215/546–4455. Reservations requested. Dress: informal. AE, DC, MC, V. Closed Sun.; closed Sat. in July and Aug.*

The Marker. Located in the Adam's Mark hotel, the Marker has been growing more popular as its menu grows more adventurous. Popular entrées include hickory-smoked crab and chicken

Dining

Alouette, **37**
Boccie Pizza, **3**
Bogart's, **12**
Bookbinder's Seafood
House, **8**
Carolina's, **5**
The Chart House, **47**
Chef Theodore, **49**
Ciboulette, **28**
The Commissary, **13**

DiLullo Centro, **27**
Downey's, **42**
The Famous
Delicatessen, **36**
The Fountain
Restaurant, **16**
Friday, Saturday,
Sunday, **4**
The Garden, **6**
Imperial Inn, **21**

Joe's Peking Duck
House, **20**
La Truffe, **46**
Le Bec-Fin, **10**
Lee's Hoagie
House, **14**
Lickety Split, **39**
The Marker, **18**
Marrakesh, **38**
Melrose Diner, **30**

The Middle East, **45**
Monte Carlo Living
Room, **41**
Morton's of
Chicago, **15**
Odeon, **25**
Old Original
Bookbinder's, **44**
Osteria Romana, **31**
Pat's King of
Steaks, **33**

Winter St.
Spring St.
20
21
Cherry St.
Arch St.
Filbert St.

Vine St.

30

Franklin Square

Broad St. Subway

Benjamin Franklin Bridge
Race St.
Quarry St.
U.S. Mint
Elfreth's Alley
Arch St.
2nd St.
Filbert St.
Commerce St. Church St.

30 **676**

Market St.

Ransted St.
Independence Hall
Ionic St.
Independence Square
Chestnut St.
Bank St.
Black Horse
46
45
Ionic St.
Sansom St.
44

Penn's Landing

Delaware Ave.

Delaware River

10th St.
Sansom St.
Walnut St.
Washington Square

Locust St.

Clinton St.

9th St.
8th St.
7th St.
6th St.
5th St.
4th St.
3rd St.
2nd St.
Front St.

Spruce St.

Delancey Place

Pine St.

Lombard St.
Rodman St.
South St.
Kater St.
Bainbridge St.
Fitzwater St.

39
38
35
37
36
43
41 **42**
40

N

47

95

31 **32** **33**
34
Fitzwater St.
48

sausage over braised spinach, sautéed fillet of red snapper in a potato crust with avocado and green onion relish, and pepper-seared tuna. The three dining rooms include intimate areas, a walk-in wine closet, and The Library, which has a fireplace and built-in bookshelves. *City Line and Monument Rds., City Line area, tel. 215/581–5000. Reservations suggested. Jackets requested. AE, DC, MC, V.*

Moderate **Carolina's.** Located a block from Rittenhouse Square, Carolina's opened in 1986 and quickly became a Center City hot spot. The dining room seats 60 at vinyl-covered tables and bentwood chairs under a stamped tin ceiling. The large menu of sandwiches, pastas, salads, a dozen appetizers, and more than a dozen entrées changes daily. Most popular are veal loaf with mashed potatoes and Cobb salad (a deep-fried tortilla shell stuffed with chicken, avocado, blue cheese, black olives, tomato, and romaine). The pastry chef's specialties are Carolina's brownie sundae and Key lime pie. *261 S. 20th St., Center City, tel. 215/545–1000. Reservations suggested. Dress: informal. AE, DC, MC, V. No lunch Sat.*

Downey's. The mahogany bar was salvaged from a Dublin bank, artwork and memorabilia cover the walls, and owner Jack Downey's antique radio collection is on display. Although the food is routine Irish fare, a lively crowd is always on hand. Irish stew and Irish whiskey cake are favorites. Downey's is popular with local athletes, especially baseball and hockey players. It has an oyster bar, outdoor sidewalk-tables, and a second-floor gaslit deck. The Sonny Troy Trio plays during Sunday brunch. *Front and South Sts., Society Hill, tel. 215/629–0525. Reservations suggested. Dress: informal. AE, DC, MC, V.*

Friday, Saturday, Sunday. When it opened 20 years ago this place was considered daring and innovative, but today it's pretty tame—almost frozen in time. Plaid fabrics drape from the ceiling; mirrors and pinlights line the walls; classical and jazz music plays in the background. The blackboard menu changes frequently. Popular entrées include rack of lamb, chicken Dijon, and hot poached salmon with sorrel sauce. All desserts are made on the premises; vanilla cheesecake with a chocolate crust and fresh berry puree topping is the most popular. The wine list is extensive. *261 S. 21st St., Center City, tel. 215/546–4232. Reservations accepted. Dress: casual. AE, DC, MC, V.*

Lickety Split. A charter member of the '70s "restaurant renaissance," Lickety Split bills itself as "South Street's longest running dinner party" and has hardly changed since it opened in 1972. It still has a plethora of plants, exposed brick walls, and pinlights; and a waterfall flows in the upstairs lounge. Much of the original menu also remains—stir-fried vegetables, avocado stuffed with crabmeat, and rack of lamb with mustard-crumbed coating. Newer offerings include the baked eggplant Montrachet with goat cheese and red bell-pepper sauce. Recommended for dessert are the chocolate cakes—the "Midnight" and the "Volcano." *4th and South Sts., Society Hill, tel. 215/922–1173. Weekend reservations advised. Dress: informal. AE, DC, MC, V.*

★ **Roller's.** A small, bustling, brightly lit place with floor-to-ceiling windows, Roller's is the best restaurant in Chestnut Hill, in the northwest corner of the city. Sit near the open kitchen and watch master chef (and owner) Paul Roller prepare duck with pear-port sauce; buffalo steak with cloves, green peppercorns, and zinfandel wine; and, the chef's personal favorite, organically farmed smoked pork chops with apple fritters. First-rate desserts include linzer torte and pear upside-down ginger-bread cake. The wine list is varied. Outdoor dining is available during the summer. *Top of the Hill Plaza, Chestnut Hill, tel. 215/242–1771. Dress: informal. Reservations advised. No credit cards. Closed Mon.; closed Sun. in July and Aug.*

Valley Green Inn. This secluded restaurant is set in the middle of the Wissahickon Valley—a forested 5½-mile-long gorge, in the northwest section of the city. Built in 1850, the inn is filled with antique tools, glassware, kitchen utensils, and Wissa-hickon memorabilia. In season, you can eat out on the porch overlooking the ducks swimming in the creek. In winter, a fire blazes inside. People used to eat here *in spite* of the food, but since Steven and Terri Bretherick took over in 1992, the cuisine complements the surroundings. The baby lamb chops Piret (grilled with a Caribbean barbecue sauce) and the scallops Julianne (named after one of the waitresses) sautéed with al-monds and served with a Brie cheese cream sauce, are two ex-amples of what the Brethericks call "American country cuisine with a touch of French." Call for directions by car or by the SEPTA R8 rail line from Center City. *Springfield Ave. and Forbidden Dr. between Chestnut Hill and Roxborough, tel. 215/ 247–1730. Reservations suggested. Dress: informal. MC, V.*

White Dog Cafe. Canine memorabilia abounds; the back of the menu explains why, telling the story of the 19th-century mystic Madame Blavatsky and how this restaurant got its name. Ging-ham and flea-market furniture give the White Dog a country-inn atmosphere. Owner Judy Wicks joins chef Kevin Von Klaus in making the White Dog *the* restaurant in University City. Ex-cellent regional cuisine uses the finest available local products, such as Bucks County broccoli, served the day it is picked. Try the whole-grain breads and the extra-tasty country terrine. Also recommended is the leg of lamb seasoned with a mixture of crushed black peppercorns, fennel, and mustard seeds. En-trées are served with an eclectic mix of vegetables. The small, lively bar serves 21 varieties of American boutique beer; the wine list is all-American. *3420 Sansom St., West Philadelphia, tel. 215/386–9224. Reservations advised. Dress: informal. AE, DC, MC, V.*

Inexpensive **The Commissary.** This gourmet café is the flagship of promi-nent Philadelphia restaurateur Steve Poses. To accompany soups, pastas, salads, and pastries, it offers a wide selection of coffees and wines. Renovated and expanded in 1991; low-fat, low-calorie items have been added to the menu. Food is avail-able for takeout. *1710 Sansom St., Center City, tel. 215/568–8055. Dress: informal. AE, DC, MC, V.*

The Restaurant School. Here's the only place in Philadelphia where you can get haute cuisine and European service at a frac-tion of the normal price: A fixed price of $13.50 buys an appetiz-er and entrée. It is managed and staffed entirely by students attending the Restaurant School, an institution that has pro-duced the chefs and owners of many Philadelphia restaurants. The menu occasionally offers Italian, Spanish, and German dishes, but is mainly French traditional, with a focus on sauces. Entrées change regularly, and may include sole Véronique gar-nished with white sauce and green grapes; or turkey rolled and stuffed with mushrooms and seasonings, and cut into medal-lions. Relocated in 1991 from a Center City brownstone to the Alison Mansion, a restored 1860 Victorian in West Philadelphia near the University of Pennsylvania, the new dining area seats 120 in an atrium setting with glass, trees, and plants. *4207 Walnut St., West Philadelphia, tel. 215/222–4200. Reservations suggested for weeknights, two weeks in advance for weekends. Jacket and tie preferred. No pipes or cigars. AE, DC, MC, V. Closed Sun. and Mon.*

Diners and Philly Food

Inexpensive **The Famous Delicatessen.** The closest thing in Philadelphia to a classic New York deli, the Famous is famous for corned beef, pastrami, and chocolate-chip cookies. Other favorites include carp, sable, Nova Scotia salmon, herring, salami, and tongue. The bickering behind the counter is a show in itself, and the waitresses have been known to sit down and schmooze with the customers. Beer is available. *4th and Bainbridge Sts., Society Hill, tel. 215/922–3274. Dress: informal. AE. Open Mon.–Sat. 7 AM–6 PM, Sun. 7 AM–4 PM.*

Lee's Hoagie House. The hoagie is Philadelphia's official sandwich, and though "heros" and "zeppelins" are available in other cities, only the Philadelphia hoagie has that certain *je ne sais quoi.* Lee's has been "hoagifying" since 1953. The original store, named after owner Lee Seitchik, is still operating in the West Oak Lane section of the city, and 23 other locations are licensed to use the Lee's name. Lee's offers a dozen different hoagies—tuna and turkey are gaining currency—but the classic is the Italian: pepper ham, genoa salami, cappacola, provolone cheese, lettuce, tomato, onions, hot peppers, spices, and oil. You can request mayonnaise, but it is considered somewhat *déclassé. 44 S. 17th St., tel. 215/564–1264. Reservations not necessary. Dress: informal. No credit cards. Closed Sun.*

Melrose Diner. A classic Philadelphia diner and more, the Melrose serves nothing elaborate but offers fresh, top-quality ingredients at diner prices. Entrées cost $5 to $9 ($13.50 for the filet mignon). You can get breakfast 24 hours a day, including the house specialty, creamed chipped beef. Popular entrées include deviled crab cutlet made from backfin crabmeat, and fried 1620 shrimp (16–20 shrimps per pound), heavily breaded. The on-premises bake shop has eight bakers. Favorite desserts are hot apple pie with vanilla sauce and butter-cream layer cake. Thirteen waitresses, most of whom are chewing gum and calling you "Hon," work 106 seats, serving 3,000 people a day. *1501 Snyder Ave., South Philadelphia, tel. 215/467–6644. Dress: informal. No credit cards. Open 24 hours.*

Pat's King of Steaks. While a hoagie is a meal, a cheesesteak is an indulgence. Thin slices of steak, fried onions, and melted cheese (your choice of American, provolone, or Cheese Whiz) served on an 8-inch roll. You get it piping hot, dripping oil and juices onto the wax paper, the outdoor metal tables, and your lap—until you acquire the proper eating stance. A side order of cheese fries, a fountain-made cherry coke, and a Tastykake for dessert—and you've had the ultimate Philadelphia culinary experience this side of Le Bec-Fin. Pat's, owned and run by the Olivieri family at this location for 63 years, claims to sell more cheesesteaks than anyone else, and they probably do. For maximum ambience, come at 3 AM. *1237 E. Passyunk Ave. (at the intersection of 9th and Wharton Sts.), South Philadelphia, tel. 215/468–1546. Reservations not necessary. No credit cards. Open 24 hours.*

★ **Reading Terminal Market.** A Philadelphia treasure, the Reading Terminal Market is a potpourri of over 80 stalls, shops, lunch counters, and food emporiums in a one-square-block indoor farmers market. You can choose from numerous cuisines—Chinese, Greek, Mexican, Japanese, Middle Eastern, Italian, soul food, and Pennsylvania Dutch. Food options include salad bar, seafood, deli, five bake shops, specialty hoagie shop, sushi bar, and Bassett's ice cream store. Lunch early to beat the rush. The Down Home Diner serves Brunswick stew made with rabbit. *12th and Arch Sts., Center City, tel. 215/922-2317. Open Mon.–Sat. 8 AM–6 PM. Closed Sun.*

Chinese

Expensive **Susanna Foo.** Susanna's is the most expensive Chinese restau-
★ rant in Philadelphia, and the best. Owners Susanna Foo and E. Hsin used to own Hunan, another top-ranked Chinese restaurant. A $1.5 million renovation in 1993 is planned to enlarge the room (a former steak house), put in a new kitchen, upstairs bar, and Chinese art—to create a space worthy of Foo's gourmet offerings. A favorite entrée is the Eight Treasure Quails, made with Chinese sausage, lotus seeds, and sweet rice. The bar has a full wine list and imported beers. Skip the Western-style desserts in favor of the chocolate-dipped fortune cookies. *1512 Walnut St., Center City, tel. 215/545-2666. Reservations required. Dress: informal. AE, DC, MC, V. Closed Sun.*

Inexpensive **Imperial Inn.** This is one of Philadelphia's larger and better-known Chinese restaurants. The decor—with white linen, flowers, and chandeliers—is fancier than that of most other restaurants in Chinatown. The menu offers Cantonese, Szechuan, and Mandarin selections. The Imperial is known for its lunchtime dim sum—"finger-food" appetizers that you choose from a cart wheeled to your table. *142 N. 10th St., Chinatown, tel. 215/627-2299. Dress: informal. AE, DC, MC, V.*

★ **Joe's Peking Duck House.** Not the best Chinese restaurant in Philadelphia but the best in Chinatown. With its friendly atmosphere and plain environment, it's like many of the other 50 or so Chinese restaurants around 10th and Race streets, but the quality is better. Joe's is known for Peking duck and barbecued pork. The Cantonese wonton soup is excellent. *925 Race St., Chinatown, tel. 215/922-3277. Reservations advised. Dress: informal. No credit cards.*

French

Very Expensive **La Truffe.** La Truffe serves both rich classic and lighter mod-
★ ern French cuisine in a French country-inn atmosphere. Specialties include appetizer—*mille-feuille de pleurotte* (wild mushrooms in a puff pastry); entrée—*carré d'agneau au thym* (rack of lamb with thyme sauce); dessert—white chocolate mousse with fresh raspberry sauce. A la carte entrées cost about $30. *10 S. Front St., Old City, tel. 215/925-5062. Reservations advised. Jacket and tie required. AE, DC, MC, V. Closed Sun.*

★ **Le Bec-Fin.** This is the best restaurant in Philadelphia. It's also the most expensive—about $100 a meal—and worth it. The mise-en-scène is fit for a French king: apricot silk walls, crystal chandeliers, and gilt-framed mirrors; and "The Fine Beak" (or more loosely "The Fine Palate") has won a zillion awards. Craig

Claiborne, of the *New York Times,* called it "the finest French restaurant in the East." Owner-chef Georges Perrier is a perfectionist who spares nothing to inject excellence into every detail. The five-course prix-fixe dinner includes choice of appetizer, fish course, entrée, sorbet and cheese, and dessert cart. This is the place to "share" dishes with your dining companions; you'll be hard pressed to say which is the most sensational. One superb meal includes *galette de crabe aux haricots verts* (crab cakes and green beans), *saumon fumé à la minute* (smoked salmon), *filet d'agneau au curry de madras et son chutney de pommes* (lamb with curry and apple chutney), and finally, the *charrette de dessert:* a three-tiered cart with more than 30 sinful temptations, of which you may succumb to as many as you wish. If you want a taste of the Beak without blowing the budget on dinner, lunch is a relatively modest $32, and Le Bar Lyonnais downstairs offers munchies with a French accent for about $10 a pop. *1523 Walnut St., Center City, tel. 215/567–1000. Reservations required. Jacket and tie advised. AE, DC, MC, V. Closed Sun.*

Expensive   **Alouette.** Alouette serves French cuisine with an Asian accent. Owner Kamol Phutlek, one of the better chefs in town, is famous for his sauces—tamarind, lime and pineapple, Thai curry, and raspberry lemon. A favorite appetizer is snails in puff pastry with white wine butter sauce. The elegant decor includes fresh flowers, candlelit tables, and a Victorian bar. The French flower-garden courtyard seats 20 people in summer. *4th and Bainbridge Sts., Society Hill, tel. 215/629–1126. Reservations advised weekdays, required weekends. Dress: informal. AE, DC, MC, V. Closed Tues.*

Ciboulette. The food has always been exceptional at Ciboulette (French for chives), and now the setting equals the fare. In 1993, owner-chef Bruce Lim moved from his 35-seat minimalist room on Spruce Street to the turn-of-the-century elegance of the former Bellevue Stratford Hotel. The restaurant now occupies the Pink and Gold rooms of what was once Philadelphia's most opulent hotel, with appointments—such as the original 1904 terrazzo mosaic floor (each tile 2½ inches deep)—that you will see in no other dining room in the city. For an appetizer, try the marinade-of-three-fish salad (sea bass, salmon, and tuna) with coriander. Chef Lim (who developed his talents at the excellent Fountain Restaurant in the Four Seasons Hotel) is proud of his rack of lamb, now done in mustard sauce. A new dessert cart offers over 20 desserts made daily on the premises. *200 S. Broad St., The Bellevue, 2nd fl., tel. 215/790–1210. Jacket and tie suggested. Reservations advised. AE, DC, MC, V.*

Moderate   **Odeon.** Among the trendiest new eateries in the city, Odeon is a posh restoration of a former flower shop, with large mirrors, green marble columns, and Art Deco sconces. The roasted eggplant with tomato, mozzarella, and sweet peppers makes a memorable first course. The sautéed crab cakes in a lemon-butter sauce is one of the specialties of the house. Recommended for dinner is the Szechuan-peppercorn–encrusted duck breast in star anise and tamari sauce. Desserts include hazelnut meringue layered with buttercream. At the bar there is a selection of over 30 single-malt whiskeys and a cruvinet serves 16 different wines by the glass. Try to sit at the balcony tables above the sweeping stairway or at the table by the window. *114 S. 12th St., Center City, tel. 215/922–5875. Reserva-*

tions required on weekends. Dress: informal. AE, DC, MC, V. Closed Sun.

Italian

Very Expensive **Monte Carlo Living Room.** Italian haute cuisine is served amid crystal chandeliers and imported furniture in two mirrored, candlelit dining rooms. Homemade pastas, pastries, and gelati are all recommended. Fish dishes are a specialty. Milk-fed veal stuffed with mozzarella and prosciutto, served with a mushroom sauce, is a popular entrée. The six-course "of the chef" dinner costs $65. Dancing in a private club upstairs is free to diners. *2nd and South Sts., Society Hill, tel. 215/925-2220. Reservations required on weekends. Jacket required. AE, DC, MC, V.*

Expensive **DiLullo Centro.** Occupying the former Locust Theater, DiLullo Centro may be the most striking restaurant in Philadelphia. The two dining areas—one dark, one better lit—have murals, etched glass, dark wood, and brass and glass partitions. Food is good to excellent, but some dishes are overpriced. Recommended pasta dishes are tortellini stuffed with crabmeat and flavored with tomato and brandy and the *tonnarelli* (mushroom pasta) with salmon. Best entrées include the rack of lamb and the medallions of tuna served on a bed of escarole and beans. For dessert try the homemade gelati "flavor of the day." The excellent wine list has some hard-to-find Italian selections, including Arneis Montebertotto Bianco. *1407 Locust St., Center City, tel. 215/546-2000. Reservations suggested on weekends. Jacket and tie advised. AE, DC, MC, V. Closed Sun.*

★ **Osteria Romana.** You'll pay more than you're used to for Italian food, but Osteria Romana is worth it. It's the finest Italian restaurant in Philadelphia. The stucco walls are trimmed in dark wood and the white tile floors are styled after a Roman *ristorante*. The friendly staff makes you feel at home. Pastas are ample enough for a relatively inexpensive entrée: Don't pass up the gnocchi. Top entrées include suckling pig; *fritto misto* (a mixture of squid, scallops, and shrimp in a delicate batter); and saltimbocca (veal, sage, and prosciutto in white wine with a dash of cream). Homemade gelato is the star dessert. The excellent wine list includes a Cervaro and a Tunina. *935 Ellsworth St., South Philadelphia, tel. 215/271-9191. Reservations advised. Dress: informal. AE, MC, V. Closed Mon.*

Tiramisu. "The name is Italian for a 'pick-me-up,'" says chef-owner Alberto Delbello, explaining the name of his restaurant and the popular dessert in which he specializes. The intimate room is narrow, with a small bar at one end and a wood-burning fireplace at the other. Oil paintings from Italy line the exposed-brick walls. Delbello describes his fare as "nouvelle Jewish-Roman cuisine," with many items on the menu taken from *The Classic Cuisine of the Italian Jews*, by Edda Servi Machlin. You'll munch on matzoh with olive oil and garlic, while you peruse the menu. For a fun appetizer try the baby artichokes with garlic. A memorable entrée is the veal scaloppine with mushrooms, rosemary, shallots, and, of course, garlic. The eponymous dessert is served in large portions and made with cream cheese, espresso coffee, chocolate shavings, ladyfinger cookies, a touch of Tiramisu liqueur and . . . no garlic. *528 S. 5th St., Society Hill, tel. 215/925-3335. Reservations recommended. Dress: informal. AE, MC, V.*

Moderate **Ristorante Primavera.** Get here early: This popular Italian bistro seats only 36 and takes reservations only for parties of six or more. Cozy touches include soft track lighting, exposed brick walls, pink table linens, and wall-to-wall carpeting. *Insalata di frutti di mare* with lemon juice, olive oil, and parsley is a huge but inexpensive seafood appetizer. If your appetite is smaller, go with the Caesar salad. Some entrées, such as the veal chop with shiitake mushroom and white wine sauce, are good, but pastas and appetizers are the strong suits. Saltimbocca (veal, prosciutto, sage, and white wine) is delicious. For dessert, try the *tiramisu*, a sweet from the recipe book of the manager's grandmother. The wine list is small; service is friendly. *146 South St., Society Hill, tel. 215/925–7832. Dress: informal. No credit cards.*

★ **Victor Cafe.** Looking for your waiter? He may be on the stairway singing a Verdi aria. At the Victor Cafe the waiters are opera singers and the kitchen plays second fiddle to the music. The northern Italian cuisine has improved now that the third generation of the Di Stefano family has taken charge, but people still come here more for the music and the atmosphere. Busts of classical music composers adorn the shelves, and framed photos of opera singers line the walls. The family's record collection consists of 25,000 78 RPMs. *1303 Dickinson St., South Philadelphia, tel. 215/468–3040. Packed weeknights; weekends booked weeks in advance. Dress: informal. AE, DC.*

Inexpensive **Boccie Pizza.** Two sparkling wood-burning ovens in a refurbished warehouse turn out both traditional and "nouveau" pizzas. Design your own from 22 ingredients. Or choose one from the menu, such as the Moroccan (topped with lamb strips, scallions, and yogurt sauce), or the Hawaiian with a pesto base. Non-pizza entrées are also available. After the meal, you can play a game of boccie on the court right in the middle of the restaurant. *4040 Locust St., University City, tel. 215/386–5500. Dress: informal. MC, V.*

Triangle Tavern. One of the many South Philadelphia neighborhood Italian bar-restaurants—only cheaper. The Triangle has lots of local color. Mussels are the specialty of the house; *calamari* (squid) with red sauce ("Italian gravy" to Philadelphia Italians) is also popular. Dusty's Trio has been providing live entertainment on Friday and Saturday nights here for 40 years. *10th and Reed Sts., South Philadelphia, tel. 215/467–8683. Dress: casual. No credit cards.*

Japanese

Moderate **Tokio.** Decor here is Japanese minimalist: A toy Godzilla
★ guards the four tables and sushi bar; Japanese rock plays in the background. Sushi and sashimi, which are attractively presented at most Japanese restaurants, are even more attractive here. Try one of the combination dishes ranging in price from $8 to $20. A $10 dish includes octopus, yellowtail, eel, and a ring of rice and is adorned with flying-fish eggs. If you can't fathom raw fish, consider the sukiyaki or the yosenabe—they're cooked on your table and you decide when they're done. Green tea ice cream is the house dessert. *124 Lombard St., Society Hill, tel. 215/922–7181. Dress: informal. AE, DC, MC, V.*

Ziggy's. So much is happening here that dining may seem incidental. The sleek black interior with its geometric neon shapes, floor-to-ceiling video screen, and—at the mahogany bar—personal TV sets, has a mysterious ambience. Your waiter may be wearing theatrical makeup. Food is served under a spotlight at your table. The menu is mostly Japanese— sashimi, sushi, and maki sushi. *Chirashi sushi* is an assortment of *surimi*, salmon roe, giant clam, and squid garnished with vegetables atop vinegared rice. "All you can eat" sushi for $19.95 is offered Thursday through Sunday. For dessert try the green tea ice cream. *1210 Walnut St., Center City, tel. 215/985– 1838. Reservations advised on weekends. Dress: informal. AE, DC, MC, V.*

Mexican

Moderate **Tequila's.** The place to go for Mexican food in Philadelphia. For
★ appetizers, skip the *nachitos obligatorios* and try one of the citric seviches (such as fish and shrimp stuffed in pineapple). The best entrée is the *pescado frito*, a whole fish (usually red snapper or grouper) marinated in citrus, fried, and served with a garlic sauce. Others to sample are *chiles rellenos*—poblano peppers stuffed with ground beef mixed with fruit or cheese— and the defatted duck baked in a ground squash seed sauce. The walls have photos of Pancho Villa and Emiliano Zapata and alcoves contain Mexican glassware and ceramics. For dessert, many favor the *crepe ve Cajeta* with goat's-milk syrup. Select from 10 different Mexican beers and 10 brands of tequila. *1511 Locust St., Center City, tel. 215/546–0181. Dress: informal. AE, DC, MC, V.*

Middle Eastern

Moderate **Marrakesh.** People who don't like eating with their hands—
★ well, they'll survive. There are no utensils here, and diners sit on low cushioned benches at hammered-brass tables. After you wash your hands with warm water and dry them on towels, you're served a $20 prix fixe seven-course banquet: salads, *bastilla* (meat pie with chicken, almonds, and scrambled eggs), chicken and lamb with honey and almonds, couscous with vegetables, fresh fruit, baklava, and sweet mint tea. A fun dining experience. *517 S. Leithgow St., Society Hill, tel. 215/925– 5929. Reservations required. Dress: informal. No credit cards. Dinner only.*

The Middle East. More than just a restaurant, the Middle East is a show. It has mirrors, Oriental rugs on the walls, and gilded portraits worthy of a sultan's harem. You might see a hula dancer or a fire-eater, but the Middle East is famous for its belly dancers. (Join them if you feel adventurous.) The owners, the Tayoun family, have filled the menu with dishes from their ancestral Lebanon and other Middle Eastern countries. Lamb is the staple—on the shank, braised with tomatoes; in moussaka; on kebabs; and ground raw in *kibbie nayee* (raw lamb and wheat germ), the national dish of Lebanon. American food, including meatless Pritikin dishes, is also available. *126 Chestnut St., Old City, tel. 215/922–1003. Reservations suggested. Dress: informal. AE, DC, MC, V.*

Inexpensive **Chef Theodore.** Chef Theodore is a cut above the other Delaware Valley Greek restaurants. The 1990 renovations added a new dining room and a bar-lounge and doubled the seating to accommodate 90 people. The bargain-priced *meze* combination platter includes *baba cunush* (roast eggplant dip), *humus* (ground chick-peas with sesame paste), *taramosalata* (salty caviar spread), *tzatziki* (whipped yogurt with cucumbers and lemon), marinated octopus, stuffed grape leaves, calamata olives, and feta cheese. Among a dozen nightly specials are braised lamb with *avgolimono* (lemon) and dill sauce, served with artichoke hearts. All entrées are served in portions that are a challenge to finish. You can end your meal with good Greek coffee and sweet but not overly rich desserts. *1100 S. Delaware Ave., South Philadelphia, tel. 215/271–6800. Dress: informal. AE, MC, V. Closed Mon.*

Seafood

Very Expensive **Old Original Bookbinder's.** This is a favorite haunt of celebrities, politicians, and athletes—many of whom appear in photos on the walls. The seafood is well prepared but not necessarily the best you'll ever eat. "Bookie's" is often criticized for being overpriced (entrées range from $17 to $30) and touristy (it runs a gift shop with Bookbinder souvenirs). You can select a lobster from a tank and have it cooked to order. This was the site of the Bookbinder family's first restaurant, opened in 1865. *125 Walnut St., Society Hill, tel. 215/925–7027. Reservations suggested. Dress: informal. AE, DC, MC, V.*

Expensive **Bookbinder's Seafood House.** Bookbinder's, the most famous name in Philadelphia restaurants, is actually two separate restaurants with different owners in different parts of town. This one is owned by the original family; the other, Old Original Bookbinder's, stands on the site of the Bookbinder family's first restaurant. Seafood House, a tad less expensive than Old Original, has typical seafood restaurant decor like stuffed swordfish mounted on the walls and fishermen's nets dangling from the ceiling. The menu features lobster Coleman (lobster stuffed with chunks of crabmeat), crab imperial, fresh stone crabs, snapper soup, and baked crabs. *215 S. 15th St., Center City, tel. 215/545–1137. Reservations suggested. Dress: informal. AE, DC, MC, V.*

Moderate **Sansom Street Oyster House.** This Philadelphia favorite serves
★ first-rate raw oysters plus clams, fish, shellfish, and grilled and blackened dishes. It's an unpretentious place with dark wood paneling and uncovered tables. The family collection of over 200 oyster plates covers the walls. In 1988 they expanded both the space and the menu, adding a bar, more seating, and non-seafood items like steaks and chicken. The menu changes daily. House-specialty desserts are the apple Brown Betty and the bread pudding with whiskey sauce. *1516 Sansom St., Center City, tel. 215/567–7683. Reservations accepted only for parties of 5 or more. Dress: informal. AE, DC, MC, V. Closed Sun.*

Steaks

Very Expensive **Morton's of Chicago.** With a tuxedoed maître d' and the atmosphere of a private club, Morton's is a steakhouse catering largely to businessmen on expense accounts. The balcony-level dining area overlooks the main dining room, which has an Art Deco bar and walls lined with bottles of wine. Choose your cut of meat or fish from raw items on a cart wheeled to your table; it will be cooked to your specifications. The house specialty, a 24-ounce porterhouse, should fill you up. *1 Logan Sq. (on 19th St.),*

Center City, tel. 215/557–0724. Reservations suggested. Jacket and tie advised. AE, DC, MC, V.

Expensive   **The Saloon.** Here's a steakhouse with Italian specialties. Everything it does is big: big pieces of meat, big drinks, big prices. Big money went into the antique turn-of-the-century decor—mahogany paneling, mirrors, and stained glass. For an appetizer, try the salad of radicchio with shiitake mushrooms, served warm. For an entrée, order the off-the-menu special risotto with abundant porcini mushrooms, or cannelloni filled with veal in one of the excellent tomato sauces. Desserts include lemon and berry tarts. *750 S. 7th St., South Philadelphia, tel. 215/627–1811. Reservations recommended. Dress: informal. AE. Closed Sun.*

Thai

Inexpensive   **Thai Garden East.** In 1988, Heng Leevongcharoen, a former ★ dishwasher, and his wife Rudee opened Thai Garden in West Philadelphia. It quickly became *the* Thai restaurant in the city. In 1990, Chef Leevongcharoen moved to Center City, next door to the new Convention Center, and created Thai Garden East. The contemporary ambience is different, but the food that made both restaurants popular is as good, and as inexpensive, as ever. The *miena cum* appetizer—toasted peanuts, coconut chips, and lime piled on spinach leaves spiced with chopped chili and a Thai plum sauce—is delectable. *Chu chee* (curried duck) and Thai-style barbecued chicken with sweet-and-sour sauce are among the excellent entrées. For dessert try the Thai custard. *101 N. 11th St., Chinatown, tel. 215/629–9939. Reservations suggested. Dress: informal. MC, V.*

Vietnamese

Inexpensive   **Van's Garden.** Van's is probably the least expensive Asian res- ★ taurant in Philadelphia, yet it's first rate. Hodgepodge decor includes flocked red and black wallpaper, linoleum floors, and blond wood wainscoting. A superb appetizer is grilled meatballs wrapped in rice paper, with carrots, radishes, cucumbers, noodles, and a thick brown bean sauce for dipping—a sort of Vietnamese hoagie. Among entrées, you can get 10 sweet-and-sour shrimp in a tempura-like batter. Barbecued shrimp on vermicelli at $6.95 is the most expensive item on the menu. Dinner here is a superb value. For a variation on a dessert theme, try the rice pudding with taro and coconut juice. *121 N. 11th St., Chinatown, tel. 215/923–2439. Dress: informal. BYOB. No credit cards.*

Brunch

Sunday brunch is a Philadelphia tradition. Scores of local establishments open their doors on Sunday mornings, serving everything from traditional bagels and lox at the Famous Deli to the more unusual rock shrimp and grits baked in cream with pepper jack cheese and roasted peppers found at the White Dog Cafe.

Brunch connoisseurs will not want to miss the Sunday-morning spread at the Four Seasons Hotel (*see* Chapter 7), where for from about $28 to $35, diners can feast on one of two sumptuous buffets amid crystal, linen, and massive floral arrangements.

The hearty buffet at the Swann Lounge Cafe features cooked-to-order omelets and waffles, as well as vegetable stir-fries, pasta, and a broccoli-and-cheese soufflé. In the adjacent, more elegant, Fountain Restaurant, diners can choose from either the menu or the buffet, which specializes in fish, including an occasional caviar dish. The menu features the "Melody of Pancakes," which includes cornbread, whole wheat, regular, and bran—the fanciest stack of flapjacks in Philly. A jazz–New Age trio plays from 11 AM to 3 PM. Children eat for half price. Reservations necessary.

Another classy (and expensive) brunch experience is to be had at Founder's on the 19th floor of the Hotel Atop the Bellevue (*see* Chapter 7). Choose from the sumptuous buffet tables and stations that fill up the Ethyl Barrymore Room, then stroll down the short hallway to a table in Founder's, the most magnificent dining room in the city. The cost is $28.50 (half price for kids under 12).

All the restaurants listed below offer Sunday brunch. Descriptions, addresses, and phone numbers appear in the Dining section above: *Alouette, Bogart's, Carolina's, Chart House, Ciboulette, Commissary, Downey's, Famous Deli, Lickety Split, The Marker, Roller's, Valley Green Inn, White Dog Cafe.*

7 Lodging

*By Rathe Miller
and Michael
Schwager*

Philadelphia hotels run the gamut from commonplace to world class, from a five-star hotel with every luxury to a 12-room country inn. While many are basic utilitarian hotels or national chains, others are experiences in themselves. Though aside from youth hostels and bed-and-breakfasts, the city has only a few moderately priced hotels; most are expensive.

Although the number of rooms—12,000—is small for a city of nearly a million and half, it usually isn't difficult to find a place to stay. The Philadelphia Marriott, adjacent to the Pennsylvania Convention Center, is scheduled to open in December 1994, and will give the downtown another 1,200 rooms. The only times you're likely to encounter problems are the weekend of the Army-Navy football game (usually the weekend after Thanksgiving weekend) and during occasional large conventions. Nevertheless, reservations are advised. The city has no central reservation office.

Hotels are listed geographically. Most hotels are downtown, grouped in three areas: the shopping/theater district, the Benjamin Franklin Parkway/museum area, and the historic district. A half-dozen hotels are clustered near Philadelphia International Airport. Several are on the campus of the University of Pennsylvania in West Philadelphia. Two are in the City Line area. One is in Chestnut Hill in the northwest part of the city.

Within geographic groupings, hotels are listed alphabetically according to the following price categories.

Unless otherwise noted, all rooms have private bath.

Highly recommended lodgings in each price category are indicated by a star ★.

Category	Cost*
Very Expensive	over $140
Expensive	$100–$140
Moderate	$50–$100
Inexpensive	under $50

All prices are for a standard double room; excluding 12% tax (7% sales tax plus 5% hotel tax).

The following credit card abbreviations are used: AE, American Express; DC, Diners Club; MC, MasterCard; V, Visa.

Philadelphia has no off-season rates, but most hotels offer discount packages for weekends when demand from business people and groups subsides. Besides substantially reduced rates, these packages often include an assortment of free features, such as breakfast, parking, cocktails, champagne, and the use of exercise facilities.

Aside from such packages, most downtown hotels charge around $14 a day for parking.

Center City

Hotels downtown are located in three areas. The shopping/theater district encompasses a few blocks on either side of Broad

Street, near Walnut Street. The Parkway/museum area runs along the Benjamin Franklin Parkway from 16th Street to the Philadelphia Museum of Art. The historic district on the east side of downtown centers on Independence Hall and extends to the Delaware River.

Very Expensive **Four Seasons.** If a director wanted a location for a romantic ho-
★ tel-room view in Philadelphia, she would choose a room here, overlooking the fountains in Logan Circle and the Benjamin Franklin Parkway. Built in 1983, the eight-story U-shaped hotel has block-long hallways that some guests don't like. Guest-room furniture is Federal style, dark and stately. Philadelphia's most expensive hotel provides terry robes and a complimentary shoeshine—hang your shoes in the bag on your doorknob and they come back shined the next morning. The Fountain Restaurant, nestled in the lobby, is the hands-down best hotel dining in town. Weather permitting, the Swann Courtyard Cafe is an excellent spot for a drink and a kiss. *1 Logan Sq. (near major museums), 19103, tel. 215/963–1500 or 800/332–3442. 371 rooms. Facilities: 24-hr room service, 24-hr concierge service, 6 nonsmoking floors, exercise room, dry sauna, massage, indoor pool, restaurant, indoor/outdoor café (health menu available from room service and in the restaurant). Weekend rates. AE, DC, MC, V.*

★ **Hotel Atop the Bellevue.** A Philadelphia institution for 90 years, the elegant Bellevue hotel was reopened in 1989 on seven floors in its original building. A three-year, $150 million renovation transformed the lower floors into office and shop space, while the 12th through 19th floors were redesigned to accommodate the hotel. The Barrymore Room, topped by a stained-glass 30-foot dome, and the seven-story Conservatory atrium are just two of the hotel's lavish public areas. Founders, with views of the city from its 19th-floor setting, is the most visually impressive dining room in the city. From the champagne toast available at registration, to the telephones and TVs in the bathrooms, a stay at the Bellevue is full of pleasant touches. Rooms are large and each has an entertainment center with color TV, stereo, and VCR (choose from a library of 75 cassettes); minibar; and computer modem data port. Guests have free use of the Sporting Club, the best health club in town. *Broad and Walnut Sts., 19102, tel. 215/893–1776 or 800/221–0833. 170 rooms. Facilities: 24-hr room service, 24-hr concierge, gourmet restaurant, lounge, wine bar, health club, three floors of shops. AE, DC, MC, V.*

Latham. This is a small, elegant hotel with a European accent and an emphasis on personal service. Doormen clad in vests and riding boots welcome you to the lobby. A concierge is on duty daily from 10 to 8. All rooms have marble-topped bureaus and French writing desks, full-wall mirrors, hair dryers, and makeup mirrors; most have minibars. The weekend package includes a deluxe room, valet parking, and gourmet breakfast. *17th St. at Walnut St. (1 block from Rittenhouse Sq.), 19103, tel. 215/563–7474 or 800/528–4261. 139 rooms. Facilities: executive floor; free use of health spa 3 blocks away; restaurant; piano lounge; business center with fax machine, copier, and secretarial service. AE, DC, MC, V.*

Philadelphia Hilton and Towers. You can sit in the four-story atrium lobby and behold one of the busiest corners of Philadelphia's shopping and theater district. Rooms are decorated in earth-tones, with modern furnishings. Opened in 1983, the

Lodging

Adam's Mark, **3**

Bank Street Hostel, **22**

The Barclay, **11**

Best Western Independence Park Inn, **24**

Chamounix Mansion, **2**

Chestnut Hill Hotel, **5**

Comfort Inn at Penn's Landing, **21**

Days Inn, **30**

Four Seasons, **8**

Guest Quarters, **27**

Holiday Inn Philadelphia International Airport, **31**

Holiday Inn Center City, **9**

Holiday Inn City Line, **4**

Holiday Inn Independence Mall, **20**

Holiday Inn Midtown, **18**

Hotel Atop the Bellevue, **16**

International House, **6**

Latham, **13**

Penn Tower, **7**

Philadelphia Hilton and Towers, **17**

Philadelphia Airport Marriott Hotel, **28**

Ramada Inn-Center City, **1**

Ramada Inn-Conference and Sports Center, **29**

Ramada Suites-Convention Center, **19**

The Rittenhouse, **10**

Ritz-Carlton, **14**

Sheraton Society Hill, **26**

Society Hill Hotel, **23**

Thomas Bond House, **25**

The Warwick, **12**

Wyndham Franklin Plaza, **15**

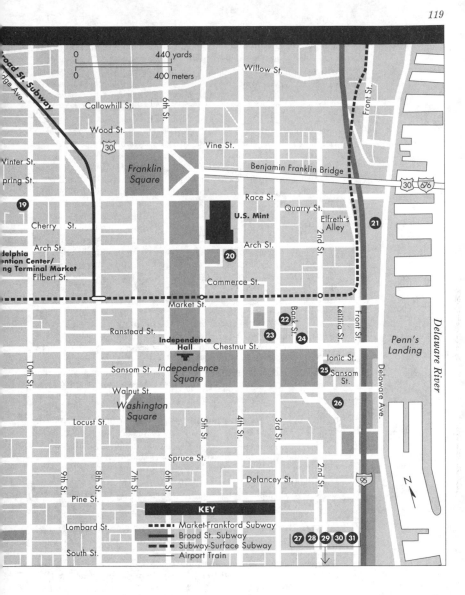

Willow St.

Broad St. Subway

Ridge Ave.

0   440 yards

0   400 meters

Callowhill St.

6th St.

Wood St.

30

Vine St.

Winter St.

Spring St.

Franklin Square

Benjamin Franklin Bridge

Front St.

30   676

19

Race St.

Cherry St.

U.S. Mint

Quarry St.

Elfreth's Alley

21

Arch St.

2nd St.

Arch St.

Philadelphia Convention Center/ Reading Terminal Market

20

Filbert St.

Commerce St.

Market St.

Ranstead St.

Bank St.

22

Letitia St.

Front St.

Penn's Landing

Independence Hall

23

Chestnut St.

24

Delaware River

Sansom St.

Independence Square

Ionic St.

25

Sansom St.

10th St.

Walnut St.

Washington Square

26

Delaware Ave.

Locust St.

5th St.

4th St.

3rd St.

Spruce St.

9th St.

8th St.

7th St.

6th St.

2nd St.

95

Pine St.

Delancey St.

N

KEY

Lombard St.

South St.

▪▪▪▪ Market-Frankford Subway
━━ Broad St. Subway
▬ ▬ Subway-Surface Subway
── Airport Train

27 28 29 30 31

hotel's sawtooth design gives each room a peaked bay window with a 180-degree view. East-side rooms get a panoramic view of the city, the Delaware River, and New Jersey. During baseball season you might be sitting next to big-league players in the lobby restaurant, Cafe Academie—many of the teams stay here when they're in town to play the Phillies. *Broad and Locust Sts., 19107, tel. 215/893–1600 or 800/HILTONS. 427 rooms. Facilities: free Continental breakfast, health club with indoor pool, saunas, tanning salon, whirlpool, weight room, snack bar, racquetball courts, gift shop, lobby lounge with live entertainment, restaurant in atrium area. AE, DC, MC, V.*

The Rittenhouse. This luxury hotel takes full advantage of its Rittenhouse Square location; many rooms and both restaurants overlook the city's classiest park. The expansive white-marbled lobby leads to the Mary Cassatt Tea Room and Lounge and a cloistered garden. The 33-story building's sawtooth design gives the guest rooms their unusual shapes, with nooks and alcoves. Each room has two TVs, three telephones, an entertainment center in an armoire, a fully-stocked minibar, and a king-size bed. Ninth-floor rooms facing the square have the best views. *210 West Rittenhouse Sq., 19103, tel. 215/546–9000 or 800/635–1042. 98 rooms, including 11 suites. Facilities: 2 restaurants, bar, 24-hr room service, concierge daily 7AM–11:30PM, health club, business center, 3 nonsmoking floors, valet parking $19. Weekend packages. AE, DC, MC, V.*

Ritz-Carlton. Ritzy it is: a "security" elevator from the arrival lobby to the main lobby; mantelpieces from Italy; silk walls in the bar; a million dollars' worth of art displayed throughout. Opened in November 1990, the 15-story building is nestled between the twin blue towers of Liberty Place and adjacent to the Shops at Liberty Place (more than 70 stores, boutiques, and restaurants). All rooms have an elegant colonial motif; most have king-size beds, although rooms with oversize twins are available. All the typical luxury amenities are here: entertainment center in armoire; honor bar; complimentary shoe shine; valet laundry service; in-the-bathroom telephone, terry robes, hair dryers, and scale. You'll also find a recent copy of *Philadelphia* magazine marked for the proper day with a Ritz-Carlton bookmark listing the hotel's special services. *17th and Chestnut Sts. (at Liberty Pl.), 19103, tel. 215/563–1600 or 800/241–3333. 290 guest rooms. Facilities: 2 restaurants, bar, lobby lounge, 24-hr room service, concierge service 7 AM to 11 PM, baby-sitting service, gift shop, health club. Weekend package. AE, DC, MC, V.*

Sheraton Society Hill. Conveniently located for visits to the historic district, this red-brick, neo-Colonial building is two blocks from Penn's Landing, three blocks from Head House Square, and three blocks from Independence Hall. Opened in 1986, its four-story atrium lobby is framed by archways and balconies, filled with trees and plants, and lit by wrought-iron lanterns. Rooms are furnished traditionally but have modern conveniences such as a bar, a remote-control TV, and coffee makers. Fourth-floor rooms facing east toward the Delaware River have the best view. Pianist Sinisha Mitrovik plays regularly in the atrium lobby. *1 Dock St., 19106, tel. 215/238–6000 or 800/325–3535. 365 rooms, 17 suites. Facilities: restaurant/ bar, 24-hr room service, indoor pool, fitness center with whirlpool, sauna, and exercise room. AE, DC, MC, V.*

Wyndham Franklin Plaza. "Please Wait for Next Available Receptionist" read the signs in the lobby of Philadelphia's biggest and busiest hotel. The 70-foot atrium lobby encompasses three restaurants, a bar, and numerous sitting areas. Hallways show the wear and tear of being the city's main convention hotel, but rooms are well cared for. Decor is modern, in gray and silver with chrome tubular purple chairs, full-length mirrors, and cable TV. *16th and Vine Sts., 19103, tel. 215/448–2000 or 800/ 822–4200. 758 rooms, including 38 suites. Facilities: room service; access to health club with 3 racquetball courts, 3 squash courts, 2 tennis courts, masseuse, exercise equipment, aerobics center, pool; beauty shop; barber shop; florist; travel service; gift shop. Weekend packages. AE, DC, MC, V.*

Expensive **The Barclay.** There's something special about having Rittenhouse Square right outside your front door *(see* Tour 3 in Chapter 3). The hotel was built in 1929 and was once one of Philadelphia's two best. The elegant, dark-paneled lobby leads to a registration area sparkling with a half-dozen crystal chandeliers and matching wall fixtures. Some guest rooms have hardwood floors and Oriental rugs. Half the rooms have fourposter beds—and many of those have canopies. Furniture is antique style throughout and in most rooms TV sets are concealed in classic armoires. *Rittenhouse Sq. E., 19103, tel. 215/ 545–0300 or 800/421–6662. 240 rooms, including 50 suites. Facilities: concierge service, restaurant, lobby lounge with jazz pianist. AE, DC, MC, V.*

Best Western Independence Park Inn. From the rooms facing busy Chestnut Street you'll hear the clop-clop of the carriage horses and the roar of the city buses. The five-story building is a former dry-goods warehouse built in 1856; it opened in 1988 as a hotel. The high-ceilinged guest rooms are modern with colonial touches and come standard and deluxe (deluxe includes king-size bed and parlor). VCRs and videos are available for a small charge. Complimentary Continental breakfast and afternoon tea are served in a courtyard dining room with a glass atrium ceiling. *235 Chestnut St., 19106, tel. 215/922– 4443 or 800/624–2988. 36 rooms. Facilities: modem ports in telephones; access to health club 3 blocks away. AE, DC, MC, V.*

Holiday Inn Center City. Centrally located between Benjamin Franklin Parkway, Rittenhouse Square, and City Hall, this is an above-average Holiday Inn with an excellent location. The 25-floor hotel opened in 1971 and completed a $9.5 million renovation in 1993. All rooms have a green-and-beige color scheme and contemporary decor. Amenities include 75-channel cable TV, telephone modem ports, and hairdryers. *1800 Market St., 19103, tel. 215/561–7500 or 800/HOLIDAY. 445 rooms, including 2 suites. Facilities: 2 no-smoking floors; 2 executive-level concierge floors; 8th-floor outdoor pool; weight room with Nautilus, rowing machines, exercise bikes; gift shop; restaurant; cocktail lounge. Weekend package. AE, DC, MC, V.*

Holiday Inn Independence Mall. "Independence Mall" in the name is no exaggeration: This is one of the hotels most convenient to the downtown historic area. To complement its location, all rooms are done in Colonial decor with Ethan Allen Georgetown furniture, including poster beds and wing chairs. *4th and Arch Sts., 19106, tel. 215/923–8660 or 800/HOLIDAY. 364 rooms, 7 suites. Facilities: outdoor pool, videogame room, gift shop, cocktail lounge, Benjamin's restaurant. Weekend package. AE, DC, MC, V.*

Holiday Inn Midtown. Rooms are more spacious than average here—perhaps because they're older (it opened in 1964). Renovated in 1992, the grey walls of the lobby are accented with cherry-wood molding and original art. All guest rooms have contemporary furnishings and a light, floral motif. Rooms facing south to Walnut Street have the best views. Drive in off Walnut Street for valet parking. The location is excellent: one block from the Broad Street Subway, near the theater and shopping district, and three blocks from the new Convention Center. *1305 Walnut St., 19107, tel. 215/735–9300 or 800/HOLIDAY. 161 rooms. Facilities: nonsmoking rooms, outdoor pool, restaurant, lounge. Weekend package. AE, DC, MC, V.*

The Warwick. The lobby, brightened by mirrors and 18-foot Palladian windows, hosts a constant stream of activity. A block of the hotel's 225 rooms are actually apartments, which makes for an interesting mix of guests in business suits and residents in shorts and sneakers. A $5-million renovation was completed in 1992. The spacious rooms are decorated in "English country style." Bathrooms are in marble, with an ivy-green motif. A complimentary shoeshine is available. You'll find the current issue of *Philadelphia* magazine in your room. *1701 Locust St., 19103, tel. 215/735–6000 or 800/523–4210. 225 rooms. Facilities: restaurant/bar, European-style coffee shop, free use of health club 2 blocks away. Weekend package. AE, DC, MC, V.*

Moderate **Comfort Inn at Penn's Landing.** The price is the most noteworthy item here. The 10-story hotel, opened in 1987, provides basic rooms and service. Decor is contemporary, with oak furniture and a mauve color scheme. A bar enlivens the small, nondescript lobby. Tucked between the Benjamin Franklin Bridge, Delaware Avenue, and I–95, the location has more noise than charm. Rooms on upper floors facing the river have a good view of the Benjamin Franklin Bridge beautifully lit up at night. *100 N. Christopher Columbus Blvd., 19106, tel. 215/627–7900 or 800/228–5150. 185 rooms, including 3 suites with hot tubs. Facilities: lobby lounge, complimentary Continental breakfast, free parking, courtesy van service to points all over Center City. AE, DC, MC, V.*

Ramada Inn–Center City. If you're willing to stay a bit away from downtown but near the museums, you'll find a bargain here. The three-story, Y-shaped building was a Quality Inn till 1991, and renovations were ongoing in 1993. Rooms are done in mauve and taupe with oak-finish furniture and individual climate control. The new security system uses electronic keycards. The best view faces south toward the Benjamin Franklin Parkway, the Rodin Museum, and the downtown skyline. *501 N. 22nd St., 19130, tel. 215/568–8300. 278 rooms, including 4 suites. Facilities: room service, restaurant, outdoor café; gift shop, outdoor pool; free parking. Weekend rates (winter only). AE, DC, MC, V.*

★ **Ramada Suites–Convention Center.** A real bargain—suite accommodations at hotel-room prices. It opened in 1985 in a historically certified 1890 building that was once the Bentwood Rocker Factory. Much of the original building was incorporated into the present decor, including exposed brick walls and overhead beams, which give rooms a rustic, homey atmosphere. Every suite has a kitchen. The environment is East meets West: Drexel Heritage furniture with Oriental prints and accent pieces. Ramada took over from Quality Inns in 1993, when this slightly out-of-the-way location suddenly became next-door neighbor to the Pennsylvania Convention Center. *1010 Race St., 19107, tel. 215/922–1730 or 800/221–2222. 92 suites. Facilities: free parking, free buffet breakfast. AE, DC, MC, V.*

Airport

Since the area has few attractions other than the airport and the hotels themselves, hotels here are less expensive than those downtown. For most attractions and entertainment, figure on heading into town, a 20-minute drive or taxi ride away. Three of the hotels are right at the airport and near a sewage-treatment plant; fortunately, their filtration systems effectively insulate guests from the noxious smells and loud noises.

Very Expensive **Guest Quarters.** This eight-story all-suite hotel has no corri-
★ dors. A glass-walled elevator whisks you to your floor, where suites front an ivy-covered balcony overlooking the light-flooded atrium lobby and restaurant. Suites are standard or deluxe: Deluxe have larger living rooms and better views. All suites have a king-size bed in the bedroom and a queen-size foldout in the living room; three telephones; two remote-control TV/clock-radios; honor bars; and coffee makers, plus complimentary in-suite coffee and daily newspaper. Packages range from Bare Bones to Honeymoon (which includes breakfast, bubble bath, and champagne). *Gateway Center, 4101 Island Ave., 19153, tel. 215/365–6600 or 800/424–2900. 251 suites. Facilities: atrium restaurant and lounge; free Continental breakfast on weekends; free hors d'oeuvres 5–7 PM; exercise room with Universal, bikes, rowing machines; indoor pool; whirlpool; steam room; free parking; free airport shuttle. AE, DC, MC, V.*

Expensive **Philadelphia Airport Marriott Hotel.** You can swim in the lobby of the Airport Marriott before jumping on a free shuttle bus for the five-minute ride to your terminal across the street. During the week, this is mostly a business travelers' hotel. Rooms have wood and wicker dressing tables and bureaus and cable TV. There are eight "Female Travelers Rooms," with special amenities and safety features. *4509 Island Ave., 19153, tel. 215/365–4150 or 800/228–9290. 330 rooms. Facilities: concierge floor, no-smoking floor, swimming pool in lobby; workout room with weights, machines, bikes, whirlpool, and saunas; 2 restaurants; sports bar; free parking; free airport shuttle. Weekend rates. AE, DC, MC, V.*

Moderate **Ramada Inn–Conference and Sports Center.** This circular high-rise building was renovated in 1992. Rooms have coffee makers, refrigerators, and cable TV with remote control. Upper floors have a good view of the city. *20th St. and Penrose Ave., 19145, tel. 215/755–6500. 194 rooms, including 3 suites. Facilities: restaurant, lounge, free shuttle to airport and sports complex. AE, DC, MC, V.*
Days Inn. Even though this new hotel is surrounded by highways and is across the street from the airport, special construction makes it quiet. The sunny, pastel-green corridors of the four-story L-shaped building lead to pleasant and spacious rooms. *2 Gateway Ctr., 4101 Island Ave., 19153, tel. 215/492–0400 or 800/325–2525. 177 rooms. Facilities: coin-operated launderette, Seasons Cafe, 32 no-smoking rooms, free airport*

shuttle. Special packages and senior-citizen rates, children under 18 free. AE, DC, MC, V.

Holiday Inn Philadelphia International Airport. A $3 million renovation in 1993 converted the lobby's "Floridian" theme to a more traditional look—with green marble, darker colors, and a fireplace. The slightly oversize rooms are pastel-colored with light-colored wood furniture. It's 3 miles west of the airport. *45 Industrial Hwy. (Rte. 291), Essington 19029, tel. 215/521–2400 or 800/HOLIDAY. 306 rooms. Facilities: restaurant, gift shop, fitness center, outdoor pool, free airport shuttle. Weekend rates. AE, DC, MC, V.*

University City

Located in West Philadelphia, just across the Schuylkill River, this area is a five- to 10-minute drive from Center City. Slightly less expensive than downtown, the hotels are on the campus of the University of Pennsylvania, near Drexel University, and across the street from the Civic Center, the city's secondary convention facility.

Expensive **Penn Tower.** The University of Pennsylvania purchased and renovated this 21-floor former Hilton in 1987. It is located on the eastern edge of the campus across the street from the university's hospital, the Children's Hospital of Philadelphia, and the Civic Center. Rooms have excellent views east to Center City and west across campus. All have cable TV, Colonial decor, and a pastel color scheme. *34th St. and Civic Center Blvd., 19104, tel. 215/387–8333 or 800/356–PENN. 175 rooms, including 7 suites. Facilities: concierge floor, restaurant, lounge, free use of U. of Penn athletic facilities, including Olympic-size pool. AE, DC, MC, V.*

Inexpensive **International House.** This residence for students and professors from around the world is located on the University of Pennsylvania campus. Rooms are available year-round, but guests must have an affiliation with an educational institution. The high-rise building has an unusual poured-concrete, tiered design and an oddly barren atrium. Both the public areas and the rooms themselves have a rough-hewn, spartan feel. No children permitted. *3701 Chestnut St., 19104, tel. 215/387–5125. 379 rooms. Single rooms share bath and living room; double rooms have 2 single beds and private bath. Facilities: cafeteria, bar. College or university affiliation required. MC, V.*

City Line

If you prefer to stay outside the bustle of downtown and get free parking, you'll like the two hotels here. It's only a 10-minute ride on the Schuylkill Expressway to Center City under favorable conditions; however, the expressway is frequently under construction and often heavily congested.

Expensive **Adam's Mark.** This 23-story hotel is one of the tallest in Phila-
★ delphia. Request a room on the upper floors facing south toward Fairmount Park and the downtown skyline. There's nothing special about the rooms, which are on the small side. The big attraction here is the nighttime activity: Quincy's, a turn-of-the-century nightclub; two restaurants; a popular lounge; and a sports bar. *City Ave. and Monument Rd., 19131, tel. 215/581–5000 or 800/444–2326. 515 rooms, including 56*

suites. Facilities: indoor and outdoor swimming pools, health club, whirlpool, aerobics classes, hair salon, gift shop, travel agency. AE, DC, MC, V.

Holiday Inn City Line. This eight-story Holiday Inn is perfectly ordinary, but it's a good value in a choice location. You could stay here to save money and just walk across the parking lot to the Adam's Mark nightclub, restaurants, and lounges. A five-minute walk takes you to six other restaurants. In the lobby you can sink into an overstuffed easy chair and watch swimmers in the glass-enclosed pool. *4100 Presidential Blvd., 19131, tel. 215/477-0200 or 800/HOLIDAY. 343 rooms. Facilities: The Glass Tree restaurant, pool off lobby. AE, DC, MC, V.*

Chestnut Hill

Staying here, about a 25-minute drive from downtown, puts you among some of Philadelphia's finest homes and shops. It has more than 120 shops—from Oriental-rug dealers to bookstores, clothing boutiques, crafts and music stores, and cheese shops. Nearby is the Wissahickon Valley of Fairmount Park.

Moderate **Chestnut Hill Hotel.** Here's a Colonial inn in the heart of Chestnut Hill. Built as a hotel in 1899, the four-story building was renovated in 1983. Ask to see the rooms first; they vary widely in size and ambience. Some have mahogany reproductions of 18th-century furniture, including four-poster beds. A packet of brochures in each room describes area shops and sights. *8229 Germantown Ave., 19118, tel. 215/242-5905. 28 rooms, including 3 suites. Facilities: 2 restaurants; adjacent to a farmers market and shopping complex. AE, DC, MC, V.*

Bed-and-Breakfasts

Bed-and-breakfasts, which follow the European tradition of a room and meal in a private house or small hotel, are less expensive alternatives to hotels. Most operate under the auspices of central booking agencies that screen homes and match guests and hosts. Host homes offer considerable diversity in urban, suburban, and rural settings.

Services and policies vary. Some accept children and pets. Some provide free transportation from airports, and bus and train terminals. Some offer monthly rates. Breakfasts range from Continental to elegant.

Bed and Breakfast, Center City. It represents a dozen homes in the city, from a posh high rise on Rittenhouse Square to a restored town house just off the square. Children permitted. Prices range from $40 to $80. *1804 Pine St., Philadelphia 19103, tel. 215/735-1137 or 800/354-8401. MC, V.*

Bed and Breakfast Connections. Its selection of more than 60 host homes and inns includes a Colonial town house, a converted 1880s bank-style barn, and an 18th-century farmhouse on the Main Line. Prices range from $30 to $125. *Box 21, Devon 19333, tel. 215/687-3565 or 800/448-3619. AE, MC, V.*

Bed and Breakfast—The Manor. This service has various locations throughout Philadelphia and surrounding areas, including Amish country. Many hosts supply transportation for a nominal fee. Some accommodate the handicapped. Prices range from $45 to $85. *Box 416, 830 Village Rd., Lampeter 17537, tel. 717/464-9564. MC, V.*

Bed and Breakfast of Philadelphia. This reservation service books over 100 host homes in Philadelphia, Valley Forge, Amish country, and New Hope. Options range from a Federal town house in the downtown historic area to a pre-Revolutionary farmhouse in Chester County and many suburban homes. Prices range from $35 to $150. *1530 Locust St., Suite K, 19102, tel. 215/735–1917. AE, MC, V.*

Society Hill Hotel. This 1832 former longshoreman's house is one of the smallest hotels in the city. Renovated in 1980, all 12 rooms are uniquely furnished with antiques, brass beds, and lamps. Fresh flowers adorn all rooms and the breakfast tray is brought to your room with fresh-squeezed juice and hand-dipped chocolates. *301 Chestnut St., 19106, tel. 215/925–1394. 12 rooms, including 6 suites. Facilities: outdoor café (voted Philly's classiest by* Philadelphia *magazine), piano bar, restaurant. AE, DC, MC, V.*

Thomas Bond House. Spend the night in the heart of Olde City the way Philadelphians did 220 years ago. Built in 1769 by a prominent local physician, this four-story house recently underwent a faithful, meticulous restoration of everything from its molding and wall sconces to its millwork and flooring. All rooms have 18th-century features such as marble fireplaces and four-poster Thomasville beds. It doesn't get any more Colonial than this. *129 S. 2nd St., 19106, tel. 215/923–8523. 12 rooms, including 2 suites. Facilities: parlor, complimentary wine and cheese. AE, MC, V.*

Youth Hostels

Youth hostels provide dormitory-style accommodations for less than you'd pay to park your car at a downtown hotel. They also offer a sense of adventure and a chance to share living, eating, and sleeping quarters with travelers from all over the world.

The American Youth Hostel Regional Office and Travel Center is at 624 South 3rd Street (tel. 215/925–6004).

Chamounix Mansion. Here's the cheapest place to stay in Philadelphia—$10 a night if you are an American Youth Hostel member, and $3 more if you are the guest of an AYH member. Located on a wooded bluff overlooking the Schuylkill River (and, unfortunately, the Schuylkill Expressway), it feels like it's out in the country. This restored 1802 Quaker country estate is loaded with character. The entrance hall is lined with flags; period rooms have antiques; walls display old maps, sketches, and paintings. Drawbacks: dormitory-style living, shared baths, hard to find. *Chamounix Dr., 19131, tel. 215/878–3676. 6 rooms for 48 people, shared baths and kitchen. Facilities: game room, outdoor sports. No credit cards. Closed Dec. 15–Jan. 15.*

Bank Street Hostel. Independently owned and managed by David Herskowitz, Bank Street opened in 1992 and, at $14 a night, is a downtown-Philly lodging bargain. It's located on the cusp of Olde City and Society Hill in a 140-year-old manufacturing building that's been combined with two neighboring buildings. *32 South Bank St., 19106, tel. 215/922–0222 or 800/392–4678. Three rooms for 54 people. Facilities: pool table, lounge area, 46-inch TV. No credit cards.*

8 The Arts and Nightlife

The Arts

For current productions and performances, check the "Guide to the Lively Arts" in the daily *Philadelphia Inquirer*, the "Weekend" section of the Friday *Inquirer*, the "Friday" section of the *Philadelphia Daily News*, and the Donnelley Directory Events Hotline (tel. 215/337–7777 ext. 2540). *Philadelphia Spotlite*, a free weekly guide listing plays, music, sports, and events, is available at the Visitors Center (16th St. and John F. Kennedy Blvd.). Check "UpStages" (tel. 215/567–0670) at the Visitors Center for tickets to some of the smaller productions and concerts around town, sometimes at a discount.

Theater

Forrest Theater (1114 Walnut St., tel. 215/923–1515) has major Broadway productions, recently *Evita*, *La Cage Aux Folles*, *Les Misérables*, and *Phantom of the Opera*.

Annenberg Center (3680 Walnut St., tel. 215/898–6791) has four stages, from the 120-seat Studio to the 970-seat Zellerbach Theater. Something is going on almost all the time—with performers like Liv Ullman and acts such as the Flying Karamazov Brothers and Avner the Eccentric.

Merriam Theater (250 S. Broad St., tel. 215/732–5446). Formerly the Shubert, and part of the University of the Arts, the Merriam presents musicals and dramas occasionally performed by touring companies.

Walnut Street Theater (9th and Walnut Sts., tel. 215/574–3550). Founded in 1809, this is the oldest English-speaking theater in continuous use in the United States. The schedule includes musicals, comedy, and drama in a lovely auditorium where almost every seat is a good one.

Wilma Theater (2030 Sansom St., tel. 215/963–0345) has gained favorable critical notices for its innovative work since adopting a policy of hiring Equity actors. The season runs from September to June.

Philadelphia Theater Company (1714 Delancey St., at Plays and Players, tel. 215/592–8333) performs Philadelphia and world premieres by contemporary American playwrights. It also has Stages, a program of new plays by American playwrights.

Society Hill Playhouse (507 S. 8th St., tel. 215/923–0210). The main stage features contemporary works; the Second Space Cabaret Theater has been showing the musical comedy *Nunsense* for the past eight years.

Theater of the Living Arts (334 South St., tel. 215/922–1010) presents a year-round season of concerts of jazz, New Age music, rock, comedians, and off-Broadway fare.

American Theater Arts for Youth (Port of History Museum, Penn's Landing, tel. 215/563–3501) features musicals and live productions of the National Theater for Children.

Philadelphia Festival Theater for New Plays (3680 Walnut St., tel. 215/222–5000) focuses on works by new playwrights; Bruce Graham is the award-winning playwright-in-residence. Their season runs from January through June.

Freedom Theater (1346 N. Broad St., tel. 215/765–2793) is the oldest and most active African-American theater in Pennsylvania. Performances are held September through May.

Concerts

Philadelphia Orchestra. The world-renowned ensemble performs at the Academy of Music (Broad and Locust Sts., tel. 215/893–1900) from September to May and at the Mann Music Center (West Fairmount Park, tel. 215/878–7707) in summer. In its nearly 100-year history, the orchestra has been dominated by two conductors—Leopold Stokowski and Eugene Ormandy. Riccardo Muti ended his 12-year tenure in 1992 and passed the baton to the new musical director, Wolfgang Sawallisch.

Concerto Soloists of Philadelphia (9th and Walnut Sts., tel. 215/574–3550), directed by Marc Mostovoy, performs chamber music from September to June.

Music from Marlboro, a classical music series, is held at the Pennsylvania Convention Center (12th and Arch Sts., tel. 215/569–4690) from October to May.

Robin Hood Dell East (Strawberry Mansion Dr., East Fairmount Park, tel. 215/477–8810) is the site for rhythm-and-blues and soul concerts on Monday, Wednesday, and Friday evenings in July and August.

Philly Pops (tel. 215/735–7506), conducted by Peter Nero, performs at the Academy of Music from October to May and, occasionally, at other local events.

All-Star Forum (tel. 215/735–7506). Impresario Moe Septee and his 53-year-old organization bring visiting orchestras, recitals by stars such as Itzhak Perlman and Isaac Stern, ballets, and special events to the Academy of Music.

Mellon Jazz Festival (tel. 215/636–1666 or 215/561–5060) presents a series of concerts (many free) in June at locations around town. The top names in jazz perform, recently Shirley Scott, Wynton Marsalis, and Chick Corea.

Mozart on the Square (tel. 215/636–1666) takes place in May in or near Rittenhouse Square and features orchestral concerts, opera, chamber music, and recitals. Tentative for 1994.

Philadelphia Folk Festival (Old Pool Farm, near Schwenksville, tel. 215/242–0150) is the oldest continuously running folk festival in the country and takes place each year during the last week in August. Performers have included Doc Watson, Taj Mahal, Joan Baez, and Judy Collins.

Opera

Opera Company of Philadelphia (tel. 215/981–1450) productions at the Academy of Music between November and April feature such stars as Luciano Pavarotti. All performances are in original languages with computerized English "supertitles" above the stage.

Pennsylvania Opera Theater (tel. 215/731–1212) stages popular and lesser-known operas; all are sung in English and are presented at the Merriam Theater, November to May.

Savoy Company (tel. 215/735–7161), the oldest amateur Gilbert and Sullivan company in the country, stages one G&S operetta each May at the Academy of Music and at Longwood Gardens.

Dance

Pennsylvania Ballet (tel. 215/551–7000), under president and artistic director Christopher D'Amboise, dances on the stages of the Academy of Music and the Merriam Theater, from October to April. The *Nutcracker* production at Christmastime is a perennial favorite.

South Street Dance Company (tel. 215/483–8482) presents modern dance at sites throughout the city.

Philadelphia Dance Company (Philadanco) (tel. 215/387–8200) performs modern dance in spring and fall at Annenberg Center (3680 Walnut St., tel. 215/898–6791) and other locations.

Waves (tel. 215/563–1545). This internationally known company blends ballet with belly dancing, break-dancing, gymnastics, and other movement forms.

Film

Along with numerous first-run commercial movie theaters, Philadelphia has several art and repertory houses. Avoid the first-run theaters on Chestnut Street west of Broad Street: They're frequented by rowdy urban youths.

Ritz Five (214 Walnut St., tel. 215/925–7900) and **Ritz at the Bourse** (4th St. north of Chestnut St., tel. 215/440–1181) are the finest movie theaters in town for avante-garde and foreign films. Both have comfortable seats, clean surroundings, a first-rate sound system, and courteous audiences and staff.

Roxy Screening Rooms (2023 Sansom St., tel. 215/561–0114) is an art house showing the intellectual and the esoteric. No Stallone or Schwarzenegger here.

Philadelphia Festival of World Cinema (3701 Chestnut St., tel. 215/895–6593) is a 10-day event every May with screenings, seminars, and events with critics, scholars, and filmmakers.

Nightlife

Nightlife in Philadelphia is far better than it used to be (when they supposedly rolled up the sidewalks at 8 o'clock). Today you can listen to a chanteuse in a chic basement nightclub; dance till 3 AM in a smoky bistro; and watch street jugglers, mimes, and magicians on a Society Hill corner.

South Street between Front and 9th streets is still the hippest street in town. One-of-a-kind shops, bookstores, galleries, restaurants, and bars attract hoards of characters (mostly young). In the past few years, **Main Street** in Manyunk, in the northwest section of the city, has become a smaller, tamer version of South Street. In the last four years a dozen new clubs have opened up along the **Delaware River waterfront,** most of them near the Benjamin Franklin Bridge; a water taxi shuttles revelers between them.

Bars and clubs can change hands or go out of business faster than a soft pretzel goes stale. For current information, check the entertainment pages of the *Philadelphia Inquirer,* the *Philadelphia Daily News,* and *Philadelphia* magazine. You can also call radio station WRTI's "Jazz Line," an extensive, up-to-the-minute listing of music in town, at 215/204–5277. For information about Penn's Landing events call 215/923–4992.

Bars, Lounges, and Cabarets

Chestnut Cabaret. Near the University of Pennsylvania campus, this concert hall/dance club features rhythm-and-blues, reggae, alternative, heavy metal, and rock 'n' roll. Crowd mostly in their 20s and early 30s. *3801 Chestnut St., University City, tel. 215/382–1201. Open Tues.–Sat. 7 PM–1 AM. AE.*

Dirty Frank's. Frank is long gone, but this place is still dirty, cheap, and a Philadelphia classic. An incongruous mixture of students, artists, journalists, and resident characters such as Jaitch DeLeon and F. Baggs Piglatano crowd around the horseshoe-shaped bar and engage in friendly mayhem. *347 S. 13th St., tel. 215/732–5010. Mon.–Sat. 11 AM–2 AM. No credit cards.*

Khyber Pass. It's small and loud, with lots of action. The music is all live, including alternative and independent labels, national and local talent. With over 115 brands, it has probably the best selection of beers in town. *56 S. 2nd St., Olde City, tel. 215/ 440–9683. Mon.–Sat. noon–2 AM. No credit cards.*

Newport Bar and Grill. This upscale "meet market" bar and restaurant off the lobby of the Warwick Hotel is a popular afterwork place for the business crowd. *17th and Locust Sts., tel. 215/546–8800. Open Mon.–Sat. 5 PM–2 AM. AE, DC, MC, V.*

Happy Rooster. Owner "Doc" Ulitsky provides the best selection of after-dinner drinks and liqueurs in the city. French, Russian, and Gypsy music plays in the background. *118 S. 16th St., Downtown, tel. 215/563–1481. Jackets required. Open daily 11:30 AM–2 AM. Closed Sun. AE, DC, MC, V.*

Swann Lounge. Dance to piano music and a trio in an elegant hotel lounge. *Four Seasons Hotel, 18th St. and Benjamin Franklin Pkwy., Center City, tel. 215/963–1500. Piano music Mon.–Fri. 6 PM–10 PM; Viennese buffet with trio and dancing, Fri. and Sat. 9 PM–1 AM. AE, DC, MC, V.*

Trocadero. This spacious rock 'n' roll club occupies a former burlesque house where W. C. Fields and Mae West performed. A lot of the old decor remains: Mirrors, pillars, and balconies surround a dance floor. Under-30 crowd. Nationally known concert acts most Monday to Wednesday nights. Local DJs host dance parties Thursday, Friday, and Saturday. *1003 Arch St., Chinatown, tel. 215/922–7776. Open Thurs. 9 PM–2 AM, Fri. 4 PM–2 AM, Sat. 7 PM–2 AM. AE.*

Woody's. Philadelphia's most popular gay bar. *202 S. 13th St., tel. 215/545–1893. Open daily 11 AM–2 AM. No credit cards.*

Comedy Clubs

Comedy Cabaret atop the Middle East. This no-smoking club presents national names and local talent. *126 Chestnut St., Olde City, tel. 215/625–JOKE. Cover: $10.*

Funny Bone. Local talent opens the show for national headliners. *221 South St., tel. 215/440–9670. Shows Tues.–Sat. Cover: $8–$11. AE, MC, V.*

Dancing and Discos

Katmandu. Outdoor Caribbean restaurant and bar with live music nightly—world, reggae, rock—and a "Wild Island" dance party on Saturday nights. *Delaware Ave. south of Spring Garden St., tel. 215/629–7400. Open daily 11:30 AM–2 AM. AE, DC, MC, V.*

Maui Entertainment Complex. Dancing indoors and out to live bands (rock, alternative, progressive) and to radio DJ danceparty broadcasts. *Pier 53 North, 1143 Delaware Ave., tel. 215/ 423–8116. Open Wed.–Sat. till 2 AM. Covers range from $5–$7.*

Monte Carlo Living Room. The DJ at this sophisticated watering hole plays Top-40 hits, European sounds, and South American music. An intimate room where all the furnishings, from the tapestries to the paintings, are European. Customers are in their 30s to 50s. *2nd and South Sts., tel. 215/925-2220. Open Tues.-Sat. 5:30-2. Jackets required. $10 cover. AE, DC, MC, V.*

Pulsations. At the biggest, highest-tech disco in the area—20 miles from downtown Philly—a 28-foot starship glides over the dance floor and an alien robot emerges. Lots of neon, lots of lasers, and hydraulically lifted lights emerging from the dance floor. It has a 25,000-watt sound system and holds more than 2,000 people, most of them in their 20s and early 30s. *Rte. 1, Glen Mills, tel. 215/459-4140. Times vary nightly. AE, MC, V.*

Quincy's. Live rock 'n' roll or dance music programmed by a DJ in a re-created turn-of-the-century atmosphere. Sunday night is live Big Band night. *Adam's Mark Hotel, City Ave. and Monument Rd., City Ave. area, tel. 215/581-5000. No jeans. Open 4:30 PM-2 AM.*

Revival. Along with New Wave and contemporary music, this dance club has performance art, fashion shows, theme nights, and rock videos. Showcases new bands. *22 S. 3rd St., Old City, tel. 215/627-4825. Open Tues.-Sun. 9 PM-3 AM. AE.*

Jazz

Liberties. Handsome restored Victorian pub features live jazz Friday and Saturday. *705 N. 2nd St., Northern Liberties, tel. 215/238-0660. Open daily 11 AM-2 AM. AE, DC, MC, V.*

Ortlieb's Jazz Haus. Hear good jazz in a 100-year-old bar. The celebrated jazz organist Shirley Scott and her quartet perform frequently. Tuesday jam session for local musicians. *847 N. 3rd St., Northern Liberties, tel. 215/922-1035. Music 9:30 PM-1:30 AM. AE, DC, MC, V.*

Zanzibar Blue. A hip restaurant and bar adjoins the hottest jazz room in town. The best local talent plays six nights, national names on selected Sunday nights. *305 S. 11th St., tel. 215/829-0300. Jazz daily 8 PM-2 AM. AE, DC, MC, V.*

Miscellaneous

Painted Bride Art Center. By day it's a contemporary art gallery showing bold, challenging works. By night it's a "multidisciplinary, multicultural performance center," featuring performance art; prose and poetry readings; folk, world, and new music; jazz, dance, and avant-garde theater. In 1994 this nonprofit educational institution celebrates its 25th season with an "Old-Time Friends of the Bride Reunion," including monologist Spaulding Gray. *230 Vine St., Old City, tel. 215/925-9914. Gallery open Tues.-Sun. noon-6 PM. Call for performance schedule. AE, MC, V.*

9 Bucks County

By Joyce
Eisenberg

*A writer and
editor whose travel
and feature
articles have
appeared in local
and national
publications,
Joyce Eisenberg, a
Philadelphia
native, is editor of
the Delaware
Valley edition of*
Travelhost
magazine.

*Updated by
M. T.
Schwartzmann*

Bucks County, about an hour's drive north of Philadelphia, could have remained 625 square miles of sleepy countryside full of old stone farmhouses, lush rolling hills, and quaint covered bridges if it hadn't been discovered in the '30s by New York's Beautiful Brainy People. Such luminaries as writers Dorothy Parker and S. J. Perelman and composer Oscar Hammerstein bought country homes here, a short drive from Manhattan. Pulitzer Prize- and Nobel Prize-winning author Pearl S. Buck chose to live in the area because it was "a region where the landscapes were varied, where farm and industry lived side by side, where the sea was near at hand, mountains not far away, and city and countryside were not enemies." Noted author James A. Michener, who won the 1947 Pulitzer Prize for his "Tales of the South Pacific," was raised and worked in Doylestown.

Over the years, Bucks County has become known for art colonies and antiques, summer theater, and country inns. And although parts of the county have fallen prey to urban sprawl and hyper-development, many areas of central and upper Bucks County remain as bucolic as ever. One of Bucks County's agrarian pursuits is a cottage vineyard industry. Five local wineries open their doors to visitors for tours and tastings.

Named after England's Buckinghamshire, Bucks County was opened by William Penn in 1681 under a land grant from Charles II. The county's most celebrated town, New Hope, was settled in the early 1700s as the industrial village of Coryell's Ferry. (One of the original gristmills is the home of the Bucks County Playhouse, which has been designated the State Theater of Pennsylvania.) The town was the Pennsylvania terminal for stagecoach traffic and Delaware River ferry traffic. Barges hauled coal along the 60-mile Delaware Canal until 1931.

Commerce built up New Hope but art helped sustain it. The art colony took root in the late 19th century and was revitalized first in the 1930s by New York theater folk and more recently with the formation of the New Hope–Lambertville Gallery Association, a cooperative network of gallery owners, artists, and the community. Today New York artists are again relocating to the region. In 1988, the James A. Michener Art Museum opened in the renovated Bucks County jail. It showcases 19th- and 20th-century American art. A $2 million-plus expansion, unveiled in 1993, more than doubled the center's exhibit space, and another two-story addition is expected to follow.

New Hope is a hodgepodge of old stone houses, narrow streets and alleys, pretty courtyards, and charming restaurants. Summer weekends can be frantic here, with shoppers wandering through the tiny boutiques and galleries along Main Street. The Delaware Canal threads through town and you can glide lazily along it in a mule-pulled barge.

Doylestown is the county seat. An important coach stop in the 18th century, the town is best known as the home of Henry Chapman Mercer, curator of American and Prehistoric Archaeology at the University of Pennsylvania Museum, master potter, self-taught architect, and writer of gothic tales. When Dr. Mercer died in 1930 at the age of 74, along with a legacy of artistic creativity he left a bizarre mansion named Fonthill, a museum displaying 50,000 implements and tools, and a pottery and tile works that still makes Mercer tiles.

American Express offers Travelers Cheques built for two.

American Express® Cheques *for Two*. The first Travelers Cheques that allow either of you to use them because both of you have signed them. And only one of you needs to be present to purchase them.

Cheques *for Two* are accepted anywhere regular American Express Travelers Cheques are, which is just about everywhere. So stop by your bank, AAA* or any American Express Travel Service Office and ask for Cheques *for Two*.

The county is also a treasure trove for Colonial history buffs. Among the most interesting sites is Pennsbury Manor, a careful reconstruction of the brick Georgian-style mansion and estate William Penn built for himself in the late 1600s. On the banks of the Delaware, the 500-acre Washington Crossing Historic Park is situated where George Washington and his troops crossed the icy river on Christmas night 1776 to surprise the Hessian mercenaries at Trenton.

The Delaware River and the canal that follows its path offer opportunities for canoeing, kayaking, and fishing. Thousands float down the river each year in inner tubes or on rubber rafts. Joggers, hikers, bicyclists, cross-country skiers, and horseback riders enjoy the 60-mile canal towpath.

The town of Lahaska is the center of antiques shopping in Bucks County. The bargain-price American treasures that made the area an antiques hunter's paradise are nowadays few and far between, but there is good prowling between New Hope and Doylestown all along U.S. 202 and in the 70 shops clustered in Peddler's Village, where you can find fine furniture, handcrafted chandeliers, handwoven wicker, and home-spun fabrics. One of three antique carousels in the county resides here as well. Another may be found at nearby Indian Walk, a mini-marketplace just south on Route 413 in Wrightstown.

For families, a premier attraction in Langhorne is Sesame Place, a theme park based on the public television series. There are shows starring Bert and Ernie, water play such as Big Bird's Rambling River raft ride, a computer gallery, and lots of colorful structures on which to climb and jump.

Although you can see all the major tourist attractions in a daylong whirlwind tour, plan to stay overnight in Bucks County. A number of houses and mills, some dating back to a half-century before the Revolution, are now quaint bed-and-breakfasts and excellent restaurants. A hearty meal, blissful sleep, and a day spent wandering along River Road (Route 32) are what make visits to Bucks County most enjoyable.

If you visit between mid-April and June, you can join in the county's annual celebration of the arts—Bucks Fever. This six-week festival features performances by local theater, dance, and music companies; exhibitions of sculpture, photography, crafts, and painting; walks and talks highlighting local history; and special events such as the Folkfest at the Mercer Museum, where more than 100 costumed craftsmen demonstrate their tinsmithing, blacksmithing, barrel-making, and wood-carving skills. In addition, there are militia drills, sheep shearing, a quilting bee, and wagon rides.

Essential Information

Getting Around

By Car Bucks County is a large area—40 miles long and up to 20 miles across—and is almost impossible to tour without a car. From Philadelphia, the most direct route is to follow I–95 north to Exit 31 (New Hope); turn left at the bottom of the exit ramp and follow to Route 532. Turn right onto 532 north, left onto

Route 32 north and travel about 7 miles to New Hope, a total of about 40 miles from Philadelphia.

By Bus   **Greyhound** (tel. 800/231–2222) has three buses a day to Doylestown from Philadelphia. The trip takes 70–75 minutes. The fare aboard is $8 one way, $15.50 round-trip.

By Train   **SEPTA** (tel. 215/580–7800) provides frequent service from Philadelphia (Market Street East, Suburban, and 30th Street stations) to Doylestown on the R5 line. The trip takes up to 90 minutes.

Guided Tours

Nancy Neely (tel. 215/822–6692) will drive you around the county in your car. A longtime Bucks County tour guide, she will take you off the main roads, show you the covered bridges, and amuse you with local color. Reservations required.

Marlene Miller of Executive Events Inc. (tel. 215/766–2211) offers customized group tours and tour groups for individual travelers in 28-passenger minivans. Some tour themes include covered bridges, historic mansions, arts, wineries, antiques, and shopping.

Bucks County Carriages (tel. 215/862–3582) offers 20-minute horse-drawn carriage tours. Horses are "parked" at Logan Inn in New Hope, near the bakery in Peddler's Village, and at the Lambertville Station in Lambertville, N.J. Daytime and evening rides vary according to season and departure location. Call for an exact schedule. Customized tours—perhaps from your B&B to dinner and back—are available by reservation.

Coryell's Ferry Ride and Historic Narrative (tel. 215/862–2050) is a half-hour sightseeing ride on the Delaware River in a 40-foot, 28-passenger pontoon boat or a 65-foot, 49-passenger stern-wheeler.

Ghost Tours of New Hope (tel. 215/357–4558) offers a one-hour lantern-led walk which explores the haunting tales of the area. The tour was designed by psychic investigator Adi-Kent Thomas Jeffrey, author of *The Bermuda Triangle* and former Bucks County resident.

Mule Barge (*see* Exploring Bucks County, *below.*).

New Hope & Ivyland Rail Road (*see* Exploring Bucks County, *below*).

Important Addresses and Numbers

Tourist   **Bucks County Tourist Commission** (Box 912, Doylestown
Information   18901, tel. 215/345–4552 or 800/836–2825). *On the Fonthill property. Open Apr.–Oct., Mon.–Fri. 8:30–5:30, Sat. 10–4.*

Central Bucks Chamber of Commerce (Fidelity Bank Building, 115 W. Court St., Doylestown 18901, tel. 215/348–3913). Free guidebooks and tourist information is available. *Open weekdays 8:30–5.*

New Hope Information Center (1 W. Mechanic St., at Main St., New Hope 18938, tel. 215/862–5880 for an automated menu of information, or 215/862–3050 for a travel counselor). It is a convenient place to stop or contact in advance for information about New Hope and its surrounding attractions. The center also offers a free lodging referral service. *Open weekdays 10–5, Saturday and Sunday 10–6.*

Emergencies Dial 911 in an emergency, or go to the emergency room, **Doylestown Hospital** (595 W. State St., Doylestown, tel. 215/345–2200).

Exploring Bucks County

Numbers in the margin correspond to points of interest on the Bucks County map.

Many Bucks County attractions are contained within the triangle formed by the towns of New Hope, Doylestown, and Newtown. Other interesting sites are located along River Road (Route 32), from Pennsbury Manor north to charming river towns such as Erwinna. If you have just one day to visit Bucks County, begin at Fonthill in Doylestown, check out the antiques shops along U.S. 202, stroll through New Hope, and head north on River Road for dinner at one of the inns. For a longer stay, you can pick and choose among the attractions listed below. We begin in the southern part of the county, closest to Philadelphia, and work our way north.

Situated on a gentle rise 150 yards from the Delaware River, ❶ **Pennsbury Manor** is the Georgian-style mansion and plantation William Penn built as his country estate. Living history demonstrations at the rebuilt manor house and work buildings on 40 of the estate's original 8,400 acres provide a glimpse of everyday life in 17th-century America. Among the antique furnishings in the house are some fine William and Mary and Jacobean pieces as well as some of Penn's furniture. Formal gardens, vineyards and orchards, an icehouse, smokehouse, bake and brew house, and collections of tools attest to the self-sufficient nature of Penn's early community. They also hint that although history portrays Penn as a dour Quaker, as governor of the colony he enjoyed the good life by importing the finest provisions and keeping a vast retinue of servants and slaves. These extravagances led to the financial difficulties that resulted in a nine-month term in debtor's prison. The house can be seen only on the tour. *Tyburn Rd. E off U.S. 13, Morrisville 19067, tel. 215/946–0400. Admission: $5 adults, $4 senior citizens, $3 children 6–17. Open Tues.–Sat. 9–5, Sun. noon–5. Last tour at 3:30.*

❷ Six miles north is **Fallsington,** the pre-Revolutionary village where William Penn attended Quaker meetings of worship. The village displays 300 years of American architecture, from a simple 17th-century log cabin to the Victorian excesses of the late 1800s. Three historic buildings, including the log cabin, have been restored and opened for guided tours. Ninety period homes surround the village, which is listed on the National Register of Historic Places. *Tyburn Rd. W off U.S. 13, Fallsington 19054, tel. 215/295–6567. Admission: $3 per person for guided tours, reservations required. Houses are open to the public on the second Sat. in Oct.*

❸ **Washington Crossing Historic Park** is the site of George Washington's 1776 crossing of the Delaware River to surprise the Hessian garrison at Trenton. Attractions are divided between the Lower and the Upper Park, which are about 5 miles apart. *Free admission to grounds. Ticket for 45-minute walking tour of 5 historic park buildings: $2.50 adults, $2 senior cit-*

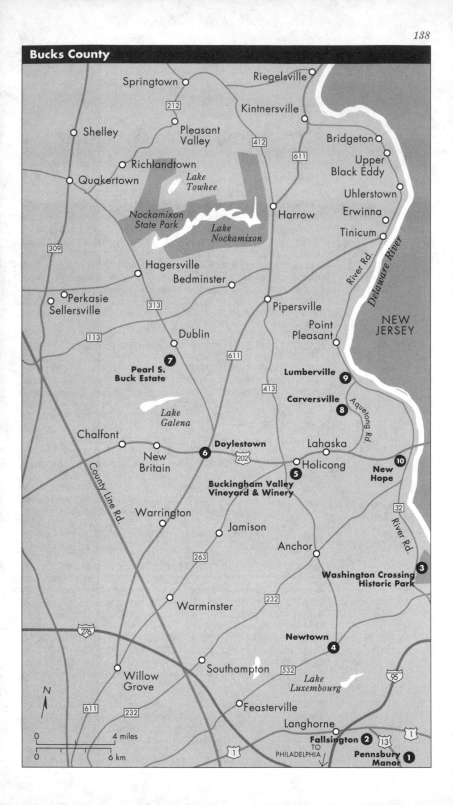

izens, 50¢ children 6–17, available at Visitors Center, Thompson-Neely House, and Bowman's Hill Tower. Tours Mon.–Sat. 9:30, 11, 12:30, 2, 3:30; Sun. 12:30, 2, 3:30. Buildings open year-round, Mon.–Sat. 9–5 and Sun. noon–5.

In the Lower Park, the fieldstone **Memorial Building and Visitors Center** (Rte. 32, 7 mi south of New Hope) displays a reproduction of Emanuel Leutze's famous painting of the crossing (the original hangs in the Metropolitan Museum of Art in New York). Even more realistic is the annual Christmas Day reenactment of the crossing when local businessmen don Colonial uniforms and brave the elements in small boats. The **McConkey Ferry Inn** where Washington and his staff had Christmas dinner while waiting to cross the river is nearby. Also open is **Taylor Mansion,** a completely restored 19th-century residence.

In the Upper Park, about 5 miles north on Route 32, stop at the landmark **Bowman's Hill Tower,** named after a surgeon who sailed with Captain Kidd. Washington used the hill as a lookout point. You can get a much better view of the countryside than he did by riding the elevator up the 110-foot-tall memorial tower. *Admission: $2.50 adults, $2 senior citizens, $2 children 6–17, $1 children 3–5. Tower gate open daily 10–4:30; to 5:30 on weekends and holidays, Apr.–Nov.*

One-half mile north of the tower, the 80-acre **Wildflower Preserve** has been planted with hundreds of species of wildflowers, trees, shrubs, and ferns native to Pennsylvania. Take the guided tour or follow short trails clearly marked so as to bring you back to your starting point. *Tel. 215/862–2924. Mar.–Oct., daily guided nature walks, $2 per person, $4 per family.* At the same location, the **Platt Bird Collection** displays more than 100 stuffed birds and 600 eggs. Also in the Upper Park is the **Thompson-Neely House,** an 18th-century farmhouse furnished just as it was when the Colonial leaders planned the attack on Trenton in the kitchen. *Washington Crossing Historic Park, Rtes. 532 and 32, tel. 215/493–4076. Free admission to grounds. Ticket for 45-min walking tour of 5 historic park buildings: $1.50 adults, $1 senior citizens, 50¢ children 6–17, available at Visitors Center, Thompson-Neely House and Tower. Tours Mon.–Sat. 9:30, 11, 12:30, 2, 3:30; Sun. 12:30, 2, 3:30. Park open Mon.–Sat. 9–5, Sun. noon–5 year-round.*

❹ Until the real estate boom of the 1980s, **Newtown** was a busy village serving the commercial needs of the surrounding rural community. Today, it's the bustling center of sprawling suburban development. The town takes pride in its many 18th- and 19th-century homes and inns; the downtown historic district is on the National Register of Historic Places. The Newtown Historic Association building (Court St. and Center Ave., tel. 215/968–4004) contains regional antiques and paintings by renowned local artist Edward Hicks. An association brochure provides a walking tour of the town.

❺ The **Buckingham Valley Vineyard & Winery** is a small family-owned winery that produces distinguished estate-bottled varietal wines. One of the state's first farm wineries, the vineyards and wine cellars are open to tours and tastings. *Rte. 413, 2 mi south of Rte. 202, tel. 215/794–7188. Free self-guided tour. Open Tues.–Fri. noon–6, Sat. 10–6, Sun. noon–4.*

❻ **Doylestown,** the county seat, is a showcase of American architecture, with the stately Federal brick buildings of Lawyers'

Row, and gracious Queen Anne, Second Empire, and Italian-ate-style homes. The historic district, with its nearly 1,200 buildings, is listed on the National Register of Historic Places. Three walking tours highlighting the architecture and history of Doylestown are mapped out in a brochure available at the **Central Bucks Chamber of Commerce** (Fidelity Bank Building, 115 W. Court St.) and at area B&Bs, inns, and bookstores. The most unusual buildings in Doylestown are those created by Henry Chapman Mercer. The three brilliantly eccentric structures on **Mercer Mile** are constructed exclusively with reinforced concrete, a method perfected by Mercer in the early part of this century.

Fonthill, Henry Chapman Mercer's home, is modeled after a 13th-century Rhenish castle replete with turrets, towers, and balconies. Inside is a multilevel labyrinth of surprise passages, sudden stairways, and built-in concrete furniture. Fonthill's wealth of books, prints, and engravings is enhanced by the setting: the ceilings and walls are embedded with tiles from Mercer's own kilns and ancient tiles from around the world. *Swamp Rd. (Rte. 313) and E. Court St., Doylestown 18901, tel. 215/ 348–9461. Admission: $5 adults, $4.50 senior citizens, $1.50 children and students. Open Mon.–Sat. 10–5, Sun. noon–5. Hour-long guided tours. Reservations suggested.*

The **Moravian Pottery and Tile Works** on the Fonthill grounds still make Mercer's unique tiles. As author and Bucks County resident James Michener described them, "Using scenes from the Bible, mythology, and history, Mercer produced wonderfully archaic tiles about 12 or 14 inches square in powerful earth colors that glowed with intensity and unforgettable imagery." Reproductions of Mercer's tiles can be bought in the Tile Works Shop. The factory, built in 1912, resembles a Spanish mission with an open-ended courtyard. *130 Swamp Rd., Doylestown 18901, tel. 215/345–6722. Admission: $2.50 adults, $2 senior citizens, $1 children 7–17. Open daily 10–5, last tour at 4. 45-min self-guided tours every half hour. Closed major holidays.*

An archaeologist, Mercer worried that the rapid advance of progress would wipe out evidence of America's productivity before the Industrial Revolution. Consequently, from 1895 to 1915 he scoured the back roads of eastern Pennsylvania buying implements, tools, and household items that might otherwise have been destroyed. His collection, representing every craft, including more than 50,000 objects from before the age of steam, is displayed at the **Mercer Museum,** which he opened in 1916. The Spruance Library on the third floor holds 20,000 volumes on Bucks County history. *84 S. Pine St., Doylestown 18901, tel. 215/345–0210. Admission: $5 adults, $4.50 senior citizens, $1.50 children and students. Open Mon.–Sat. 10–5 (Tues. until 9), Sun. noon–5. Self-guided tours.*

Across the street is the new **James A. Michener Art Museum,** endowed by Michener, a native of Doylestown. The arts museum occupies the buildings and grounds of the former Bucks County Jail, which dates from 1884. A 23-foot-high fieldstone wall surrounds seven exhibition galleries, an outdoor sculpture garden, and a Gothic-style warden's house. The collection and changing exhibits (photography, crafts, textiles, sculpture, and painting) focus on 19th- and 20th-century American art and Bucks County art. A $2.2 million expansion in 1993 renovated the two original galleries and added five new ones, including a re-creation of Michener's Doylestown study. Yet another addition, the Hall of Artists, is scheduled to debut in 1994. *138 S. Pine St., Doylestown 18901, tel. 215/340–9800. Admission: $5 adults, $4.50 senior citizens, $1.50 students 12–18. Open Tues.–Fri. 10–4:30, weekends 10–5.*

From Doylestown, you can detour to Green Hills Farm, Pearl S. Buck's country home (built in 1835) where she wrote nearly 100 novels, children's books, and works of nonfiction while raising seven adopted children and caring for many others. The house still bears the imprint of the girl who grew up in China and became the only American woman to win both the Nobel and Pulitzer prizes. She is best known for *The Good Earth*. The **Pearl S. Buck Estate** is filled with her collection of Asian and American antiques and personal belongings. The Pearl S. Buck Foundation, which supports Amerasian children in seven Asian countries, operates out of offices on the property. *520 Dublin Rd., Perkasie, PA 18944, tel. 215/249–0100 or 800/220–2825. Admission: $5 adults, $4 senior citizens and students 6–17, $12 families (parents with children under 19). Tours Tues.–Sat. 10:30, 1:30 and 2:30; Sun. 1:30 and 2:30. Closed major holidays.*

The road from Doylestown to New Hope (Rte. 202) is studded with antiques shops, especially around Lahaska. (*See* Shopping, *below*).

Before you get to New Hope, take a scenic detour by making a left turn onto Aquetong Road. Wind through fields and woods dotted with old houses and barns to the tiny old mill village of **Carversville.** Stop in at the **Carversville General Store** where locals gather for gossip and take-out coffee and pick up picnic supplies. Then continue past the ball field to Fleecydale or Old Carversville roads. (Ignore the "Road Closed" sign; it's been there for years.) Both of these back-country roads lead to River Road (Route 32) in **Lumberville,** where you can picnic along the canal or on Bull's Island, accessible by the footbridge across the Delaware River. Open since 1770, the **Lumberville Store** in Lumberville is the focus of village life, the place to mail letters, buy groceries, and rent a bicycle. Across the street the **Black Bass Hotel** is a British-style pub with a stunning river view from the indoor dining room and the new outdoor deck. Past Lumberville are the towns of Point Pleasant (*see* Outdoor Activities and Participant Sports, *below,* for information on renting a canoe or inner tube), Erwinna, and Upper Black Eddy. The **Homestead Store** in Upper Black Eddy scoops out great big ice cream cones and makes hearty sandwiches till 9 each night.

The cosmopolitan village of **New Hope** is a mecca for artists, shoppers, and lovers of old homes. Listed on the National Register of Historic Places, the town is easy to explore on foot; the most interesting sights and stores are clustered along four blocks of Main Street and on the cross streets—Mechanic, Ferry, and Bridge streets—which lead to the river. (Bridge St. leads to a bridge spanning the Delaware to the New Jersey village of Lambertville, another assemblage of shops and galleries.) For a good orientation to New Hope, take the Bucks County Carriages horse-drawn tour (*see* Guided Tours, *above*) which starts by the cannon alongside the Logan Inn.

The **Parry Mansion** is a stone house built in 1784 by wealthy lumber-mill owner Benjamin Parry and occupied by five generations of his family. The furnishings reflect decorative changes from 1775 to the Victorian era—including candles, white-washed walls, oil lamps, and wallpaper. *S. Main and Ferry Sts., tel. 215/862–5148. Admission: $4. Open May–Oct. Fri.–Sun. 1–5.*

Time Out Family-owned **Gerenser's Exotic Ice Cream** has been making ice cream—with 14% butterfat—since 1943. "Exotic" is no exaggeration: We recommend German peach brandy, Amaretto with roasted almonds, and peanut butter chocolate chip. *22 S. Main St., New Hope, tel. 215/862–2050.*

Beginning in 1832, coal barges plied the Delaware Canal. Today, the mules pull barges filled with relaxing tourists. The **Mule Barge Ride** is a one-hour narrated excursion past Revolutionary-era cottages, gardens, and artists' workshops. A barge historian/folk singer is often aboard. *New and S. Main Sts., New Hope, tel. 215/862–2842. Price: $6.95 adults, $6.50 senior citizens, $5.50 students over 11, $4.25 children under 12. Runs Apr., Wed., Sat., Sun. 11:30, 1, 2, 3, 4:30; May 1–Oct. 15, daily 11:30, 1, 2, 3, 4:30, 6; Oct. 16–Nov. 15, Wed., Sat., Sun. 11:30, 1, 2, 3, 4:30.*

The **New Hope & Ivyland Rail Road** makes a 9-mile, 50-minute scenic run from New Hope to Lahaska. The train crosses a trestle used in the rescue scenes in the old "Perils of Pauline" movies. The New Hope depot is an 1891 Victorian gem embellished with a witch's hat on the roof. Theme trains include wine-and-cheese trains, Halloween haunted trains, Santa trains at Christmas, and murder mystery trains. *W. Bridge and Stockton Sts., tel. 215/862–2332. Admission: $6.95 adults, $5.50 senior citizens, $3.50 children 3–11. Open daily Apr.–Nov., weekends Dec.–Mar., with trains running every 75 min. beginning at 11 AM or 12:15. Reservations required for theme trains.*

North of New Hope, the two-lane River Road (Route 32) winds scenically along the Delaware. It is a lovely drive with charming old inns, a winery, and ancient stone houses hidden around bends in the road. You'll pass through a series of tiny river towns along the way, many with a general store, inn, and restaurant. Stop for lunch at an inn or picnic along the river and take a walk or ride a bike along the towpath.

What to See and Do with Children

Mule Barge (*see* Exploring Bucks County, *above*).
New Hope & Ivyland Rail Road (*see* Exploring Bucks County, *above*).
Sesame Place. A recreation park designed for children aged from 3 to 15, Sesame Place has recently expanded, with the additions of Sesame Island and Twiddlebug Land, to offer even more fun for older children and adults. More than 40 outdoor activities on 9 acres include Sesame Neighborhood, a replica of the street on the popular public TV show; animal shows and a Big Bird musical revue; lots of water activities—shallow pools, slides, fountains, and lazy rivers (bring a swimsuit); a computer gallery with high-tech puzzles and games; and lots of clever apparatus, such as Cookie Mountain and Ernie's Bed, on which

to climb and jump. *100 Sesame Rd. (off Oxford Valley Rd.),
Langhorne, tel. 215/757–1100. Admission: $19.95 all ages.
Parking $4. Open daily mid-May–mid-Sept., weekends only
May 1–15 and mid-Sept.–mid-Oct. Call for hours.*

Sportland America. Just up the road from Sesame Place in
Langhorne, this huge indoor arcade offers batting cages, miniature golf, roller skating, bumper cars, and more. *9 Cabot
Blvd. E, Langhorne, tel. 215/547–7766. Open Sun.–Thurs. 10–
10, Fri. and Sat. 10–1 AM.*

Quarry Valley Farm. This Bucks County farm has a barnyard
full of animals, a petting zoo, cow milking, a hayloft to jump in,
and pony rides. The farm shop sells homegrown goodies. *Street
Rd. near Peddler's Village, Lahaska, tel. 215/794–5882. Admission: $6 adults, $5.50 children, under 1 free. Open Apr.–
Dec., daily 10–5.*

Off the Beaten Track

Eleven covered bridges are all that remain of the 36 originally
built in Bucks County. Although the romantically inclined call
them "kissing bridges" or "wishing bridges," the roofs were actually intended to protect the supporting beams from the rav-
ages of the weather. The bridges are examples of the lattice-
type construction of overlapping triangles, without arches or
upright beams. They are delightful to stumble upon, but if
you're serious about seeing them, the Bucks County Tourist
Commission (tel. 215/345–4552 or 800/836–2825) the "Bucks
County Covered Bridges Tour" brochure, which provides directions, driving distances, and a brief history of each bridge.

Trained as an architect, the late Bucks County woodworker
George Nakashima crafted furniture from the souls of trees for
more than 40 years. His work is distinguished by free-flowing
natural contours that express his philosophy that trees are objects of "the highest artistic and spiritual worth." His furniture
has been featured at the Metropolitan Museum of Art and the
American Craft Museum in New York. His children are continuing the business. *293 Aquetong Rd., tel. 215/862–2272. Show-
room open to public every Sat. except holidays, 1–4:30 PM.*

In 1966 President Lyndon B. Johnson greeted nearly 100,000
pilgrims who had come to Doylestown for the dedication of a
new shrine—**The National Shrine of Our Lady of Czestochowa.**
Since then, millions, including Pope John Paul II, many U.S.
presidents, and Lech Walesa, have made a pilgrimage to this
Polish spiritual center in Doylestown. The complex includes a
modern church with huge panels of stained glass depicting the
history of Christianity in Poland and the United States. The
gift shop and bookstore sell religious gifts, many of them handcrafted and imported from Poland, and the cafeteria serves hot
Polish and American food on Sunday. *Ferry Rd. (off Rte. 313)
in Beacon Hill (mailing address: Box 2049, Doylestown
18901), tel. 215/345–0600. Open daily 9–4:30; most principal
holidays are celebrated Sun. at noon at the Polish mass.*

Shopping

Antiques

Bucks County has long been known for its antiques shops featuring everything from fine examples of early American craftsmanship to fun kitsch. There are formal and country furnishings plus American, European, and Oriental antiques. Many shops (and another winery) are located along a 4-mile stretch of U.S. 202 between Lahaska and New Hope and on intersecting country roads. Shops are generally open on weekends with weekday hours by appointment: It's best to call first.

Hobensack & Keller (Bridge St., New Hope, tel. 215/862–2406), old garden ornaments, cast-iron furniture, fencing and Oriental rugs; **Olde Hope Antiques** (U.S. 202 and Reeder Rd., tel. 215/862–5055), hooked rugs, Pennsylvania German textiles, hand-painted furniture, and folk art; **Katy Kane** (34 West Ferry St., New Hope, tel. 215/862–5873), antique and vintage designer clothing, jewelry and accessories, and fine linens; **Lahaska Antique Courte** (U.S. 202 opposite Peddler's Village, tel. 215/794–7884 or 215/794–8695), 12 shops of American and European furniture and decorations.

The **Heritage Collectors' Gallery** (161 Peddler's Village, Lahaska, tel. 215/794–0901) exhibits and sells such historical artifacts and original documents as a baseball inscribed by Babe Ruth, letters signed by Lincoln and Douglas, a signed copy of Amelia Earhart's book, and a handwritten order by Oliver Hazard Perry after the British surrendered to him during the War of 1812, selling for $13,500. Prices range from $10 to $300,000.

Art Galleries

Many New York artists have relocated to Bucks County and more than 30 galleries in New Hope and neighboring Lambertville (across the river in New Jersey) showcase paintings, prints, and sculpture. The New Hope–Lambertville Gallery Association (tel. 215/862–5529) publishes a guide to member galleries, available at the Association and at the New Hope Information Center.

Auctions

At **Brown Brothers** (Rte. 413 south of Rte. 263, Buckingham, tel. 215/794–7630), Saturday auctions start with box lots and move on to bigger and better things acquired at estate sales—jewelry, silver, linens, tools, books, frames, furniture, and other household items. It opens Saturdays at 8 AM and runs until 3, September–May; auctions take place 4–10 Thursday evenings June through August.

Flea Markets

Rice's Sale and Country Market (Green Hill Rd. near Peddler's Village, Solebury, tel. 215/297–5993) has been in operation for more than a century. It opens Tuesdays at 6 AM, when the local antiques dealers check out the goods, and closes at 1 PM. There

are bargains on canned goods, clothing, linens, shoes, back-is-
sue magazines, and plants. *Call for additional holiday open-
ings.*

Gift Ideas

New Hope's streets are lined with shops selling handmade
crafts, art, and contemporary wares. **Peddler's Village** (U.S.
202 and Rte. 263, Lahaska, tel. 215/794–4000) began in the early '60s when Earl Jamison bought a 6-acre chicken farm, moved
local 18th-century houses to the site, and opened a Carmel, California–inspired collection of 70 specialty shops and restaurants. Today, the 42-acre village peddles books, cookware,
toys, leather goods, clothes, jewelry, dried wreaths, posters,
candles, and a host of other decorative items. Crowd-drawing
seasonal events include a Strawberry Festival in May, an All-
American Teddy Bear's Picnic in July, and a Scarecrow Festival from mid-September through October. On the grounds is
the Golden Plough Inn (tel. 215/794–4004), a 60-room country
inn decorated with Early American country furnishings.

Sports and the Outdoors

Ballooning

Keystone State Balloon Tours organizes hot air balloon flights
over Bucks County followed by a champagne reception back on
land. Flights are scheduled at dawn or in late afternoon, when
the winds are best. *Van Sant Airport, just off Rte. 611, Headquarters and Cafferty Rds., Erwinna, tel. 215/294–8034. Cost:
$150 per person. Open daily year-round, weather permitting.
Reservations required.*

Biking

Kiddle Cyclery (Rtes. 413 and 202, Buckingham, tel. 215/794–
8958) rents three- to 10-speed road bicycles. Closed some Sundays. **Lumberville Store Bicycle Rental Co.** (River Rd., 8 mi
north of New Hope, tel. 215/297–5388) rents mountain bikes
with wide tires. They can direct you to scenic bike routes.

Camping

In the northern part of the county many of the parks have canoes for rent, trails for biking and hiking, and camping facilities. The largest and best-equipped is **Nockamixon State Park**
(Rte. 563, Quakertown), which has a 1,450-acre lake, boating
and boat rental, swimming pool, bike path and bike rental, hiking trails, ice skating and sledding in winter, trap shooting, and
picnic areas. Other fine parks include **Tohickon Valley Park**
(Point Pleasant) and **Ralph Stover Park** (Pipersville), county
and state parks respectively, joined along Tohickon Creek near
Point Pleasant; and **Lake Towhee** east of Applebachsville. In
the south, **Core Creek Park** (Langhorne) is a 1,200-acre facility
with fishing and boating on Lake Luxembourg; and **Neshaminy
State Park** is near Croydon. Call the County Parks (tel. 215/
757–0571) or State Parks (tel. 215/257–3646).

Canoeing/Tubing

Over a hundred thousand people a year—from toddlers to grandparents in their 80s—negotiate the Delaware River on inner tubes or canoes from **Point Pleasant Canoe & Tube**. It also rents rafts and kayaks. The Point Pleasant site on River Road (tel. 215/297–TUBE) is open daily April through October. A bus transports people upriver to begin three- or four-hour tube or raft rides down to the base. No food, cans, or bottles are permitted on the tube rides. Wear sneakers you don't mind getting wet and lots of sunscreen. Life jackets are available at no charge. Reservations are required.

Fishing

Fishermen are drawn to the Delaware River and Lake Nockamixon for small-mouth bass, trout, catfish, and carp. The most popular event is the annual shad run (early April to early June), which has spawned a festival and street fair in Lambertville, NJ, the last weekend in April. The required fishing license can be purchased at any area sporting-goods shop; a five-day tourist license costs $20.50; a trout stamp costs an extra $5.50. For a license and tips on where to fish, try the **Nockamixon Sports Shop** (Rte. 313 and 5th St., Perkasie, tel. 215/257–3133) or **Dave's Sporting Goods** (1127 N. Easton Rd., Rt. 611, north of Doylestown, tel. 215/766–8000).

Glider Rides

Good thermals in the area make **Country Aviation** glider rides thrilling. Gliders seat one or two passengers (no more than 340 pounds combined) plus the pilot. Flights are priced at $65 for one person and $98 for two, for a 3,000-foot tow (15–20 min. ride), or $85 for one and $140 for two, for a 5,000-foot tow (30–40 min. ride). You can also fly in an open-cockpit biplane; 20-minute rides cost $90 for one, $150 for two. Aerobatic biplane flights are available at $99 for one person only. *Van Sant Airport, just off Rte. 611, Headquarters and Cafferty Rds., Erwinna, tel. 215/847–8401. Open year-round, daily 8:30–5:30. Call for reservations.*

Horseback Riding

Haycock Riding Stables (Old Bethlehem Rd., Perkasie, tel. 215/257–6271) escorts riders on one- and two-hour trips through Nockamixon State Park. *Call for reservations.*

West End Farm (River Rd. in Phillips Mill, north of New Hope, tel. 215/862–5883) offers one-hour escorted trail rides along the Delaware Canal. *Call ahead for reservations.*

Towpath

The 60-mile towpath at the **Delaware Canal State Park** is used for biking, hiking, jogging, and, in the winter, cross-country skiing. In winter the canal freezes over to form a great ice-skating rink. A recommended 6-mile route for hikers and bikers starts at Lumberville.

Dining and Lodging

Dining

Bucks County has no regional specialties to call its own. What makes dining here unique is the variety of food and settings in which diners can enjoy a fine meal: Continental, American, regional, nouvelle, and ethnic cuisine all served with a dollop of history in restored mills, pre-Revolutionary taverns, stagecoach stops, and elegant Victorian mansions.

Category	Cost*
Very Expensive	over $30
Expensive	$20–$30
Moderate	$10–$20
Inexpensive	under $10

per person for a 3-course meal, without wine, tax (6%), or service

Lodging

Although Bucks County has limited lodging options for families, it offers numerous choices to couples. Accommodations ranging from modest to elegant can be found in historic inns, small hotels, and bed-and-breakfasts. Most hostelries include breakfast with their room rates. Plan and reserve early—as much as three months ahead for summer and fall weekends. Unless otherwise stated, all accommodations listed below require a two-night minimum stay on weekends and a three-night minimum stay on holiday weekends. Many inns prohibit or restrict smoking. Unless otherwise indicated, all rooms have private bath and hotels are open year-round. Since many inns are historic homes furnished with fine antiques, they often bar young children.

Category	Cost*
Very Expensive	over $105
Expensive	$85–$104
Moderate	$60–$84
Inexpensive	under $60

double occupancy, based on peak (summer) rates, not including sales and room tax (8%)

The following credit card abbreviations are used: AE, American Express; D, Discover; DC, Diners Club; MC, MasterCard; V, Visa.

The most highly recommended restaurants and hotels are indicated by a star ★.

Carversville

Dining **The Carversville Inn.** Its out-of-the-way location has made this
★ circa-1813 inn one of the area's best kept secrets. Chef Will
Mathias's regional American cuisine with a southern flair is
now a favorite among locals. The menu changes seasonally, but
you can always count on interesting and innovative sauces such
as roast red pepper horseradish on a grilled filet mignon or
rosemary-maple-walnut sauce on roast duck. On Friday evenings look for complimentary hors d'oeuvres at the bar.
*Carversville and Aquetong Rds., tel. 215/297–0900. Dress: ca-
sual. Closed Mon. AE, MC, V. Expensive.*

Doylestown

Dining **Cafe Arielle.** This French bistro serves delicious grilled seafood
★ dishes (including tuna steak), prime meats, and spit-roasted
duckling in an open kitchen atmosphere amid country French
furnishings and striking artwork. *100 S. Main St. in the
Doylestown Agricultural Works, tel. 215/345–5930. Reservations requested. Dress: casual. Closed Mon. AE, DC, MC, V.
Very Expensive.*

Russell's 96 West. The chef-proprietor Russell Palmer artisti-
cally presents classical French cuisine—with an accent on
Southern France—in a restored 1846 town house. The seasonally changing menu may include rack of lamb, Norwegian
salmon with a tomato, scallion, bacon-reduction sauce, and sautéed duck with soy and ginger. Vegetables are bought from local organic farmers. Dinner and the lighter lunch are also
served on the patio in warm weather. Russell will prepare a
surprise six-course dinner for $55 per person. *96 W. State St.,
tel. 215/345–8746. Reservations recommended. Jackets requested. Closed Sun. AE, D, DC, MC, V. Very Expensive.*

Lodging **Pine Tree Farm.** A Colonial farmhouse dating from 1730 was redecorated with cheerful country antiques in light and airy
rooms. The glass-enclosed rear of the house, which includes the
dining room, indoor-outdoor patio, and solarium, overlooks 16
acres of pine trees, a pond, and the pool. Breakfast, served
poolside in summer, features poached eggs Florentine and
homemade apple muffins. Room 1 is a favorite. *2155 Lower
State Rd., 18901, tel. 215/348–0632. 4 rooms. Facilities: lighted
tennis court, outdoor pool, pond. No smoking. No children.
AE, MC, V. Very Expensive.*

★ **Highland Farms.** This Bucks County estate was the home of
lyricist Oscar Hammerstein from 1941 to 1961. The 1840s federal-style country home is set on 5 acres and is elegantly furnished with antiques and Hammerstein family memorabilia.
The video library is stocked with Rogers and Hammerstein
films. A four-course country breakfast is served in the formal
dining room or on the brick patio overlooking the 60-foot pool.
*70 East Rd., 18901, tel. 215/340–1354. 4 rooms, 2 with bath. Fa-
cilities: outdoor pool, tennis courts. Children over 12 welcome.
AE, MC, V. Very Expensive.*

Doylestown Inn. Located in the middle of town at the crossroads of U.S. 611 and 202, this witch's-hat-topped Victorian
hotel dates to 1902. Renovated in 1990, some guest rooms feature richly stained furnishings and moldings while others
are furnished with painted country-pine armoires and hand-
stenciled walls. Mercer tiles are found in the lobby and there's

one in each bathroom floor. Two corner rooms, No. 205 and No. 305, incorporate a circular tower as rounded window bays. *18 W. State St., Doylestown, 18901, tel. 215/345–6610, fax 215/ 345–4017. 21 rooms and one suite. No minimum stay. AE, D, DC, MC, V. Expensive–Very Expensive.*

The Inn at Fordhook Farm. The Burpee family (of seed catalogue fame) country estate is now a B&B loaded with family memorabilia and antiques. Built in 1760 and purchased in 1888 by W. Atlee Burpee, the house has high-ceilinged spacious bedrooms (one with a Mercer tile fireplace) brightened with floral prints, a large Federal-style living room, and a dining room with another Mercer tile fireplace. The full country breakfast featuring oatmeal buttermilk pancakes, cheese-filled French toast, and homegrown berries is served in the Burpee family dining room. The carriage house, with its dark wood paneling and vaulted cathedral ceiling, is a more modern alternative to the main house. *105 New Britain Rd., 18901, tel. 215/345–1766. 5 rooms, 3 with private bath in the main house, 2 in carriage house. Facilities: marked paths through 60 acres, lawn bowling, badminton, croquet. Children over 12 allowed. AE, MC, V. Expensive–Very Expensive.*

Erwinna

Dining **Evermay on-the-Delaware.** Ron Strouse, who has cooked at La
★ Varenne in Paris and with the late James Beard in New York, serves an unforgettable prix fixe six-course dinner in an elegant Victorian mansion. The contemporary American menu changes constantly and offers guests a choice of two entrées. Specialties include grilled tuna with fresh tomato salsa or chicken on linguine with basil and pine nuts. The meal includes champagne, hors d'oeuvres, and a cheese course. *River and Headquarters Rds., 13 mi north of New Hope, tel. 215/294–9100. Jackets required. Reservations required about a month in advance. Dinner Fri.–Sun. and holidays at 7:30. MC, V. Very Expensive.*

Lodging **Isaac Stover House.** Talk-show host Sally Jesse Raphael's 1837 brick mansion is a delightful B&B full of personality. Theme rooms include: Shakespeare & Co., Cupid's Bower, Emerald City with Wizard of Oz memorabilia, the Amore Room adorned with watercolor prints of Italy, more. The opulent Victorian sitting room features pink swag curtains; innkeeper Susan Tettemer describes it as "reminiscent of a French brothel." Full breakfast is served on a sunny porch or in the breakfast room. The inn is set on 13 acres of woods and meadows overlooking the Delaware River. *Box 68, River Rd., 18920, tel. 215/ 294–8044. 7 rooms, 5 with private bath. Smoking only on first floor. Children over 12 welcome. AE, MC, V. Very Expensive.*

★ **Evermay on-the-Delaware.** A three-story Victorian mansion has been transformed into a small elegant hotel overlooking the Delaware River. The rooms in the cream-colored clapboard building and nearby carriage house are filled with antiques and fresh flowers. Guests take pre-dinner sherry and afternoon tea in a stately parlor warmed by twin fireplaces. Breakfast of fresh fruit compote, croissants, juice, and coffee is served in the glassed-in conservatory overlooking great sweeps of lawn. Request a room with a river view. *River and Headquarters Rds., 13 mi north of New Hope, 18920, tel. 215/294–9100. 11*

*rooms in main house, 4 in carriage house; and a 1-bedroom
cottage. No children. MC, V. Expensive–Very Expensive.*

Holicong

Lodging **Barley Sheaf Farm.** At the end of a long, maple-fringed drive-
★ way is Barley Sheaf Farm, playwright George S. Kaufman's
"Cherchez la Farm" from 1936–1953, Bucks County's theatrical heyday. A 1740 fieldstone mansion, the inn's 30-acre park-
like setting includes a duck pond, a swimming pool, and a
meadow full of sheep. The bedrooms are a medley of floral
prints, brass, and four-poster beds. A hearty breakfast is
served on the glass-enclosed sun porch. Rooms in the adjacent
cottage are smaller but share the same country antique decor.
*Box 10, U.S. 202, 18928, tel. 215/794–5104. 10 rooms. Facili-
ties: outdoor pool, badminton, croquet, conference center for
25. Children over 8 welcome. AE, DC, MC, V. Very Expensive.*
Ash Mill Farm. A handsome 18th-century fieldstone manor
house set on 10 acres is a country B&B. The parlor has high ceilings, ornate moldings, and deep-silled windows; rooms feature
Irish and American antiques and thoughtful extras such as
thick terry-cloth robes, hair dryers, and down comforters on
canopy or four-poster beds. Full country breakfast is served to
the strains of Mozart or Vivaldi. Afternoon tea and homebaked
treats are offered by a cozy fire, in the garden, or on the sunny
front porch with a view of resident sheep. *Box 202, U.S. 202,
18928, tel. 215/794–5373. 6 rooms with 1 suite, 4 with bath. Facilities: golf privileges at a local country club. Children over 14
welcome. No credit cards. Moderate–Very Expensive.*

Lahaska

Dining **Jenny's.** American regional cuisine is served in country French
rooms. Lobster and crab sauté and filet Chesterfield (filet mignon with cheddar cheese, bacon, and horseradish sauce) are
favorites. Live jazz and blues are featured Friday and Saturday nights and Dixieland music during brunch on Sunday. *U.S.
202, Peddler's Village, tel. 215/794–4020. Reservations recommended. Dress: casual. AE, D, DC, MC, V. No dinner Mon.
Expensive.*
The Spotted Hog. This casual country bistro in the Golden
Plough Inn serves American cuisine such as New York strip
steak, grilled chicken with macadamia lime butter, Philadelphia cheesesteaks, interesting pizzas, and sundaes. Live bands
play folk, country, and pop Thursday, Friday, and Saturday
evenings and Sunday afternoons. *Peddler's Village, Rte. 202
and Street Rd., tel. 215/794–4030. No reservations. Dress: casual. AE, D, DC, MC, V. Moderate.*

Lodging **Golden Plough Inn.** Spacious guest rooms with four-poster
★ beds, rich fabrics, and cozy window seats evoke 19th-century
Bucks County. All rooms are equipped with air-conditioning,
remote control TV, a small refrigerator, and a complimentary
bottle of champagne, and some have a fireplace or a Jacuzzi.
The main inn has 22 rooms; the other 38 are scattered about the
village, in an 18th-century farmhouse, a historic carriage
house, and Merchant's Row above some of the Peddler's Village
shops. *Peddler's Village, Rte. 202 and Street Rd., Box 218,
18931, tel. 215/794–4004, fax 215/794–4001. 60 rooms, including 22 suites. Facilities: complimentary Continental breakfast*

or *$4.95 credit toward à la carte menu. Children welcome. AE, D, DC, MC, V. Expensive–Very Expensive.*

New Hope

Dining
★

La Bonne Auberge. For two decades, La Bonne Auberge has kept its title as Bucks County's most elite and expensive restaurant, thanks to the owners Chef Gerard Caronello, a native of Lyon, France, and his wife, Rozanne, of Great Britain. Consistently excellent, classic French cuisine is served in this pre-Revolutionary farmhouse. A small parlor features the original hearth and low beamed ceilings. The Terrace Room, used for dining, has a modern country-French ambience. Specialties include grilled salmon with a light lobster sauce served on the side and rack of lamb. A four-course table d'hôte menu, available Wednesday and Thursday evenings in addition to the regular menu, is a bargain. *Village 2 off Mechanic St., tel. 215/ 862–2462. Reservations required. Jackets required. Closed Mon. and Tues. AE. Very Expensive.*

Hotel du Village. Diners partake of country French fare in a converted private school. Chef-owner Omar Arbani prepares tournedos Henri IV, fillet with bearnaise sauce; sweetbreads with mushrooms in madeira sauce; and fillet of sole in curried butter, topped off by extravagant desserts. Dinner is served in a Tudor-style room with working fireplaces or on the sun porch. *Phillips Mill and N. River Rds., tel. 215/862–5164 or 215/862–9911. Reservations suggested on weekends. Jackets suggested. AE, DC. Closed Mon. and Tues. Closed for lunch. Expensive.*

Martine's. Reminiscent of a quaint English pub with a beamed ceiling, plaster over stone walls, and an oversize fireplace, Martine's is more popular with locals than with visitors. The eclectic menu features filet Mignon au poivre, pasta, duckling, and seafood paella. Outdoor dining is on a small patio. *7 E. Ferry St., tel. 215/862–2966. Reservations recommended weekends. Dress: casual. AE, DC, MC, V. Expensive.*

Mother's. One of New Hope's most popular dining spots, Mother's main claims to fame are sinful desserts representative of which are the chocolate mousse bombe and mocha Amazon. Homemade soups, pasta, and unusual pizzas stand out among the selections on the extensive menu. In summer, meals are also served in the garden. Expect to wait; it's always crowded here. *34 N. Main St., tel. 215/862–9354. Reservations recommended for dinner. Dress: informal. AE, D, MC, V. Expensive.*

Odette's. In 1961, Parisian actress Odette Myrtil Logan converted a former canal lock house into a stylish restaurant. The atmosphere is French country bistro; the cuisine, Continental with a menu that changes seasonally. A "Lite-Bites" menu also is available during most serving hours. Belgian waffles and eggs Benedict are made table-side during Sunday buffet brunch. Some of the dining rooms command a view of the river. Entertainment consists of a piano bar, cabarets, and art shows. *S. River Rd., 4 mi south of New Hope, tel. 215/862–2432. Reservations advised; request a river view. Dress: casual. AE, DC, MC, V. Expensive–Very Expensive.*

Havana Bar and Restaurant. The American regional and contemporary fare offered by the Havana is enhanced by its hickory-grilled specialties. Dishes featured are sesame onion rings, a Chinese vegetable sandwich, and Jane's boned roast duck.

The bar serves exotic elixirs enlivened by jazz bands Thursday through Sunday nights and karaoke Monday nights. The view of Main Street is ideal for people-watching, especially from the outdoor patio. *105 S. Main St. tel. 215/862–9897. No reservations. Dress: informal. AE, D, DC, MC, V. Moderate.*

The Logan Inn. The saloon in New Hope's oldest building dates to 1727, when it opened as the Ferry Tavern. The Logan, circa 1993, serves from four menus—lunch (11:30–4), café (after 4), dinner (4:30–close), and a popular all-day Tavern Menu with such favorites as nachos, wings, salads, burgers, and pizzas. *10 W. Ferry St., tel. 215/862–2300. Reservations advised. Dress: informal. AE, D, DC, MC, V. Inexpensive–Expensive.*

Lodging ★ **The Whitehall Inn.** Guest rooms at the 18th-century manor house of what was once a gentleman's horse farm are furnished with period antiques, canopy beds, and patterned wallpaper. Guests get a bowl of fresh fruit and bottle of regional wine upon arrival and will find chocolate truffles and velour robes in their room. The spacious parlor has sofas and rocking chairs facing a blazing fireplace. The four-course candlelit gourmet breakfast is served at tables set with white linen, English china, and heirloom silver; in the afternoon, high tea is served. *1370 Pineville Rd., 18938, tel. 215/598–7945. 6 rooms, 4 with bath. Facilities: outdoor pool, tennis, 12 secluded acres, dressage horses. Children over 12 welcome. No smoking. AE, D, DC, MC, V. Very Expensive.*

The Logan Inn. A 1988 face-lift of one of the oldest inns in continuous operation in North America has restored its original Colonial charm. Established in 1727 as an extension of the Ferry Tavern, the Ferry Inn accommodated passengers who used the Delaware River ferry to Lambertville. George Washington is said to have stayed here at least five times. Rooms are decorated with original and reproduction Colonial and Victorian furnishings, including canopy beds, plus original paintings by local artists. Some rooms have river views. Full or Continental breakfast from the restaurant downstairs is included. Ask Gwen the innkeeper about haunted room No. 6! *10 W. Ferry St., 18938; tel. 215/862–2300. 16 rooms. Children welcome. AE, D, DC, MC, V. Moderate–Very Expensive.*

★ **The Wedgwood Inn.** Three buildings comprise the Wedgwood Inn B&B lodgings: a blue "painted lady" 1870 Victorian house with frilly woodwork, a gabled roof, wraparound porch, and a porte-cochere; a Federal-style 1840 stone manor house; and the Aaron Burr House, another 1870 Victorian building added in 1990 to the inn's properties. Minutes from downtown, the collection of inns grace 2.5 acres of landscaped grounds with gazebos and gardens. Wedgwood pottery, antiques, fireplaces, and wood-burning stoves add to its charm. Continental-plus breakfast and afternoon tea are served in the sun porch, gazebo, or guest room. *111 W. Bridge St., 18938, tel. 215/862–2570. 19 rooms, all with private bath including 4 suites and a carriage house. Facilities: pool and tennis club privileges; 4 rooms accommodate children. Mid-week discount. Pets allowed on a limited basis. AE, MC, V. Moderate–Very Expensive.*

Hotel du Village. Flower-filled grounds surrounding the large, old stone boarding school create the feeling of an English manor house. The 20 guest rooms are decorated with country furniture and a Continental breakfast is served in the parlor. *Phillips Mill and N. River Rds., tel. 215/862–5164 or 215/862–*

9911. Facilities: 2 tennis courts; outdoor pool. No children on weekends. AE, DC. Expensive.

Holiday Inn. This comfortable motel is a few minutes from New Hope and 30 minutes from Sesame Place. It is one of the few spots in Bucks County that welcomes children. *Box 419 (U.S. 202), 18938, tel. 215/862–5221 or 800/465–4329. 159 rooms. Facilities: restaurant, lounge with entertainment Fri. and Sat. nights, outdoor pool, tennis, playground. AE, DC, MC, V. Moderate–Expensive.*

New Hope Motel in the Woods. A clean, modern, one-story motel, with wood-paneled guest rooms, offers the lowest rates in the area and welcomes families. *400 W. Bridge St., 18938, tel. 215/862–2800. 28 rooms. Facility: outdoor pool. D, DC, MC, V. Inexpensive.*

Newtown

Dining **Jean Pierre's.** Owner/chef Jean Pierre Tardy, formerly execu-
★ tive chef at Philadelphia's distinguished Le Bec-Fin, prepares classic French cuisine in a quaint country French setting. Salmon stuffed with lobster and salmon mousse in puff pastry and a combination plate of stuffed loin of lamb with boneless breast of duck are two of the chef's favorites. *101 S. State St., tel. 215/968–6201. Reservations required. Jackets requested, no jeans or sneakers. AE, DC, MC, V. Closed Mon.; dinner only weekends. Very Expensive.*

Temperance House. Continental cuisine is served in a meticulously restored 1772 inn. Homemade soup stocks and an in-house charcuterie ensure an appealing range of dishes featuring rack of lamb, roast Long Island smoked duck, and slow-roasted pork; beef, fresh-catch, and chicken preparations change each day. Request hearthside seating in the room adorned with reproductions of artwork by Edward Hicks of "Peaceable Kingdom" fame. Listen to live jazz Wednesday, Friday, and Saturday nights, and enjoy a Cajun brunch accompanied by Dixieland jazz on Sunday. *5–11 S. State St., tel. 215/860–0474. Reservations accepted. Dress: casual. AE, DC, MC, V. Open for lunch Mon.–Sat. Expensive.*

Lodging **Temperance House.** Each room in this 1772 inn is decorated with a different style of furniture: the Benetz Suite has bent willow-and-twig furniture; the Edward Hicks Suite has rich period mahogany and walls stenciled in a pattern derived from "Peaceable Kingdom" mosaic tile. Continental breakfast is served buffet style in the dining room. *5–11 S. State St., 18940, tel. 215/860–0474. 13 rooms and suites. Facilities: restaurant, access to Newtown Racquetball and Fitness Club. No minimum stay. AE, DC, MC, V. Expensive–Very Expensive.*

Quakertown

Dining **Sign of the Sorrel Horse.** Fresh game dishes make this one of Bucks County's most unusual and memorable dining experiences. The drive to the 1749 fieldstone farmhouse skirts Lake Nockamixon. Chef Jon Atkin grows his own herbs and vegetables here in season, while his wife Monique combs state stores for the best varietals (wines). A mid-week special includes dinner for two from a bistro menu and overnight accommodations at the inn upstairs for $99. This mid-week special is available Wednesday and Thursday, plus Sunday based on availability.

243 Old Bethlehem Rd., tel. 215/536-4651. Reservations accepted. Jackets required. Smoking at the bar only. AE, DC, MC, V. Very Expensive.

Lodging **Sign of the Sorrel Horse.** Tucked away in the less-frequented northern corner of the county, this inn affords visitors an escape from the crowds of New Hope and access to the many outdoor recreational choices at nearby Nockamixon State Park. A list of activities, from boating to bicycling, is available from the innkeepers. Be sure to ask for the Henry Mercer room with its exposed stone wall. *243 Old Bethlehem Rd., tel. 215/536-4651. 6 rooms, all with private bath. Children over 12 and pets welcome. AE, DC, MC, V. Expensive-Very Expensive.*

Upper Black Eddy

Lodging **Bridgeton House on the Delaware.** Wide, screened porches and a terrace provide close-up views of the Delaware River and the bridge to Milford, New Jersey. Guest rooms are decorated with wall and ceiling folk murals by the self-described artist-in-residence. The informal sitting room has white wood walls, and a glass wall overlooking the river. Two-course gourmet country breakfast is served, as is afternoon tea and sherry. Request a river view: Riverfront rooms feature French doors to private screened porches; in the penthouse, the marble fireplace and huge windows are delightful. *Box 167, River Rd., 18972, tel. 215/982-5856. 11 rooms, including 3 suites. Children under 8 welcome weekdays only. AE, MC, V. Moderate-Very Expensive.*

The Arts

Theater

The **Bristol Riverside Theatre** (120 Radcliffe St., Bristol, tel. 215/788-SUBS), a professional regional theater, has five major shows a year along with a holiday production. Children's theater is offered on Saturday mornings throughout the season with other production companies using the space during the off-season.

The **Bucks County Playhouse** (S. Main St., New Hope, tel. 215/862-2041). Housed in an historic mill, the Playhouse has been in continuous use as a theater since 1939 when it featured summer stock. After several years of non-Equity productions, the annual April through December season now has eight performances a week of Equity shows with stars from TV and stage. The 1993 season saw Loretta Swit in *Shirley Valentine* and William Shatner and Leonard Nimoy together on stage in a production of *Harry and Arthur.*

The **New Hope Performing Arts Festival** (held at various locations in the New Hope area, tel. 215/862-9894 July and August, 215/862-3347 for off-season information or to be put on the mailing list) is dedicated to original and innovative works in theater, music, and performing arts. The summer festival, with scheduling varying from year to year, includes classical music and children's programming almost every evening during the July and August season.

10 Lancaster County

By Joyce
Eisenberg

Updated by
M. T.
Schwartzman

The plain and fancy live side by side in Lancaster County, some 65 miles west of Philadelphia. This is Pennsylvania Dutch Country, where horse-drawn buggies and horn-tooting cars jockey for position on picturesque country roads.

The tourists come to see the Old Order Amish, one of the most conservative of the Pennsylvania Dutch sects. Clinging to a centuries-old way of life, the Amish shun the amenities of modern civilization, using kerosene or gas lamps instead of electric lighting, horse-drawn buggies instead of automobiles. Ironically, in turning their backs on the modern world, they have attracted the world's attention.

This bucolic region can be hectic, especially on summer weekends and in October, when the fall foliage attracts crowds. Its main arteries, U.S. 30 (also known as the Lincoln Highway and Lancaster Pike) and Route 340 (sometimes called the Old Philadelphia Pike), are lined with souvenir shops and outlet stores. The farmers markets and family-style restaurants are often crowded with busloads of tourists. But there is still much charm here in the general stores, one-room schoolhouses, country lanes, and picture-perfect farms, many of which welcome overnight guests. There are pretzel factories to tour, quilts to buy, and a host of attractions for railroad buffs. The trick is to visit the top attractions and then get off the beaten path. If possible, plan your trip for early spring, September, or Christmas season, when it is less crowded.

Note: Although many restaurants, shops, and farmers markets close Sunday for the Sabbath, commercial attractions are open.

Pennsylvania Dutch is a collective phrase for more than 35 Amish, Mennonite, and Brethren sects. Despite their name, they aren't Dutch at all. Rather, they are descendants of German and Swiss immigrants who came to the Lancaster area to escape religious persecution. "Dutch" is a corruption of "Deutsch," meaning German.

The Mennonite movement, named after its leader Menno Simons, began in Switzerland in the 16th century, the time of the Reformation. It was a radical religious group that advocated nonviolence, separation of church and state, adult baptism, and individual freedom in choosing a religion. Nicknamed Anabaptists, the Mennonites were persecuted and killed by the thousands for not conforming to either Catholic or Protestant tenets. In 1710, eight families led by Mennonite Bishop Hans Herr accepted William Penn's invitation to settle in Lancaster County.

In 1693, Swiss Mennonite Bishop Jacob Amman, whose stricter beliefs and interpretation of church tenets had attracted a following, broke off from the movement. His followers, the Amish, also settled in Lancaster. Today, there are 135,000 Amish people living in North America; Lancaster County has the second-largest Amish community in the nation, with 16,000 people. (Holmes County, Ohio, is first.) That the number of Amish has doubled in the last two decades suggests that theirs is still a viable alternative lifestyle.

The Amish religion and way of life stress separation from the world, caring for others of the faith, and self-sufficiency. What may appear as odd behavior results from religious convictions based on Biblical interpretation. The Amish, who reject compulsory school attendance and military registration, do not accept social-security benefits or purchase life or property insurance. Barn-raising is probably the best example of the Amish spirit. If a new family barn is needed, hundreds of men gather to supply the labor to build it while the women cook the meals. The job is completed in a day or two.

Old Order Amish send their children to one-room schoolhouses with eight grades to a room. They avoid larger public schools to prevent the exposure of their children to the influence of "outsiders." The Supreme Court has ruled that Amish children need not attend school beyond the eighth grade.

Telephones, television, radio, and electric appliances are not permitted. Farmers work with teams of mules to plow, plant, and harvest their crops. Families ride in horse-drawn buggies. Men and women wear plain clothing which has remained unchanged for centuries.

Although some changes have been thrust upon them by the government, the Amish do change and update some rules themselves. Some have telephones in their barns or on the edge of their property for emergency use only; many will accept a ride in an automobile or take public transportation. They live a lively, rich life of discipline and caring. They seek to be at peace with themselves, their neighbors, their surroundings, and their God.

Although the Amish are a prime attraction, they are not the only lure to Lancaster County. Lancaster (which the English named after Lancashire) is an intriguing city to explore. Very residential, with blocks of charming row houses, it served as the nation's capital for one day during the American Revolution when Congress fled Philadelphia after the Battle of Brandywine. It is also the nation's oldest inland city, dating from 1710. Historic sites in the area include Wheatland, the home of James Buchanan, Pennsylvania's only contribution to the White House.

One can spend a full day following Oregon Pike (Rte. 272) northeast from the Landis Valley Museum, an exhibit devoted to rural life before 1900. Ephrata Cloister provides a look at a religious communal society of the 1700s. It was founded in 1728, when dissident brethren split from a group that had arrived in 1724. And Main Street in Lititz, founded in 1756, offers an architectural treat for strollers.

Western Lancaster County, which includes the towns of Marietta, Mount Joy, and Columbia, is a quieter part of the county where visitors can bicycle down winding lanes, sample local wines and authentic Mennonite cooking, and explore friendly uncrowded villages. Its history is rooted in the Colonial period. The residents are of Scotch and German descent, and architecture varies from log cabins to Victorian homes. There are a number of good restaurants, inns, and farms that accept guests.

If you've brought your children as far as Lancaster, you may want to continue north to Hershey, the "Chocolate Town" founded in 1903 by Milton S. Hershey. Here the street lights are shaped like giant Hershey Kisses and the number one attraction is Hersheypark, an 87-acre theme park with kiddie rides and thrill rides, theaters, and live shows. Hershey's

Chocolate World offers tours into the simulated world of chocolate production.

The battlefields and museums of Gettysburg also are within driving distance.

Essential Information

Getting Around

By Car From Philadelphia, take the Schuylkill Expressway (I-76) west to the Pennsylvania Turnpike. Lancaster County attractions are accessible from Exits 20, 21, and 22. For a more scenic route, follow U.S. 30 (Lancaster Pike) west from Philadelphia. It's about 65 miles; allow 90 minutes.

By Bus **Greyhound/Capital Trailways** (tel. 800/231-2222) has three runs daily between Philadelphia and the R&S Bus Terminal (22 West Clay St.) in Lancaster. The ride takes two hours, 20 minutes. Fares are $10.50 one way, $20 round-trip.

By Train **Amtrak** (tel. 215/824-1600 or 800/USA-RAIL) has regular service from Philadelphia's 30th Street Station to the Lancaster Amtrak station, 53 McGovern Avenue. Trips take 80 minutes. Fares are $11 one way, $17 round-trip.

Guided Tours

Amish Country Tours (Rte. 340 between Bird-in-Hand and Intercourse, tel. 717/768-7063 or 800/441-3505) has a variety of large bus or minivan tours. Most popular is the four-hour Amish farmlands trip. Featured are stops at an Amish farmhouse, wine tasting and food tasting, and shopping for crafts. Also available are tours to Hershey.

Brunswick Tours (National Wax Museum, U.S. 30 E, Lancaster, tel. 717/397-7541) provides private guides who will tour with you in your car.

The Mennonite Information Center (2209 Millstream Rd., Lancaster, tel. 717/299-0954) has local Mennonite guides who will join you in your car. These knowledgeable guides will lead you to country roads, produce stands, and craft shops, and also acquaint you with their religion.

Rutts Tours (3466 Old Philadelphia Pike, Intercourse, tel. 717/768-8238) has guides who will join you in your car.

For an aerial tour, try **Glick Aviation** at Smoketown Airport (311 Airport Dr. off Rte. 340, Smoketown, tel. 717/394-6476). Eighteen-minute flights in a four-seater plane (pilot plus three) provide a splendid view of rolling farmlands.

You can rent or purchase a cassette tape for the self-guided **Auto Tape Tour of Pennsylvania Dutch Country.** Minimum driving time is 90 minutes. *Available at Dutch Wonderland and the National Wax Museum (2249 U.S. 30 E, Lancaster).*

Tapetours, another self-guided auto tour, begins at the Pennsylvania Dutch Convention & Visitors Bureau on Greenfield Road. The 28 stops take about three hours. *Available from Brunswick Tours (see above).*

Important Addresses and Numbers

Tourist Information   **The Pennsylvania Dutch Convention & Visitors Bureau** (Greenfield Rd. exit of U.S. 30 E, Dept. 2201, 501 Greenfield Rd., Lancaster 17601, tel. 717/299–8901 or 800/735–2629) has many brochures and maps, direct phone connections to local hotels, and a 14-minute multi-image slide presentation, "There Is a Season," a visual journey through picturesque Pennsylvania Dutch Country which serves as a good introduction to the area. *Open daily 9–5, later in summer. Slide presentation: $2 adults, $1 children 6–12.*

The Mennonite Information Center (2209 Millstream Rd., Lancaster 17602–1494, tel. 717/299–0954) serves mainly to "interpret the faith and practice of the Mennonite Church to all who inquire." It has information on local inns and Mennonite guest homes as well as a video about the Amish and Mennonite people, shown every half-hour. *Open Mon.–Sat. 8–5.*

Intercourse Tourist Information Center (3564 Old Philadelphia Pike, Intercourse 17534, tel. 717/768–3882) provides travel advice on one of the Dutch Country's most popular towns. *Open Mar.–Dec., Mon.–Sat. 9:30–5.*

Emergencies   Dial 911 for assistance, or go to one of the three emergency rooms in the city of Lancaster: **Community Hospital of Lancaster** (1100 E. Orange St., tel. 717/397–3711), **Lancaster General Hospital** (555 N. Duke St., tel. 717/299–5511), **St. Joseph's Hospital** (250 College Ave., tel. 717/291–8211). For non-emergency referrals, call the Lancaster City & County Medical Society, tel. 717/393–9588.

Pharmacy   **Weis Pharmacy** (1603 Lincoln Hwy. E, Lancaster, tel. 717/394–9826). *Open Mon.–Fri. 9–9, Sat. 9–6.*

Strasburg Pharmacy (326 Hartman Bridge Rd., Rte. 896, 2 mi south of Rte. 30, Strasburg, tel. 717/687–6058). *Open Mon.–Fri. 9–9, Sat. 9–5.*

Exploring Lancaster County

Most visitors come to Pennsylvania Dutch Country to get a glimpse of the Amish and their lifestyle. Below are suggestions for one-day tours, plus itineraries for additional touring. Train lovers will appreciate the Strasburg attractions; history and architecture buffs will enjoy the sites in and around the city of Lancaster. There is information on a tour following Oregon Pike north from Lancaster and some suggestions for seeing the western part of Lancaster County. For an extended tour of south-central Pennsylvania, the sites and attractions of Gettysburg and Hershey are also included.

Day 1

Numbers in the margin correspond to points of interest on the Lancaster County map.

❶ **People's Place,** a "people-to-people interpretation center," provides an excellent introduction to the Amish, Mennonites, and Hutterites. A 30-minute multiscreen slide show titled "Who

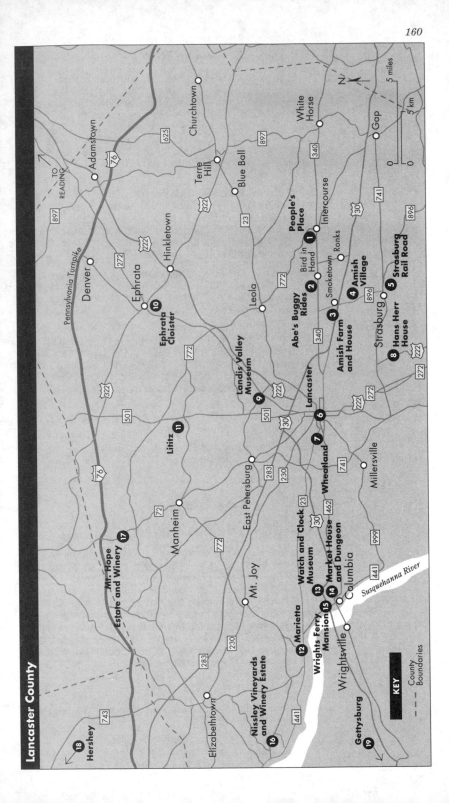

Lancaster County

KEY

- - - County
Boundaries

Are the Amish?" features close-ups of Amish life and perceptive narration. Geared toward children, **Amish World** is a hands-on exhibit on transportation, dress, schools, the effects of growing old, and mutual aid. Children can try on bonnets and play in the "feeling box." Don't miss the collection of wood sculptures by Aaron Zook. "Hazel's People," a feature film starring Geraldine Page and set in the Mennonite community, is shown Monday through Saturday from Memorial Day through Labor Day at 7:30 PM; separate admission fee. *Rte. 340, Intercourse, tel. 717/768-7171. Admission: $3 adults, $1.50 children. Open Memorial Day–Labor Day, Mon.–Sat. 9:30– 9:30, until 5 in winter.*

2 Following Route 340 west to Bird-in-Hand will bring you to **Abe's Buggy Rides**. Abe chats about the Amish during a 2-mile spin down country roads in an Amish family carriage. *No phone. Price: $10 adults, $5 children 3–12. Open Mon.–Sat. 8 AM–dusk.*

For lunch (actually, they serve dinner all day) try one of the family-style Pennsylvania Dutch restaurants (**Amish Barn** on Rte. 340; **Good 'N Plenty** on Rte. 896). You'll share a table with about a dozen other customers and be treated to hearty regional fare, including traditional "sweets and sours." There's no menu; they just bring out the food (*see* Dining and Lodging, *below*). Although it doesn't serve family style, **Bird-in-Hand Family Restaurant** on Rte. 340 is an excellent place to sample local specialties.

Several furnished farmhouses offer a simulated, up-close look at how the Amish live. Note that these are commercial, not Amish-run, enterprises.

3 **The Amish Farm and House** offers 40-minute tours through a 10-room circa 1805 house furnished in the Old Order Amish style. A map guides visitors to the farmstead's animals, waterwheel, and barns. *2395 Lincoln Hwy. E (U.S. 30), Lancaster, tel. 717/394-6185. Admission: $4.50 adults, $4 senior citizens, $2.75 children 5–11. Open daily 8:30–5, until 4 in winter, 6 in summer.*

4 **The Amish Village** also offers guided tours through an authentically furnished Amish house. Afterward, visitors may wander about the grounds of the village, which includes a one-room schoolhouse, blacksmith shop, and operating smokehouse built for the Amish Village by Amish craftsmen. *Rte. 896 between U.S. 30 and Rte. 741, Strasburg, tel. 717/687-8511. Admission: $5 adults, $1.50 children 6–12. Open daily 9–5 spring and fall, 9–6 in summer. House tours weekends 10–4 in winter.*

Save an hour or two to explore the country roads on your own. Many Amish farms (they're the ones with windmills and green blinds) are clustered in the area between Ephrata and New Holland. Drive the side roads between routes 23 and 340; visit the roadside stands and farms where hand-painted signs entice you with quilts or farm-fresh produce and eggs. Drive in and chat with the Amish—they always welcome polite inquiries. For take-home goodies and gifts, stop at a farmers market.

Time Out To sample the local ice cream, order one of the 18 farm-fresh flavors at **Lapp Valley Farm**. It also sells homemade root beer and has animals to entertain the children. *Mentzer Rd., be-*

tween New Holland and Intercourse (from Intercourse, follow Rte. 340 1 mi east, turn left on New Holland Rd., left on Peters Rd., and right on Mentzer Rd.), tel. 717/354–7988. Open Mon.–Thurs. noon–dark, Fri. 8 AM–dark, Sat. 8 AM–7 PM, or later.

Day 2. Strasburg

Train lovers could easily spend an entire day in Strasburg. To get from U.S. 30 to Strasburg, head south on Route 896 and turn left on Route 741.

⑤ The Strasburg Rail Road is a scenic 9-mile round-trip excursion from Strasburg to Paradise on a rolling antique chartered in 1832 to carry milk, mail, and coal. Passengers can chug along in the open coach featured in *Hello Dolly.* Called America's oldest short line, the wooden coaches are pulled by an iron steam locomotive. You can buy the makings for a picnic at the Strasburg Country Store (Rtes. 896 and 741) and alight at Groff's Grove in Paradise for a picnic lunch. *Rte. 741, Strasburg, tel. 717/687–7522. Round-trip: $6.50 adults, $3.50 children 3–11. Open daily Apr.–Nov., weekends only Dec.–Mar., closed first two weeks in Jan. Trains depart every 30–60 min. depending on the season, call for an exact schedule.*

Across the road from the Strasburg Rail Road, the **Railroad Museum of Pennsylvania** features 75 pieces of train history, including 13 colossal engines built between 1888 and 1930; 12 railroad cars including a Pullman sleeper that operated from 1855 to 1913; sleighs; and railroad memorabilia documenting the history of Pennsylvania railroading. An expanded Hall of Rolling Stock is envisioned for late 1994 or early 1995. *Rte. 741, Strasburg, tel. 717/687–8628. Admission: $6 adults, $5 senior citizens, $4 children 6–17. Open Mon.–Sat. 9–5, Sun. noon–5. Closed Mon. from Nov.–Apr.*

On a smaller scale, antique and 20th-century model trains are on display at the **Toy Train Museum,** the showplace for the Train Collectors Association. There are five operating layouts plus hundreds of locomotives and cars in display cases, nostalgia films, and many "push-me" buttons. *Paradise La., just north of Rte. 741, Strasburg, tel. 717/687–8976. Admission: $3 adults, $2.75 senior citizens, $1.50 children 5–12. Open daily, 10–5, May–Oct. and Christmas week, weekends only Apr. and Nov.–mid-Dec., closed Jan.–Mar.*

Just down the road at the **Red Caboose Motel** N-5 cabooses have been converted into motel units and a casual restaurant. **Abe's Buggy Rides** depart from the motel for 20- to 30-minute horse-drawn-carriage rides along scenic back roads. *Rte. 896, 1½ mi south of U.S. 30, Strasburg, tel. 717/687–0360. Rides: $8 adults, $4 children 10 and under. Departures June–Aug., Mon.–Sat.; Sept.–May, Sat. only.*

If you fancy fancy cars, **Gast Classic Motorcars Exhibit** has a changing display of more than 50 antique, classic, sports, and celebrity cars. *Rte. 896, Strasburg, tel. 717/687–9500. Admission: $6 adults, $3.50 children 7–12. Open Memorial Day–Labor Day, daily 9–9; Labor Day–Memorial Day, Sun.–Thurs. 9–5, Fri. and Sat. 9–9.*

Day 3. Lancaster

If you have another day to spend in Pennsylvania Dutch Coun-
6 try, tour the city of **Lancaster** and surrounding attractions or
follow Oregon Pike north along the route described below.

The Historic Lancaster Walking Tour, a 90-minute stroll
through the heart of this charming old city, is conducted by costumed guides who impart lively anecdotes about local architecture and history. *Tours leave from the downtown visitor center
at S. Queen and Vine Sts., near Penn Sq., tel. 717/392–1776.
Price: $4 adults, $3.50 senior citizens, $2 students. Tours
Mon.–Fri. 10 and 1:30, Sat. 10, 11, 1:30, Sun. 1:30 Apr.
through Oct., by reservation only the rest of the year.*

Central Market began with open-air stalls in 1742. The current
Romanesque building was constructed in 1889, and is one of the
oldest covered markets in the country. This is where the locals
shop for fresh fruit and vegetables, meats (try the Lebanon bo-
logna), and baked goods such as sticky buns and shoofly pie.
It's a good place to pick up food for a picnic. *Penn Sq., tel. 717/
291–4723. Open 6–4:30 Tues. and Fri., 6–2 on Sat.*

The **Demuth Foundation** includes the restored 18th-century
home, studio, and garden of Charles Demuth, one of America's
first modernist artists. *114 E. King St., tel. 717/299–9940. Free
admission. Open Tues.–Sat. 10–4, Sun. 1–4. Closed Jan.*

The Old City Hall, reborn as the **Heritage Center Museum,**
shows the work of Lancaster County artisans and craftsmen—
clocks, furniture, homemade toys, *fraktur* (ornate paintings),
and Pennsylvania long rifles. Some exhibits are on display per-
manently, while some exhibits change. *King and Queen Sts.,
tel. 717/299–6440. Donation requested. Open Tues.–Sat. 10–4.*

Rock Ford Plantation and Kauffman Museum show antiques
and folk art. The antiques are in a 1792 Georgian-style house
once owned by Edward Hand, one of George Washington's generals; the Zoe and Henry Kauffman collection of pewter, brass,
firearms, and furniture is displayed in the restored barn. *Lancaster County Park at 881 Rock Ford Rd., tel. 717/392–7223.
Admission: $3.50 adults, $2.50 senior citizens, $1.50 children
6–18. Guided 45-min. tours. Open Apr.–Nov., Tues.–Sat.
10–4, Sun. noon–4. Closed Dec.–Mar.*

7 **Wheatland** was the home of the only president from Pennsylvania, James Buchanan. The restored 1828 Federal mansion displays the 15th president's furniture just as it was during his
lifetime. A one-hour tour includes an entertaining profile of the
only bachelor to occupy the White House. *1120 Marietta Ave.
(Rte. 23), 1½ mi west of Lancaster, tel. 717/392–8721. Admission: $4.50 adults, $4 senior citizens, $3.25 students, $1.75
children 6–12. Open daily 10–4:15, Apr.–Nov. The home is
open for a Victorian Christmas exhibit the first 2 weeks of Dec.
Closed mid-Dec.–Mar.*

Artist Andrew Wyeth's ancestors were members of the Herr
8 family and the **Hans Herr House** is the subject of several Wyeth
paintings. Today, the house is owned by the Lancaster Mennonite Historical Society, which aims to correct misconcep-
tions about the Mennonite religion with exhibits about their
way of life in its Visitors Center. The 45-minute tours cover the
grounds and the 1719 sandstone house, a former Mennonite

meeting place. The house, the oldest in Lancaster County, is considered the best example of medieval German architecture in North America. *1849 Hans Herr Dr., 5 mi south of Lancaster off U.S. 222, tel. 717/464–4438. Admission: $3 adults, $1 children 7–12. Open Mon.–Sat. 9–4, Apr.–Dec. Closed Jan.– Mar.*

9 Follow Oregon Pike (Rte. 272) north from Lancaster to the **Landis Valley Museum,** an outdoor museum of Pennsylvania/ German rural life and folk culture before 1900. Owned by brothers Henry and George Landis, the farm and village is now operated by the Pennsylvania Historical and Museum Commission. From May through October, you can visit over 15 historical buildings, from a farmstead to a country store, and see daily demonstrations of such skills as spinning and weaving, pottery making, and tinsmithing, the products of which are for sale in the Weathervane Shop. There are guided tours from November to April. *2451 Kissel Hill Rd. (just off Oregon Pike), Lancaster, tel. 717/569–0401. Admission: $7 adults, $6 senior citizens, $5 children. Open Tues.–Sat. 9–5, Sun. noon–5.*

10 In the 1730s, a radical religious communal society took root in the town of Ephrata. A living example of William Penn's Holy Experiment, the monastic Protestants of the **Ephrata Cloister** lived an ascetic life of work, study, and prayer. They ate one meal a day of grain, fruit, and vegetables, and encouraged celibacy (the last sister died in 1813). The society was best known for a cappella singing, fraktur (ornate paintings), medieval German architecture, and its publishing center. Robed guides lead 45-minute tours of three restored buildings; then visitors can tour the stable, print shop, and craft shop by themselves. *Rtes. 272 and 322, Ephrata, tel. 717/733–6600. Admission: $5 adults, $4 senior citizens, $3 children 6–17. Open Mon.–Sat. 9–5, Sun. noon–5.*

11 The town of **Lititz,** west of Ephrata, was founded by Moravians who settled in Pennsylvania to do missionary work among the Indians. It's a lovely town with a tree-shaded main street lined with 18th-century cottages and shops selling antiques, crafts, clothing, and gifts. Around the main square are the Moravian communal residences, a church dating from 1787, and a hospital that treated the wounded during the Revolutionary War. Pick up a Historical Foundation walking tour brochure at the General Sutter Inn (*see* Dining and Lodging, *below*).

Time Out   **The General Sutter Inn** (Main St. and Rte. 501, tel. 717/626–2115) was named after the man who founded Sacramento in 1839, 10 years before the discovery of gold on his California property started the gold rush. A Victoriana lover's delight, this inn has a pretty coffee shop and a more formal restaurant. In summer, you can linger on the brick patio.

At the nation's oldest pretzel bakery, the **Julius Sturgis Pretzel House,** you can see pretzels twisted by hand and baked in brick ovens the same way Julius Sturgis did it in 1861. At the end of the 20-minute guided tour, visitors can try their hand at the almost extinct art of pretzel twisting. *219 E. Main St., Lititz, tel. 717/626–4354. Admission: $1.50. Open Mon.–Sat. 9–4:30.*

The first thing you'll notice in Lititz is the smell of chocolate. It emanates from the **Wilbur Chocolate Company's Candy Ameri-**

cana **Museum and Factory Candy Outlet** (48 N. Broad St., Lititz, tel. 717/626–1131), which features a candy-making demonstration (with free samples), a small museum of candy-related memorabilia, and a retail store. *Open Mon.–Sat. 10–5.*

Western Lancaster County

Some visitors avoid the crowds and commercialism of eastern Lancaster County by staying in the sleepy towns along the Susquehanna River—Columbia, Marietta, Maytown, Bainbridge, Mount Joy, and Elizabethtown.

 With architecture ranging from log cabins to more recent Federal and Victorian homes, 48% of the town of **Marietta** is listed on the National Historic Register. The restored river town, now seeing life as an artists' community, is perfect for strolling along, admiring the well-preserved facades and peeking into the art galleries and antiques shops.

Time Out Between Marietta and Columbia, pull off Route 441 at **Chickies Rock County Park.** Follow the trail from the parking area to Chickies Rock, an outcropping high above the water, for a commanding view of the Susquehanna River as it snakes through the valley.

⑬ The Watch and Clock Museum of the National Association of Watch and Clock Collectors displays a large and varied collection of timepieces, specialized tools, and related items from the primitive to the modern. There's a 19th-century Tiffany globe clock, a German Black Forest organ clock with 94 pipes, and the showstopper—the Engle Clock—an 1878 timepiece, which took clockmaker Stephen D. Engle 20 years to complete, intended to resemble the famous monument clock of Strasbourg, France. It has 48 moving figures. *514 Poplar St., Columbia, tel. 717/684–8261. Admission: $3 adults, $2.50 senior citizens, $1 children 6–17. Open Tues.–Sat. 9–4.*

⑭ The **Market House and Dungeon,** built in 1869, is one of the oldest continuously operating farmers markets in the state. You can buy handcrafted jewelry, baked goods, meat, fruits, and vegetables from local farms. The basement of the house used to be a dungeon; you can still see the ground-level windows through which prisoners were shoved down a chute into the darkness. *308 Locust St. (off of Rte. 441), Columbia, tel. 717/684–2468. Farmers market open Fri. 7–5, Sat. 7–noon. Dungeon open by appointment only; contact the Susquehanna Heritage Visitors Center, 3rd and Linden Sts., Columbia 17512, tel. 717/684–5249.*

⑮ Wrights Ferry Mansion is the former residence of English Quaker Susanna Wright, a silkworm breeder whose family helped open Colonial Pennsylvania west of the Susquehanna. The 1738 stone house showcases period furniture in the William & Mary and Queen Anne styles and a great collection of English needlework, ceramics, and glass, all pre-dating 1750. *38 S. 2nd St., Columbia, tel. 717/684–4325. Admission: $5 adults, $2.50 students 6–18. Open May–Oct., Tues., Wed., Fri., Sat. 10–3.*

Two wineries operate in the western part of the county. At the **⑯** 52-acre **Nissley Vineyards and Winery Estate,** you can review the grape-growing and wine-making process on a self-guided wine tasting tour. *Northwest of Columbia near Bainbridge, 1½ mi off Rte. 441, R.D. 1, tel. 717/426–3514 or 800/522–2387. Admission free. Open Mon.–Sat. 10–5, Sun. 1–4.*

⑰ At the **Mt. Hope Estate and Winery,** you tour not vineyards but an elegant circa 1800 mansion with turrets, hand-painted 18-foot ceilings, Egyptian marble fireplaces, gold-leaf wallpaper, and crystal gas chandeliers. Tours are led by costumed guides and followed by a formal wine tasting of Mt. Hope Wines. There are lovely estate gardens for strolls. *North of Manheim on Rte. 72, ½ mi from Exit 20 of the Pennsylvania Turnpike, tel. 717/665–7021. Admission: $5 adults, $2 those under 21. Tours May and June, weekends; July–Sept., daily.*

The **Pennsylvania Renaissance Faire** (tel. 717/665–7021) runs weekends from July to mid-October on the grounds of the Mt. Hope Estate and Winery. The winery is transformed into a 16th-century English village with human chess matches, jousting and fencing tournaments, street performances, craft demonstrations, jesters, and Shakespearean plays. *Admission: $14.95 adults, $7 children 5–11. Open July 4 weekend–Labor Day, Sat.–Mon. 11:30–7; Sept.–mid-Oct., weekends 10:30–6.*

Hershey

⑱ **Hershey** celebrates chocolate without guilt, from streetlights shaped like foil-wrapped kisses to avenues named Chocolate and Cocoa. Situated about 30 miles northwest of Lancaster, its attractions offer activities for kids of all ages (call 800/HERSHEY for brochures).

At **Hersheypark** they take the saying, "You are what you eat," seriously. Where else can you find walking Hershey Bars and talking Reese's Peanut Butter Cups? Only here, living on 87 acres that include 50 rides, games of chance, and five theaters. The park originated in 1907 as a playground for Hershey chocolate-factory employees. Among its historic attractions are the Comet, a 1946-vintage wooden roller coaster, and a carousel built in 1919 with 66 hand-carved wooden horses. *Rte. 743 and U.S. 422, Hershey, 17033, tel. 717/534–3090. Admission, including ZooAmerica: $22.95 adults, $14.95 senior citizens and children 3–8. Open Memorial Day–Labor Day, daily 10:30–10 (some earlier closings); May and Sept., weekends only.*

Within the grounds of Hersheypark is **ZooAmerica,** an 11-acre wildlife park. On display are more than 250 animals from throughout North America in re-creations of their natural habitats. *Tel. 717/534–3860. Admission: $4 adults, $3.50 senior citizens, $2.75 children 3–12 (or Hersheypark admission). Open mid-June–Aug., daily 10–8; Sept.–May, daily 10–5.*

An automated ride through **Hershey's Chocolate World** has taken the place of touring the actual factory, which stopped welcoming visitors when the crowds became too large. Chocolate pilgrims may learn how Hershey products are made, taste-test their favorite Hershey confection, and buy gifts. Chocolate World also serves as the town's official visitors center. *Tel. 717/534–4900. Admission free. Open Mon.–Sat. 9–4:45, summers until 6:45 or later; Sun. noon–4:45.*

The **Hershey Museum,** preserves the story of Milton Snavely Hershey, who founded the town bearing his name and just about everything in it. The main exhibit, "Built on Chocolate," displays Hershey artifacts and memorabilia. Chocolate bar wrappers and cocoa tins show their evolution through the years, while black and white photos of the town from the '30s, '40s, and '50s are hung side by side with color photos of the same sites today. *Tel. 717/534–3439. Admission: $4 adults, $3.50 senior citizens, $1.75 children 3–15. Open Memorial Day–Labor Day, daily 10–6; Labor Day–Memorial Day, daily 10–5.*

Hershey Gardens began with a single 3½-acre plot of 8,000 rose bushes and has grown to include 10 themed gardens on 23 landscaped acres. The gardens come to life in spring as 20,000 bulbs bloom. Flowering displays last until fall, when late roses open their petals. *Hotel Rd. near the Hotel Hershey, tel. 717/534– 3439. Admission: $4 adults, $3.50 senior citizens, $1.75 children 3–15. Open Apr.–Oct., daily 9–5.*

Chocolatetown Square is a one-acre park downtown where free concerts are held. *Look for the wooden gazebo just off the intersection of Cocoa and E. Chocolate Aves. For information on upcoming events, call the park coordinator at 717/534–3411.*

The **Hotel Hershey** (*see* Lodging, *below*) dates back to 1933, when Milton Hershey embarked upon his own personal jobs program to lift his town out of the depression, as does the downtown **Hershey Theater,** located in the rear of the Community Building. Before each showing, the theater ceiling is transformed into the nighttime sky as images of clouds drift across star-filled heavens. Other depression-era projects Milton Hershey launched are the 9,000-seat **Hersheypark Arena** and 25,000-seat **Hersheypark Stadium,** both on the theme park grounds.

Gettysburg

If you continue west from Lancaster on U.S. 30 to Adams County, about 55 miles distant, you will arrive at the site where Confederate dreams of independence died. From July 1 to 3, 1863, 51,000 Americans were killed, wounded, or counted as missing ⑲ in battle. **Gettysburg** honors these casualties with more than 1,000 markers and monuments, 20 museums, and a 5,000-acre national park.

The **Gettysburg Travel Council** (35 Carlisle St., tel. 717/334– 6274, fax 717/334–1166) offers free brochures and maps of attractions surrounding the battlefield. The **Gettysburg National Military Park Visitors Center** (Box 1080, Emmitsburg Rd., tel. 717/334–1124) offers a free map with an 18-mile driving tour through the battlefield. Private, licensed guides may also be hired at the center. Narrated tours aboard open-air, double-decker buses depart every 15 to 45 minutes from the **Gettysburg Tour Center** (778 Baltimore St., tel. 717/334–6296).

To best understand the battle, begin at the military park visitors center, where an **Electric Map** uses colored lights to illustrate deployments and clashes during the three days of fighting. Sit on the south side for the best view. *Admission: $2 adults, $1.50 senior citizens, children 15 and under free. Showings start every 45 minutes, 8:15–4:15.*

The **Cyclorama Center** contains a 19th-century, in-the-round painting that puts viewers in the center of Pickett's Charge, the South's ill-fated frontal assault during the last day of the battle. *Admission: $2 adults, $1.50 senior citizens. Showings daily every 30 minutes 9–4:30.*

To stand near the site where the Gettysburg Address was delivered, cross the street to the **National Cemetery.** *Admission free. Open daily dawn-dusk.*

Facing the battlefield entrance, the **National Civil War Wax Museum** exhibits 200 life-size figures in 30 scenes, a reenactment of the Battle of Gettysburg, and an animated Abraham Lincoln delivering his Gettysburg Address. *297 Steinwehr Ave., tel. 717/334–6245. Admission: $4.50 adults, $2.50 children 13–17, $1.75 children 6–12. Open daily 9–7.*

The **Hall of Presidents** re-creates in wax the nation's chief executives from Washington to Clinton, as well as their wives. *789 Baltimore St., tel. 717/334–5717. Admission: $4.95 adults, $3 children 6–11. Open summer, daily 9–9; spring and fall, daily 9–5; closed Dec.–Feb.*

Soldier's National Museum depicts the 10 major battles of the Civil War in miniature dioramas plus a life-size encampment scene from the night of July 2, 1863. *777 Baltimore St., tel. 717/ 334–4890. Admission: $4.95 adults, $3 children 6–11. Open summer, daily 9–9; spring and fall, daily 9–5; closed Dec.– Feb.*

The **Lincoln Train Museum** brings to life Lincoln's journey from Washington to Gettysburg in 1863. A 12-minute ride simulates the sights, sounds, and most of all the feel of traveling on a period railcar. *Bus. Rte. 15, tel. 717/334–5678. Admission: $4.95 adults, $3 children 6–12. Open summer, daily 9–9; spring and fall, daily 9–5; closed Dec.–Feb.*

Along U.S. 30, which runs through the center of town, the **Lincoln Room Museum** houses the bedroom where the president finished writing his famous address. **General Lee's headquarters** may also be found along this road, west of town. *Lincoln Room: 12 Lincoln Sq., tel. 717/334–8188. Admission: $3 adults, $2.75 senior citizens, $1.75 children 9–18. Open summer, Sun.–Thurs. 9–7, Fri. and Sat. 9–9; reduced hours off-season. Lee's headquarters: Rte. 30 W (near the Quality Inn), tel. 717/334–3141. Admission free. Open Mar.–Nov., daily 9–9.*

A general and president from a later time, Dwight D. Eisenhower, was also associated with Gettysburg. Ike's retirement farm adjoining the battlefield is administered by the park service as the **Eisenhower National Historic Site.** *Tel. 717/334– 1124. Admission: $3.60 adults, $1.60 children 13–16, $1.05 children 6–12. Open Apr.–Oct., daily 9–5; Nov.–Mar., Wed.– Sun. 9–5; closed Jan. 10–Feb. 10.*

What to See and Do with Children

Abe's or **Ed's Buggy Rides** (*see* Days 1 and 2 in Exploring, *above*).

Dutch Wonderland. With 44 acres of games and rides, the amusement park is ideally suited for families with younger children. Most rides are tame. The rides are supplemented by diving shows, an animated bear show, and concerts. *U.S. 30, east of Lancaster, tel. 717/291–1888. Admission: $11 for 5 rides; $16 for unlimited rides; children 2 and under free. Open daily 10–7*

*or later, Memorial Day–Labor Day. Weekends only Easter–
Memorial Day, Labor Day–Oct. 31.*

Indian Echo Caverns is one of the largest caves in the north-
eastern United States. A 45-minute guided walking tour explores the underground wonderland. Bring a sweater; no
strollers are allowed. *Off U.S. 322, Hummelstown, tel. 717/
566–8131. Admission: $6.50 adults, $3.25 children 4–11. Open
daily 9–6 in summer, shorter hours the rest of the year.*

National Wax Museum. Wax figures represent important people in Lancaster County history. Visitors view scenes from daily life and watch a simulated barn raising. *2249 Lincoln Hwy.
E, Lancaster, tel. 717/393–3679. Admission: $4.50 adults, $4
senior citizens, $3 children 5–11. Open daily 9–6, or later, un-
til 9 in summer.*

People's Place (*see* Day 1 in Exploring, *above*).

Strasburg Rail Road (*see* Day 2 in Exploring, *above*).

Toy Train Museum (*see* Day 2 in Exploring, *above*).

Off the Beaten Track

Choo Choo Barn, Traintown, USA, is a family hobby that got
out of hand. What started in 1945 as a single train chugging
around the Groff family Christmas tree is now a 1,700-square-
foot display of Lancaster County in miniature with 14 trains
and 140 figures and vehicles in O-gauge. Every five minutes a
house catches on fire and fire engines turn on their hoses to ex-
tinguish the blaze; flag bearers march in a Memorial Day parade; animals perform in a three-ring circus. Periodically, the
overhead lights dim and it is nighttime; streetlights glow and
locomotive headlights pierce the darkness. *Rte. 741,
Strasburg, tel. 717/687–7911. Admission: $3 adults, $1.50 children 5–12. Open Apr.–Oct., daily 10–5 (later in summer);
Nov., Dec., weekends 10–5. Closed Jan.–Mar.*

The **Green Dragon Farmers Market and Auction** is an old traditional agricultural market with a country carnival atmosphere.
Each week livestock and agricultural commodities are auctioned in the morning. Local Amish and Mennonite farmers
tend many of the 450 indoor and outdoor stalls selling meats,
fruits, vegetables, fresh-baked pies, and dry goods. One of the
state's largest farmer's markets (occupying 30 acres), it also
has a flea market and an evening auction of small animals. Try
the sticky buns at Rissler's Bakery and the sausage sandwiches
at Newswanger's. *R.D. 4 just off Rte. 272, Ephrata, tel. 717/
738–1117. Open Fri. 9 AM–10 PM.*

Shopping

Crafts

Although craftspeople in the Lancaster County area produce
fine handiwork, folk art, quilts, and needlework, much of the
best work is sold to galleries nationwide and never shows up in
local shops. Among the few places to see fine local crafts are the
Weathervane Shop at the Landis Valley Museum (2451 Kissel
Hill Rd., Lancaster, tel. 717/569–9312). Craftsmen sell the
wares they make in on-site demonstrations—tin, pottery,
leather, braided rugs, weaving, and chair-caning.

The Tin Bin (20 Valley Rd. off Rte. 501, Neffsville, tel. 717/569–6210) features handmade tinware and pottery, and reproductions of 18th-century lighting devices. **The Artworks at Doneckers** (100 N. State St., Ephrata, tel. 717/738–9503) houses studios where you can watch painters, sculptors, and potters at work. There are also art, fine crafts, and antiques galleries. For antique quilts made in Lancaster County, try **Pandora's** (Rte. 340 just east of U.S. 30, Lancaster, tel. 717/299–5305, call ahead) or **Witmer's Quilt Shop** (1070 W. Main St., New Holland, tel. 717/656–9526). Though pricey, old quilts have proven to be good investments.

The Mennonite Central Committee operates **Selfhelp Crafts of the World Gifts and Tea Room** (Rte. 272 north, just north of the Cloister in Ephrata, tel. 717/738–1101). A job-creation program designed to aid developing countries, the store has more than 3,000 items—including jewelry, Indian brass, onyx, needlework, baskets, toys, handwoven Pakistani rugs, and odd musical instruments—from Bangladesh, Botswana, Brazil, and about 30 other countries. You can dig up some bargains; for example, hand-woven wool rugs from Nepal, originally priced at $500, were on sale for 50% off. Each week for lunch the Tea Room features the cuisine of a different country.

Kitchen Kettle Village (Rte. 340, 10 miles east of Lancaster, in Intercourse, tel. 717/768–8261 or 800/732–3538) consists of 32 shops showcasing local crafts, including decoy carving; furniture making; leather tooling; relish, jam, and jelly making; and tin punching. Sample the homemade fudge and funnel cakes. Closed Sunday.

Outlets

It appears that Lancaster is trying to compete with Reading as the Factory Outlet Capital of the Universe. U.S. 30 is lined with outlets: Some are factory stores, which offer first-quality goods at large discounts; others call themselves outlets but don't have real bargains. It's a good idea to find out the retail prices of whatever you want before you leave home. With 95 stores and counting, from Lenox to London Fog and the huge Reading China & Glass, **Rockvale Square Factory Outlet Village** (U.S. 30 and Rte. 896, tel. 717/392–9595) is the largest outlet center in Lancaster. The latest addition to outlet row is **MillStream Factory Shops** (Rte. 30 west of Rockvale, near Dutch Wonderland, tel. 717/392–9202), a collection of 42 designer outlets including Ann Taylor and Brooks Brothers.

Antiques

On Sundays, antiques hunters frequent the huge antiques malls located on Route 272 between Adamstown and Denver, 1 mile west of Pennsylvania Turnpike Exit 21. As many as 5,000 dealers may turn up on summer festival Sundays. **Renninger's Antique and Collector's Market** (tel. 215/267–2177), **Barr's Auctions** (tel. 215/267–2861), and **Stoudt's Black Angus** (tel. 215/484–4385) all feature indoor and outdoor booths. Dealers display old books and prints, Victorian blouses, corner cupboards, pewter and local stoneware, and lots of furniture. Barr's is open on Saturdays, also. Several antiques cooperatives (Log Cabin Antique Center, Weaver's, Southpoint) also line the stretch.

Americana

Genuine Civil War artifacts and stirring canvases depicting the battle are the spoils of a visit to Gettysburg. The town's artist-in-residence, **Dale Gallon,** may be found at **Old Gettysburg Village** in the center of the tourist district (777 Baltimore St., tel. 717/334–8666). For a shopping experience that is more like visiting a museum, **The Horse Soldier,** another village shop, sells authentic Civil War mementos ranging from swords to photographs. For Civil War histories stop by **Farnsworth Military Impressions** (401 Baltimore St., tel. 717/334–8838).

Farmers Markets

Farmers markets offer the most unusual shopping experiences in the area. The **Central Market** in Lancaster (*see* Day 3 in Exploring, *above*) and **Green Dragon Farmers Market and Auction** in Ephrata (*see* Off the Beaten Track, *above*) are the best; if you can't shop there, try **Bird-in-Hand Farmer's Market** (Rte. 340, Bird-in-Hand, tel. 717/393–9674), a conveniently located market with produce stands, baked goods, gift shops, and outlets. Market open Wednesday through Saturday; Friday and Saturday only in winter. **Meadowbrook Farmer's Market** (Rte. 23, Leola, tel. 717/656–2226) is popular for its edible goodies as well as its flea-market items, crafts, collectibles, and country store. Open Friday and Saturday year-round, more days in summer. The county's newest farmers market may be found at the **Artworks at Doneckers** (*see* Crafts, *above*).

Sports and the Outdoors

Ballooning

Great Adventure Balloon Club offers a bird's-eye view of Pennsylvania Dutch Country. As part of the crew, you help inflate the balloon, maneuver the controls, and land the craft in a farmer's field. You spend an hour airborne, about three hours total. A chase van drives you back to the starting point. *Rheems exit of Rte. 283, Mount Joy, tel. 717/653–2009. Price: $135 per person. Open daily year-round, weather permitting. One-day advance reservation required.*

Bicycling

The Pennsylvania Department of Transportation (tel. 717/787–5248 or 717/787–6746) offers a free map with detailed bicycle routes statewide (ask for publication No. 22). Regional maps are available by quadrant (NE, SE, NW, and SW sections of the state) for $1.25.

Camping

The Pennsylvania Dutch Visitors Bureau has a complete list of area campgrounds. Some of the best include:

Mill Bridge Village and Campresort, which is attached to a restored 18th-century village. *One-half mi south of U.S. 30 on Ronks Rd., tel. 717/687–8181 or 800/645–2744. Snack shop, summer entertainment, free buggy rides, stream fishing.*

Muddy Run Park offers lovely campgrounds in the southern end of the county set among 700 acres of woodland and rolling fields which surround a 100-acre lake. Environmental programs include nature walks, bird-watching, and fly-fishing workshops. *172 Bethesda Church Rd. W, Holtwood, tel. 717/ 284-4325. Snack bar, general store, playground, boating, fishing.*

Spring Gulch Resort Campground is a glorious farmland and forest setting with 400 sites (pleasantly shaded) and rental cottages. A full schedule of weekend activities includes country dances and chicken barbecues. *Rte. 897 between Rtes. 340 and 322, New Holland, tel. 717/354-3100 or 800/255-5744. Lake, two heated pools and a spa, miniature golf, tennis and volleyball courts, fishing, game room, square dances, exercise classes.*

In Gettysburg, **Artillery Ridge Campground** provides a place to pitch a tent or park an RV one mile south of the military park visitors center. *610 Taneytown Rd., tel. 717/334-1288. Swimming, fishing, horse and bicycle rentals.*

Golf

The **Lancaster Host Resort and Conference Center** (U.S. 30, Lancaster, tel. 717/299-5500) has 27 holes for regulation golf; carts are not required. *Greens fees: $28 for 18 holes, $11.50 per person for a cart. Rental clubs available.*

The **Hershey Country Club** maintains two 18-hole courses open to the public (greens fees: $60) and **Hershey Parkview Golf** offers another 18 holes (green fees: $13). **Spring Creek Golf,** a nine-hole course, was originally built by Milton Hershey for youngsters to hone their stroke (greens fees: $15). The **Hotel Hershey** offers nine holes on the hotel grounds (greens fees: $16). *Tel. 800/900-GOLF (for all four).*

Hiking and Walking

The National Park Service provides free walking tour maps of the **Gettysburg National Military Park,** available at the Visitors Center (Emmitsburg Rd., tel. 717/334-1124). Short one-mile loops include the sites of some of the battle's most pivotal engagements. Longer 9- and 3.5-mile trails also are marked. In western Lancaster County, **Chickies Rock County Park,** between Marietta and Columbia, offers stunning views of the Susquehanna River.

Dining and Lodging

Dining

Like the German cuisine that influenced it, Pennsylvania Dutch meals are hearty and are prepared with ingredients from local farms. To sample regional fare, eat at one of the several bustling restaurants in the area where diners sit with perhaps a dozen other people and the food is passed around in bowls family style. Meals are plentiful and basic—fried chicken, ham, roast beef, dried corn, buttered noodles, mashed potatoes, chowchow, bread, pepper cabbage, shoofly pie—and that's only a partial listing. Entrées are accompanied by traditional "sweets and sours," vegetable dishes made with a vinegar-and-sugar dressing. This is the way the Amish, who hate to throw things out, preserve leftover vegetables. Lancaster County has numerous smorgasbords and reasonably priced family restaurants along with a number of Continental and French restaurants in contemporary settings and quaint historic inns. Unless otherwise noted, liquor is served.

Category	Cost*
Very Expensive	over $30
Expensive	$20–$30
Moderate	$10–$20
Inexpensive	under $10

per person for a 3-course meal, without wine, tax (6%), or service

Lodging

Lancaster County lodgings are much like the people themselves—plain or fancy. You can rough it in one of the many campgrounds in the area, meet a family by staying in their B&B or on their farm, or indulge yourself at a full-frills resort. A good selection of moderately priced motels cater to families. The Pennsylvania Dutch Visitors Bureau has a listing of all area B&Bs and farms that welcome guests. Rates are highest in summer; at most hotels off-season rates are greatly reduced. Unless otherwise indicated, all rooms have private bath and hotels are open year-round.

Category	Cost*
Very Expensive	over $100
Expensive	$80–$100
Moderate	$60–$79
Inexpensive	under $60

double occupancy, based on peak (summer) rates, without tax (6%)

Highly recommended restaurants and hotels in each price category are indicated by a star ★.

The following credit card abbreviations are used: AE, American Express; D, Discover; DC, Diners Club; MC, MasterCard; V, Visa.

Adamstown

Dining **Stoudt's Black Angus.** Prime rib cut from certified angus beef is the specialty of this popular Victorian-style restaurant, adjacent to the Black Angus antiques mall. Also notable are its raw oyster bar and German dishes such as weiner schnitzel (veal) and schwabian (pork). Stoudt's beer, brewed right next door, is on tap. On weekends from mid-July through Labor Day, a Bavarian Beer Fest featuring German bands, a pig roast, and ethnic food takes over Brewery Hall. *Rte. 272, tel. 215/484–4385.*

Reservations advised Fri.–Sun. Dress: casual. Brewery tours Sat. at 3 and Sun. at 1. AE, DC, MC, V. Closed lunch except Sun. Expensive.

Bird-in-Hand

Dining **Amish Barn Restaurant.** Pennsylvania Dutch cuisine is served family style, which means generous helpings of meat and produce, breads, and home-baked pies. Apple dumplings are a specialty. You can choose from an à la carte menu or order a family-style meal, except on Sunday afternoon when service is family-style. No liquor is served. *Rte. 340 between Bird-in-Hand and Intercourse, tel. 717/768–8886. Reservations advised on summer weekends. Dress: informal. AE, D, MC, V. Open Apr.–Dec. daily; Fri.–Sun. only in winter. Moderate.*

★ **Bird-in-Hand Family Restaurant.** This family-owned, diner-style restaurant enjoys a good reputation for hearty Pennsylvania Dutch home cooking. The menu is à la carte. There is a lunch buffet weekdays. No liquor is served. *2760 Old Philadelphia Pike, tel. 717/768–8266; Reservations not required. Dress: informal. No credit cards. Closed Sun. Inexpensive.*

Lodging **Village Inn of Bird-in-Hand.** The Victorian flavor of this three-story country inn, built in 1852, is tempered by the modern comforts of down-filled bedding, cable TV, and phones. Continental breakfast, an evening snack, and a two-hour tour of the area are complimentary. *Box 253, 2695 Old Philadelphia Pike (Rte. 340), 17505, tel. 717/293–8369. 11 rooms, including 2 deluxe suites with Jacuzzis. Facilities: access to pool and tennis courts at nearby Bird-in-Hand Family Inn. AE, D, MC, V. Moderate–Very Expensive.*

Bird-in-Hand Family Inn. Plain, clean, comfortable rooms in a family-owned motel praised for its friendly staff. *Box 402, 2740 Old Philadelphia Pike, 17505, tel. 717/768–8271 or 800/537–2535. 100 rooms. Facilities: restaurant, tennis courts, playground, indoor and outdoor pool. AE, D, DC, MC, V. Moderate.*

Churchtown

Lodging **Churchtown Inn.** This restored 1735 fieldstone mansion, over-
★ looking an Amish farm, has two beautiful Victorian parlors, a collection of handmade quilts and antique music boxes, and cozy, elegant bedrooms with pencil post canopies, brass, and high-back Victorian beds. The day dawns in the glass-enclosed garden room with a five-course breakfast including goodies such as Grand Marnier French toast, oatmeal and granola pancakes, and homemade coffee cake and ends in the parlor with an evening beverage hour, during which one of the innkeepers, a former music director, plays the piano and sings. Guests are invited to a nearby Amish home for dinner. Special-event weekends are held from mid-November through May, featuring road rallies, murder mysteries, barbecues, a formal Victorian costume ball, and professional concerts. *On Rte. 23 between Morgantown and New Holland, 5 mi from Pennsylvania. Turnpike exit 22., 2100 Main St., Churchtown, PA 17555, tel. 215/445–7794. 8 rooms, 6 with private bath; carriage house. Children over 12 welcome. Two-night minimum stay on weekends, 3-night minimum on holiday weekends. D, MC, V. Inexpensive–Very Expensive.*

Denver

Dining **Zinn's Country Diner.** Local specialties are served here daily from 6 AM to 11 PM. On the property are a gift shop, 27-hole miniature golf course, batting cages, basketball courts, and an arcade. Antiques malls are nearby. No liquor is served. *Rte. 272 north at Pennsylvania Turnpike exit 21, tel. 215/267–2210. No reservations required. Dress: informal. D, MC, V. Inexpensive.*

Lodging **Black Horse Lodge and Suites.** The lodge has contemporary rooms with balcony or patio overlooking spacious grounds. It is convenient to antiques malls and offers a free Continental breakfast. *Rte. 272, 1 mi north of Pennsylvania Turnpike exit 21. Box 343, 17517, tel. 215/267–7563. 74 rooms. Facilities: restaurant, outdoor pool, basketball, playground, fitness stations, picnic pavilion, and barbecue area. AE, D, DC, MC, V. Moderate–Very Expensive.*

East Petersburg

Dining **Haydn Zug's** offers American-Continental dining in an 1850s
★ house with tasteful Williamsburg furnishings. Its specialties include lamb tenderloins, veal Vienna, crab cakes, and fresh fish. James Beard wrote about their cheesy chowder; *Bon Appetit* profiled the establishment. A tavern menu is also available. *Rte. 72 and State St., Lancaster, tel. 717/569–5746. Reservations advised. Dress: casual. AE, MC, V. Moderate–Expensive.*

Ephrata

Dining **The Restaurant at Doneckers.** Classic and country French cuisine is served downstairs amid Colonial antiques and upstairs in a country garden. It is known for its chateaubriand for two, sautéed whole Dover sole, daily chef's veal special, and salmon. The service is fine; the wine cellar is extensive. From 2:30 to 4 light fare is served. *333 N. State St., tel. 717/738–9501. Reservations advised. Dress: casual. AE, D, DC, MC, V. Closed Wed. Moderate–Expensive.*

Lodging **The Inns at Doneckers.** Four properties dating from the 1770s to 1920s have been tastefully furnished with French country antiques and decorated by hand-stenciling. Rooms are light and airy, and the price includes Continental breakfast. *318–324 N. State St., 17522, tel. 717/738–9502. 40 rooms, including 13 suites with fireplace, Jacuzzi, or both. AE, D, DC, MC, V. Moderate–Very Expensive.*
★ **Smithton Inn.** The B&B is in a historic former stagecoach inn with seven lovingly furnished guest rooms and one four-room suite. The rooms have handmade antiques, fireplaces, and canopy beds. Three rooms with whirlpool; third floor has skylights, cathedral ceiling, Franklin stove fireplace. Nice touches abound: oversize goose-down pillows, nightshirts, magazines, and fresh flowers. Outside there's a lily pond, fountain, English lawn furniture, and lovely garden. Full breakfast is included. *900 W. Main St., 17522, tel. 717/733–6094. 8 rooms. Well-behaved children and pets welcome by prearrangement. There's a two-night minimum for stays including a Sat. or holiday. AE, MC, V. Moderate–Very Expensive.*

Gettysburg

Dining **Farnsworth House Inn.** Housed in a building that still shows bullet holes from the battle, the restaurant at this B&B serves up Civil War-era dishes such as game pie, peanut soup, and spoon bread. The outdoor garden, with sculptures, fountains, and a waterfall, provides a tranquil setting in which to ponder the events of 1863. *401 Baltimore St, tel. 717/334–8838. Dress: casual. AE, D, MC, V. Moderate.*

Lodging **Best Western Gettysburg Hotel 1797.** The hotel is a pre–Civil War structure in the heart of the historic downtown district, but the interior was completely rebuilt in 1991. Ask about the cannonball from the Battle of Gettysburg still embedded in the brick wall across the street. *1 Lincoln Sq., 17325, tel. 717/337–2000. 83 rooms. Suites have whirlpool tubs and fireplaces. D, MC, V. Expensive–Very Expensive.*

Hershey

Dining **Pippin's.** Pub-style food in an early American setting is a good value at this family-oriented restaurant, located in Tudor Square just outside Hersheypark. The restaurant remains open year-round, even when the park is closed. Its convenient location is also a short walk away from Chocolate World, Hershey Museum, and the arena and stadium. *100 W. Hershey Park Dr., tel. 717/534–3821. Dress: casual. AE, D, MC. Inexpensive–Moderate.*

Lodging **Hershey Lodge & Convention Center.** This bustling, expansive, modern resort caters to families and has two casual restaurants where kids can be kids, plus a more formal room for adult dining. *W. Chocolate Ave. and University Dr., 17033, tel. 717/533–3311 or 800/533–3131. 457 rooms. Facilities: 3 restaurants, indoor and outdoor pools, lighted tennis courts, chip-and-putt golf, bicycle rental, playground, volleyball, nightclub with DJ, movie theater. AE, D, DC, MC, V. Very Expensive.*

Hotel Hershey. This gracious Spanish-style hotel surrounded by a golf course and a landscaped garden is a quiet and sophisticated resort with lots of options for recreation. Opened in 1933 as part of Milton S. Hershey's building program to lift his town out of the Great Depression, all 241 rooms were refurbished in time for the hotel's 60th anniversary. Ask for one of the recently renovated rooms—they've still got their Old World feel. Across the street from Hersheypark and popular with families. It now offers a choice between the formal dining room and the casual Clubhouse Café. AP, MAP, and EP available. *Hotel Rd. Box 400, 17033, tel. 717/533–2171 or 800/533–3131. 241 rooms. Facilities: 2 restaurants, indoor/outdoor pool, tennis, carriage rides, golf. AE, D, DC, MC, V. Very Expensive.*

Intercourse

Dining **Kling House.** The Kling family home has been converted into a charming, casual restaurant featuring American cuisine at breakfast and lunch. Cranberry chicken, London broil, and snitz and knepp (dried apple and potato dumpling) entrées come with complimentary appetizer of red-pepper jam and cream cheese with crackers. The soups are homemade, and the desserts are luscious. A children's menu is available. *Kitchen*

Kettle Village, Rtes. 340 and 772, tel. 717/768-8261. Reservations advised. Dress: casual. MC, V. Closed Sun. Dinner served Sat. nights only. Inexpensive.

Stoltzfus Farm Restaurant. Homemade Pennsylvania Dutch foods, including meats butchered right on the farm, are served family style in a small country farmhouse, providing a less hectic alternative to Good 'N Plenty (*see* Smoketown, *below*). *Rte. 772 E, ½ mile east of Rte. 340, tel. 717/768 8156. Reservations not required. Dress: casual. Open May–Oct., Mon.–Sat.; Apr. and Nov., Sat. only; closed Dec.–Mar. MC, V. Moderate.*

Lancaster

Dining **The Log Cabin.** Steak, lamb chops, and seafood are prepared on
★ a charcoal grill in this 1928 expanded log cabin which was a speakeasy during Prohibition. The atmosphere is elegant and the setting is embellished with an impressive art collection. *11 Lehoy Forest Dr. (off Rte. 272), Leola (5 mi north of Lancaster), tel. 717/626–1181. Jackets and reservations suggested. AE, MC, V. Expensive–Very Expensive.*

Windows on Steinman Park. French-Continental cuisine is presented in elegant surroundings—lots of marble, fresh flowers, and huge windows overlooking an inviting red-brick courtyard. Its specialties include Caesar salad, Dover sole, and chateaubriand. There's piano music Tuesday through Saturday. *16–18 W. King St., tel. 717/295–1316. Reservations advised. Jackets required. AE, DC, MC, V. Closed Sat. lunch. Expensive–Very Expensive.*

Market Fare. The cuisine is American, and steaks, seafood, and veal are served in a cozy dining room with upholstered armchairs and 19th-century paintings, drawings, and photographs. Homemade soups and breads highlight the diverse menu. A children's menu and a light menu are also available. The café upstairs offers light breakfast, quick lunch, and carryout. *Market and Grant Sts. (across from the Central Market), tel. 717/299–7090. Reservations suggested. Dress: casual. AE, DC, MC, V. Expensive.*

Olde Greenfield Inn. Continental cuisine and a fine wine cellar form part of the attraction in this gracious circa-1780 restored farmhouse. House specialties include roast duckling with raspberry sauce, Cajun beef with shrimp, and jumbo lump crab cakes. Lighter entrées, like seafood crêpes, are also available. A piano player is in the lounge on weekends. Guests can dine on the patio. *595 Greenfield Rd., tel. 717/393–0668. Reservations suggested. Dress: casual. AE, D, DC, MC, V. Closed Sun. night. Moderate–Expensive.*

Center City Grill. This casual but elegant bar and restaurant has a convenient downtown location for those exploring the city center. The decor is eccentric Victorian: Framed pictures are mounted on the ceiling and doors are suspended on chains to create partitions between tables. The satisfying American menu ranges from steaks to chicken to pastas. A children's menu is available. *10 S. Prince St., tel. 717/299–3456. Dress: casual. AE, D, DC, MC, V. Moderate.*

Lancaster Dispensing Co. Fajitas, salads, sandwiches, and nachos are served until midnight in this stylish Victorian pub. The selection of imported beers is extensive. On the weekend, live music is played. *33–35 N. Market St., tel. 717/299–4602. No reservations. Dress: informal. AE, MC, V. Inexpensive.*

Lodging **Best Western Eden Resort Inn.** Spacious contemporary rooms
★ (request a room at poolside) and attractive grounds contribute
to a pleasant stay here. It has a stunning tropical indoor pool
and whirlpool under a retractable roof. The award-winning
chef in Arthur's is noted for seafood and pasta; the Sunday buffet brunch in the skylit Eden Courtyard is excellent. Fun food
is presented in Garfield's. Encore provides live entertainment.
*222 Eden Rd. (U.S. 30 and Rte. 272), 17601, tel. 717/569-6444
or 800/528-1234. 275 rooms and 40 residential-style Club
Suites with full kitchens and fireplaces. Facilities: 2 movie theaters, indoor and outdoor pool, lighted tennis court. AE, D,
DC, MC, V. Very Expensive.*
King's Cottage. This elegant Spanish mansion, which is on the
National Register of Historic Places, has been transformed
into a B&B furnished with antiques and 18th-century English
reproductions, and has an outdoor goldfish pond. Full breakfast and afternoon tea are included. It's only 2 miles from the
heart of downtown Lancaster. *1049 E. King St., 17602, tel. 717/
397-1017 or 800/747-8717, 7 rooms. Air-conditioning. Children over 12 only. Two-night minimum on weekends. MC, V.
Expensive-Very Expensive.*
Hilton Garden Inn. An new, elegant hotel popular with corpo-
rate travelers offers oversize rooms, many with cathedral ceilings and large desks. The "BounceBack Weekend" package
with breakfast is a bargain. *Intersection of Rtes. 72 and 283,
17601, tel. 717/560-0880 or 800/HILTONS. 155 rooms. Facilities: restaurant, fitness center, indoor pool, whirlpool. AE, D,
DC, MC, V. Moderate-Very Expensive.*
Lancaster Host Resort and Conference Center. This sprawling
family resort sports a striking marble lobby and comfortable,
contemporary rooms with cherrywood furnishings, bathrobes,
and minibars. The golf course and grounds are beautifully landscaped. A camp program for children ages 1–12 takes place daily during the summer and on weekends throughout the year. A
variety of packages are available. *2300 Lincoln Hwy. E (Rte.
30), 17602, tel. 717/299-5500 or 800/233-0121. 330 rooms. Facilities: 2 restaurants, indoor and outdoor pool, 27 holes of
golf, 4 indoor and 8 outdoor tennis courts, game room, bike
rental, miniature golf, DJ in lounge for dancing, piano bar.
MAP and EP available. AE, DC, MC, V. Moderate-Very Expensive.*
Willow Valley Family Resort and Conference Center. This mom-
and-pop operation has blossomed into a large and stylish family
resort. The striking skylit atrium lobby is surrounded by attractive rooms. There are moderately priced rooms, but the
ones overlooking the atrium are the most attractive and most
expensive. Since it is Mennonite owned, there is no liquor permitted on the premises. Several packages offer seasonal discounts. *2416 Willow St. Pike, 17602, tel. 717/464-2711 or 800/
444-1714, fax 717/464-4784. 353 rooms. Facilities: 3 restaurants, 9-hole golf course, lighted tennis courts, small lake, adjacent gift mall, 2 indoor and 1 outdoor pools, whirlpool. AE,
D, DC, MC, V. Expensive.*
Your Place Country Inn. This small new hotel close to the outlets and attractions has country furnishings handmade by
Amish and local craftsmen. Continental breakfast is included.
*2133 Lincoln Hwy. E, 17602, tel. 717/393-3413. 79 rooms. Fa-
cilities: restaurant, outdoor pool. AE, D, MC, V. Expensive.*
Olde Hickory Inn. A quiet one-story motel whose rooms feature

attractive oak furnishings. Many open onto a spacious lawn with a pool. The inn is across from the Landis Valley Museum. *2363 Oregon Pike, 17601, tel. 717/569-0477 or 800/255-6859. 83 rooms. Facilities: dinner theater, restaurant, outdoor pool, volleyball, playground, access to Olde Hickory Racquet Club with 9-hole golf course, shops nearby. AE, D, DC, MC, V. Moderate.*

Lititz

Lodging   **General Sutter Inn.** The oldest (1764) continuously run inn in
★   the state is a Victoriana lover's dream reminiscent of "Grandma's house." Its decor ranges from Pennsylvania folk art to Louis XIV sofas and marble-topped tables. Located at the crossroads of town, the inn is within easy walking distance of the Wilbur Chocolate Factory, Julius Sturgis Pretzel House, and the many 18th-century buildings of the historic district. The dimly lit tavern is a good place to mingle with local folks. Children are welcome. *Corner of Rtes. 501 and 772, 17543, tel. 717/626-2115. 12 rooms, including 2 family suites. Facilities: dining room, coffee shop, cocktail lounge. AE, D, MC, V. Moderate-Expensive.*

Swiss Woods. Innkeepers Werner and Debrah Mosimann designed this Swiss-style chalet while they were still living in Werner's native Switzerland. They planted it on 30 acres in Lititz, creating a comfortable, friendly, European-style bed-and-breakfast with light pine wood furnishings, a contemporary country decor, and goose-down comforters. The setting is sublime; the chalet is nestled on the edge of the woods overlooking Speedwell Forge Lake. *500 Blantz Rd., 17543, tel. 717/627-3358 or 800/594-8018. 6 rooms, 1 suite. Facilities: some rooms have Jacuzzis, canoeing, access to hiking, fishing, bird-watching, and biking. No smoking. Children welcome. Two-night minimum stay on weekends from Easter to Thanksgiving, 3-night minimum holiday weekends. D, MC, V. Moderate-Expensive.*

Marietta

Dining   **Railroad House.** In a historic hotel on the east bank of the Susquehanna River, this restaurant has a split personality. Upstairs, classic American cuisine reigns, with steaks, seafood, veal, poultry, and pastas flavored with herbs from the on-premises garden; downstairs, a light tavern menu offers gourmet pizza, wings, sandwiches, soups, and salads. In warm weather, you can dine out on the patio in the garden. On Saturday nights, the Victorian era is re-created with strolling minstrels. *W. Front and S. Perry Sts., tel. 717/426-4141. Reservations advised. Dress: casual. MC, V. Moderate-Expensive.*

Lodging   **Railroad House Bed & Breakfast.** Built in 1820 to service canal and river traffic, the Railroad House now welcomes guests to Victorian-style rooms refurbished with antiques and Oriental rugs. Full breakfast is served. *W. Front and S. Perry Sts., 17547, tel. 717/426-4141. 12 rooms, 8 with private bath, including 1 suite with kitchenette. Facilities: restaurant, tours of the area in a 19th-century surrey can be arranged. Children over 12 welcome. MC, V. Moderate-Expensive.*

Mount Joy

Dining   **Cameron Estate Inn.** American cuisine is presented with French service in the candlelit, Federal-style dining room of this country inn. Specialties include veal Cameron (medallions sautéed with wine and capers served over pasta) and fresh fish of the day. *Donegal Springs Rd., tel. 717/653–1773. Reservations required. Dress: casual, but no jeans. AE, DC, MC, V. Expensive.*

★   **Groff's Farm.** Abe and Betty Groff's 1756 farmhouse restaurant has received national attention for its hearty Mennonite fare. Candlelight, fresh flowers and original Groff Farm country fabrics and wall coverings contribute to the homey ambience. House specialties include chicken Stoltzfus, farm relishes, and cracker pudding. Dinner begins with chocolate cake. Lunch is à la carte, dinner à la carte or family style served at your own table. A new rooftop deck allows alfresco dining. *650 Pinkerton Rd., tel. 717/653–2048, fax 717/653–1115. Reservations required for dinner, suggested at lunch. Dinner seatings Tues.–Fri. at 5 and 7:30, Sat. 5 and 8. Dress: casual, but no shorts. D, DC, MC, V. Closed Sun. and Mon. Moderate–Expensive.*

Bube's Brewery. The only intact, pre-Prohibition brewery in the United States contains three unique restaurants. **The Bottling Works** in the original bottling plant of the brewery serves steaks, light dinners, salads, burgers, and subs. *No reservations. Dress: informal.* **Alois's** offers prix fixe six-course international dinners in a Victorian hotel attached to the brewery. *Reservations required. Jacket and tie advised. Closed Mon.* **The Catacombs** serves traditional steak and seafood dishes in the brewery aging cellars 43 feet below street level. A feast master, with his wenches, presides over a medieval-style dinner on Sunday nights. Wine and ale flow, musicians entertain, and diners participate in the festivities. $30 per person. *Reservations are required. Jackets are preferred. An outdoor beer garden is open in summer. 102 N. Market St., tel. 717/653–2056. AE, MC, V. Inexpensive–Expensive.*

Lodging   **Cameron Estate Inn.** This sprawling Federal red-brick mansion
★   set on 15 wooded acres was the summer home of Simon Cameron, Abraham Lincoln's first secretary of war. The rooms are equipped with Oriental rugs, antique and reproduction furniture, and canopy beds; seven have working fireplaces. The lovely porch overlooks the grounds. Continental breakfast is included. *Donegal Springs Rd., 17552, tel. 717/653–1773, fax 717/653–9432. 18 rooms, 16 with private bath. Facilities: restaurant, access to tennis courts and swimming pool nearby. No children under 12. AE, DC, MC, V. Moderate–Very Expensive.*

Ronks

Dining   **Miller's Smorgasbord.** Miller's presents a lavish spread with a
★   good selection of Pennsylvania Dutch foods. Breakfast is sensational here with omelets, pancakes, and eggs cooked to order, fresh fruits, pastries, bacon, sausage, potatoes, and much more. It's one of the few area restaurants open on Sundays. *2811 Lincoln Hwy. E (U.S. 30), tel. 717/687–6621 or 800/669–3568. Reservations for dinner only. Dress: casual. Breakfast weekends only Dec.–May. AE, MC, V. Moderate.*

Lodging **Hershey Farm.** This continually expanding motel overlooks a picture-perfect pond and a farm. Ask for one of the large rooms in the new building. *240 Hartman Bridge Rd., Ronks 17572, tel. 717/687–8635 or 800/827–8635. 59 rooms, 28 nonsmoking. Facilities: outdoor pool, family-style and smorgasbord restaurant, bakery, gift shops. D, MC, V. Expensive.*

Smoketown

Dining **Good 'N Plenty.** An Amish farmhouse has been remodeled into a bustling, family-style restaurant that seats and serves more than 650. Pennsylvania Dutch cuisine. *Rte. 896 (½ mile north of U.S. 30), tel. 717/394–7111. No reservations. Dress: informal. MC, V. Closed Sun. and mid-Dec.–Jan. Moderate.*

Lodging **Mill Stream Motor Lodge.** This popular motel was redecorated in 1990. Request a rear room, overlooking the stream. It is owned by Mennonites, so no alcohol is served. *Rte. 896, 17576, tel. 717/299–0931. 52 rooms. Facilities: restaurant serves breakfast and lunch; guests may use game room, exercise room, and indoor and outdoor pools at Willow Valley, a sister property. Two-night minimum on weekends. AE, D, MC, V. Moderate.*

★ **Smoketown Motor Lodge.** In the carriage house behind this red-brick Federal-style motel lies one of the Pennsylvania Dutch Country's best-kept secrets. Three ground floor rooms are finished in rough-hewn pine paneling, exposed ceiling beams, queen-size beds, and plush carpeting. The Carriage Room, largest of the three, features a huge bathroom with sunken tub and separate shower and dressing areas. Rooms in the main motel building are a good value as well. *109 E. Brook Rd. (Rte. 896), 17576, tel. 717/397–6944. 10 rooms. MC, V. Inexpensive.*

Strasburg

Dining **Iron Horse Restaurant.** This charming, rustic, candlelit restaurant is housed in the original 1780s Hotel Strasburg. Best bets are the catch-of-the-day, the daily veal special, the homemade breads, and, for dessert, the great, warm apple pie. There's live entertainment on weekends and an extensive wine list. *135 E. Main St. (Rte. 741), tel. 717/687–6362. Reservations suggested on weekends. Dress: casual. AE, D, DC, MC, V. Closed Mon. Dec.–May. Expensive.*

Washington House Restaurant. This restaurant at the Historic Strasburg Inn offers fine candlelight dining in two Colonial-style dining rooms. The American menu features roast turkey with stuffing, flounder stuffed with crabmeat, and filet Mignon. The lunch buffet is bountiful. *Rte. 896 (Historic Dr.), tel. 717/687–7691 or 800/872–0201. Dress: casual. AE, D, DC, MC, V. Moderate.*

Lodging **Timberline Lodges.** Beautiful lodges nestled on a hillside put you close enough to Strasburg to hear the train whistles but far away enough to hear the birds. The lodges, which sleep from two to eight people, have stone fireplaces, balconies, TV, and furnished kitchens. *44 Summit Hill Dr., 17579, tel. 717/687–7472. 11 lodges and 5 motel units. Facilities: lounge, outdoor pool, playground. Two-night minimum on weekends. AE, MC, V. Lodge Expensive–Very Expensive; Motel Inexpensive.*

★ **Strasburg Village Inn.** This historic circa-1788 house has rooms elegantly appointed in the Williamsburg style. Most have canopy or four-poster beds; two have Jacuzzis. A sitting/reading room is on the second floor; an old-fashioned porch overlooks Main Street. Full breakfast in the adjacent ice cream parlor is included, except on Sunday, when it's Continental only. *1 W. Main St., 17579, tel. 717/687–0900 or 800/541–1055. 11 rooms. AE, D, MC, V. Moderate–Very Expensive.*

★ **Fulton Steamboat Inn.** At Lancaster's busiest intersection, across from rows of outlet stores, sits a small lake, man-made waterfalls, piped-in sounds of a river, and a hotel that looks just like a steamboat. Named after the Lancaster native Robert Fulton, who built the first successful passenger steamer in the late 1700s, the hotel has three levels: The uppermost deck features whirlpool baths and private outdoor decks, the middle level has staterooms with two queen-size beds, and the bottom level has cabins with nautical themes and some bunk beds, making it a good choice for families with children. Rooms have Victorian-style furnishings, microwaves, remote control TV, and mini-refrigerators. The costumed staff look right at home in the Victorian lobby. Package plans include meals and admission to area attractions. *Rtes. 30 and 896, Box 333, 17579, tel. 717/299–9999 or 800/922–2229 outside PA, fax 717/299–9992. 95 rooms. Facilities: restaurant, indoor pool, Jacuzzi, exercise room, game room. Two-night minimum stay on weekends, 3-night minimum on holidays. AE, MC, V. Expensive.*

Historic Strasburg Inn. The newly renovated, Colonial-style inn is set on 58 peaceful acres overlooking farmland. The rooms come with double beds only. Full breakfast is included. *Rte. 896 (Historic Dr.), 17579, tel. 717/687–7691 or 800/872–0201. 103 rooms. Pets are allowed. Facilities: restaurant, tavern, outdoor pool, bicycles, volleyball. AE, D, DC, MC, V. Moderate.*

Red Caboose Motel. The motel consists of 37 railroad cabooses that have been converted into a string of rooms: a unique place to stay, especially for railroad buffs. Half a caboose sleeps two; a family gets a whole car (one double bed, four bunks). TV sets are built into pot-bellied stoves. *303 Paradise La. (off Rte. 741), 17579, tel. 717/687–6646. 40 units, including 7 efficiency suites. Facilities: restaurant, playground, buggy rides. AE, D, MC, V. Inexpensive.*

Wrightsville

Dining **Accomac Inn.** A stone building with a magnificent Susquehan-
★ na River setting, the inn offers American cuisine with French flair. Tableside cooking is featured with dishes such as duck flambéed in orange Curaçao, bananas Foster, and crepes Suzette. Specialties include fresh rack of New Zealand lamb, veal, venison, and seafood; the wine list boasts 250 selections. Queen Anne furnishings are reminiscent of Williamsburg. *Across Susquehanna River from Marietta (take Rte. 30 west to Wrightsville exit, turn right and follow signs), tel. 717/252–1521. Reservations suggested. Most men wear jackets. AE, D, MC, V. Very Expensive.*

Farm Vacations

A number of farm families open their homes to visitors and allow them to observe, and even participate in, day-to-day farm life. Your hosts may teach you how to milk a cow and feed chickens. They serve you breakfast with their family, and invite you to church services. Make reservations weeks in advance: Most farms are heavily booked during the summer tourist season.

Jonde Lane Farm. Breakfast with the family is served every day but Sunday at this working dairy and poultry farm. There are four guest rooms including one family room, which can sleep up to seven people; two shared baths. Ponies, chickens, and cats are conspicuous. Guests can fish on the property. *1103 Auction Rd., Manheim 17545, tel. 717/665–4231. Open Easter–Thanksgiving. No credit cards. Inexpensive.*

Olde Fogie Farm. An organic farm specializing in asparagus, berries, lamb, and beef offers bed and breakfast in an old-frame home with an Amish cookstove, a petting farm, a goat to milk, a creek, a pond, and a new stable for horseback riding. *106 Stackstown Rd., Marietta 17547, tel. 717/426–3992. 2 rooms, 1 with private bath, the other shares bath with family; 2 efficiency apartments. No credit cards. Inexpensive.*

Rocky Acre Farm. Sleep in a 200-year-old stone farmhouse, which was once a stop on the Underground Railroad. This is a dairy farm with calves to feed, cows to milk, and dogs, kittens, roosters, and sheep—in the meadow, of course—to enjoy. Guests can go fishing and boating in the creek. A full hot breakfast is served daily. *1020 Pinkerton Rd., Mt. Joy 17552, tel. 717/653–4449. 5 rooms with private bath and 2 efficiency units with shared bath. No credit cards. Inexpensive.*

Verdant View Farm. Don and Virginia Ranck's 1896 farmhouse sits on about 122 acres devoted to dairy and crop farming. Guests use five rooms on the second floor, one with a private bath. Hearty breakfasts are served in the family dining room every day but Sunday. *429 Strasburg Rd., Paradise 17562, tel. 717/687–7353. No credit cards. Inexpensive.*

The Arts

Theater

Dutch Apple Dinner Theater (510 Centerville Rd. at U.S. 30, Lancaster, tel. 717/898–1900). A candlelight buffet plus Broadway musicals and comedies are the draws in this 400-seat theater. Recent seasons have included *Camelot*, *Nunsense*, and *Fiddler on the Roof*. Matinees and dinner shows. Call for reservations.

The **Fulton Opera House** (12 N. Prince St., Lancaster, tel. 717/397–7425). This restored 19th-century Victorian theater is America's oldest theater in continuous use, and a National Landmark. The stage is busy, with a theater series, a series geared to families, and a music series with big-band concerts, pop, and jazz as well as performances by the Lancaster Symphony Orchestra and the Lancaster Opera.

Sight & Sound Entertainment Centre (Rte. 896, Strasburg, tel. 717/687–7800) is a 1,372-seat, state-of-the-art theater—the largest Christian entertainment complex in the nation—presenting concerts and biblically-based theatrical productions with lavish costumes, special effects, and live animals.

11 Excursions

Brandywine Valley

By Joyce
Eisenberg

Updated by
Rathe Miller

The Brandywine River flows lazily from West Chester, Pennsylvania, to Wilmington, Delaware. Although in spots it's more a creek than a river, it has nourished many of the valley's economic and artistic endeavors and has inspired the du Ponts and the Wyeths, the families most often associated with the Brandywine Valley.

The Wyeths, who captured the beauty of the local landscape on canvas, and the du Pont family, who recontoured it with grand gardens, mansions, and mills, have bequeathed much to visitors in this scenic region 25 miles south of Philadelphia. The Brandywine Valley actually incorporates parts of three counties in two states: Chester and Delaware counties in Pennsylvania, and New Castle County in Delaware.

This is the kingdom of the du Ponts, the French bureaucratic family (originally named du Pont de Nemours) whose patriarch, Pierre-Samuel du Pont, escaped with his family from post-Revolutionary France and settled in northern Delaware. The Du Pont company was founded in 1802 by his son Éleuthère Irénée (E. I.), who made the family fortune first in gunpowder and iron, and later in chemicals and textiles.

E. I. and five generations of du Ponts lived in Eleutherian Mills, the stately family home on the grounds of a black-powder mill that has been transformed into the Hagley Museum. The home, from which Mrs. Henry du Pont was driven after accidental blasts at the powder works, was closed in 1921. Louise du Pont Crowninshield, a great-granddaughter of E. I., restored the house fully before opening it to the public.

Louise's brothers were busy, too. Henry Francis was filling his country estate, Winterthur, with furniture by Duncan Phyfe, silver by Paul Revere, decorative objects, and interior woodwork salvaged from entire homes built between 1640 and 1840. More than 200 rooms were added to display his outstanding collection of American decorative arts.

Pierre devoted his life to horticulture. He bought a 1,000-acre 19th-century arboretum and created Longwood Gardens, where he entertained his many friends and relatives. Today, 350 acres of the meticulously landscaped gardens are open to the public. Displays range from a tropical rain forest to a desert; acres of heated conservatories, where flowers are in bloom year-round, create eternal summer. Pierre also built the grand Hotel du Pont in downtown Wilmington adjacent to company headquarters. No expense was spared; more than 18 French and Italian craftsmen labored for two years carving, gilding, and painting.

Alfred I. du Pont's country estate, Nemours, was named after the family's ancestral home in north-central France. It encompasses 300 acres of French gardens and a mansion in the Louis XVI style.

The Brandywine Valley is also Wyeth country, where three generations of artists have found landscapes worthy of their talents. Although American realist Andrew Wyeth is the most famous local artist, the area's artistic tradition started long before when artist/illustrator Howard Pyle started a school in the valley. He had more than 100 students, including Andrew's father, N. C. Wyeth; Frank Schoonover; Jessie Willcox Smith; and Harvey Dunn. It was that tradition which inspired Andrew and his son Jamie.

In 1967, local residents formed the Brandywine Conservancy to prevent industrialization of the area and pollution of the river. In 1971, they opened the Brandywine River Museum in a preserved 19th-century gristmill. It celebrates the Brandywine School of artists in a setting much in tune with their world.

The valley is also the site of one of the more dramatic turns in the American Revolution, the Battle of Brandywine, and an offbeat museum, which celebrates the mushroom. The region is dotted with antiques shops, fine restaurants, cozy country inns, and reliable bed-and-breakfasts. Because there is a lack of agencies that offer guided tours, your best bet is to rent a car and explore on your own with the help of a map from one of the tourist information agencies listed below.

Getting Around

By Car Take U.S. 1 south from Philadelphia; Brandywine Valley is about 25 miles from Philadelphia and many attractions are on U.S. 1. To reach Wilmington, pick up U.S. 202 south just past Concordville, or take I–95 south from Philadelphia.

By Bus From Philadelphia, **Greyhound/Trailways** (tel. 800/231–2222) has about 10 daily departures to the Wilmington terminal at 101 North French Street. The trip takes one hour.

By Train **Amtrak** (tel. 215/824–1600 or 800/872–7245) has frequent service from Philadelphia's 30th Street Station to the Wilmington Station at Martin Luther King Jr. Boulevard and French Street on the edge of downtown. It's a 25-minute ride.

Guided Tours

Colonial Pathways (Box 879, Chadds Ford, PA 19317, tel. 215/ 388–2654) guides escort you—in your car—for full-day excursions. You can plan the itinerary, or have them do it for you. Call for reservations.

Important Addresses and Numbers

Tourist **The Brandywine Valley Tourist Information Center** (U.S. 1
Information north of Kennett Sq., tel. 215/388–2900 or 800/228–9933) in the Longwood Progressive Meeting House at the entrance to Longwood Gardens has information on attractions, lodging, and restaurants. Open daily, May–Sept. 10–6; Oct.–Apr. 10–5. The center is run by the **Chester County Tourist Bureau**, which has its main office at the Government Services Center, 601 Westtown Rd., West Chester, PA 19382, tel. 215/344–6365.

For good road maps and visitors' guides, contact the **Delaware County Convention and Visitors Bureau** (200 E. State St., Suite 100, Media, PA 19063, tel. 215/565–3679 or 215/565–3666 for tape of events) and the **Greater Wilmington Convention and Visitors Bureau** (1300 Market St., Suite 504, Wilmington, DE 19801, tel. 302/652–4088).

Exploring

Numbers in the margin correspond to points of interest on the Brandywine Valley map.

If you start early enough, you can tour the valley's top three attractions—the Brandywine River Museum, Longwood Gardens, and Winterthur—in one day. If you have more time to spend in the valley, you can stop in to see the additional sites in Pennsylvania and then move on to Delaware.

❶ Franklin Mint Museum, a private mint that creates heirloom-quality collectibles, displays uniquely designed coins, precision die-cast model cars, masterpieces from the House of Igor Carl Fabergé, paintings by Andrew Wyeth and Norman Rockwell, and sculpture in porcelain, crystal, pewter, and bronze. *U.S. 1, Franklin Center, PA 19091, tel. 215/459–6168. Admission free. Open Mon.–Sat. 9:30–4:30, Sun. 1–4:30.*

❷ Brandywine Battlefield State Park, in Chadds Ford, is a popular stop for history buffs. Nearby is the site of the Battle of Brandywine, where British General William Howe and his troops defeated George Washington on September 11, 1777. The Continental Army then fled to Lancaster, leaving Philadelphia vulnerable to British troops. The Visitors Center has audiovisual materials and displays about the battle. On the site are two restored farmhouses that once sheltered Washington and Lafayette. *U.S. 1, Chadds Ford, PA 19317, tel. 215/459–3342. Admission: no charge to enter park; house tours $3.50 adults, $2.50 senior citizens, $1.50 children 6–17, children under 6 free. Open Tues.–Sat. 9–5, Sun. noon–5.*

❸ In a converted Civil War–era gristmill, the **Brandywine River Museum** showcases the art of Chadds Ford native Andrew Wyeth, a major American realist, and his family: his father, N. C. Wyeth, illustrator of many children's classics; his sisters Henriette and Carolyn; and his son Jamie. The collection also emphasizes still life, landscape painting, and American illustration. Glass-walled lobbies display the river and countryside which inspired the Brandywine School. The museum uses a system of filters, baffles, and blinds to direct natural light. Outside the museum visit a garden with regional wildflowers and follow a nature trail along the river. *U.S. 1 and Rte. 100, Chadds Ford, PA 19317, tel. 215/388–7601. Admission: $5 adults, $2.50 senior citizens, $2 students, children under 6 free. Open daily 9:30–4:30. Closed Christmas Day.*

❹ Longwood Gardens has established an international reputation for its colorful gardens featuring flowers and blossoming shrubs. In 1906, Pierre Samuel du Pont bought a simple Quaker farm, famous for its trees, and turned it into the ultimate estate garden. Fabulous seasonal attractions include magnolias and azaleas in spring, roses and water lilies in summer, fall foliage and chrysanthemums, and winter camellias, orchids, and palms. Bad weather is no problem as 3½ acres of exotic foliage, cacti, ferns, and bonsai are housed in heated conservatories. There are illuminated fountain displays on Tuesday, Thursday, and Saturday evenings at 9:15 in summer. *U.S. 1, Kennett Square, PA 19348, tel. 215/388–6741. Admission: $10 adults ($6 Tues.), $6 youths 16–20, $2 children 6–15, children under 6 free. Open daily 10–5, plus some evenings in summer and from Thanksgiving to Christmas.*

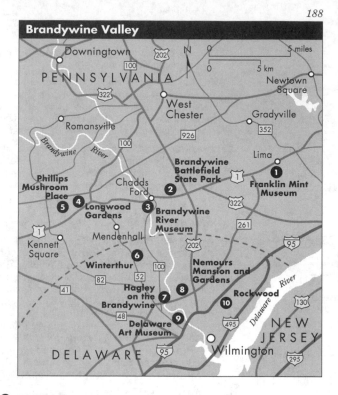

Brandywine Valley

---

⑤ **Phillips Mushroom Place** is a small museum devoted exclusively to a fungus—the mushroom. Mushrooms are Pennsylvania's number one cash crop and most are grown in Kennett Square. The history, lore, and growing process of mushrooms is explained with dioramas, exhibits, and an 18-minute film. The gift shop sells a variety of mushrooms. *U.S. 1, ½ mi south of Longwood Gardens, Kennett Square, PA 19348, tel. 215/388–6082. Admission: $1.25 adults, 75¢ senior citizens, 50¢ children 7–12, children under 7 free. Open daily 10–6.*

⑥ Henry Francis du Pont housed his 89,000 objects of American decorative art in a nine-story mansion called **Winterthur.** The 1640–1860 furniture, silver, paintings, and textiles are displayed in period room settings. Surrounding the museum are 1,000 acres of landscaped lawns, gardens, and virgin forest. "Winterthur's Yuletide Tour" (Nov. 15–Dec. 31) showcases the holiday traditions of early America. The Galleries, opened in 1992, houses permanent displays and changing exhibits of decorative arts and crafts. *Rte. 52, Winterthur, DE 19735, 5 mi south of U.S. 1, tel. 302/888–4600. Children under 12 not permitted on reserved tours. Admission: A variety of tours ranges from $7–$20, with discounts for senior citizens and children. The garden tram tour runs all year and is included in all tours. Open Tues.–Sat. 9–5, Sun. 11–5.*

⑦ **Hagley on the Brandywine** offers a glimpse of the du Ponts at work. A restored, mid-19th-century mill community on 240 landscaped acres, Hagley is the site of the first Du Pont blackpowder mills. The museum's exhibits, including a restored workers' community, depict the dangerous work of the early explosives industry. The tour includes stops at Eleutherian Mills, an 1803 Georgian-style home which was furnished by five generations of du Ponts, and a French Renaissance-style garden. Allow about two hours for your visit. The coffee shop is open for lunch except in winter. *Rte. 141 between Rte. 100 and U.S. 202, Wilmington, DE 19807, tel. 302/658-2400. Admission: $9.75 adults, $7.50 senior citizens and students, $3.50 children 6-14, children under 6 free, $26.50 household. Open Mar. 15-Dec., daily 9:30-4:30; Jan.-Mar. 14, Sat. and Sun. 9:30-4:30. In winter, weekday tours at 1:30.*

8 **Nemours Mansion and Gardens,** a 300-acre country estate built for Alfred I. du Pont in 1910, is a modified Louis XVI château showcasing European and American furnishings, rare rugs, tapestries, and art. The gardens, reminiscent of Versailles, are landscaped with fountains, pools, and statuary. The estate can only be seen on the guided two-hour tours. *Rockland Rd., between Rte. 100 and U.S. 202, Wilmington, DE 19899, tel. 302/651-6912. Admission: $8; visitors must be over 16. Open May through Nov. Tours Tues.-Sat. 9, 11, 1, and 3; Sun. at 11, 1, and 3. Reservations recommended.*

9 **Delaware Art Museum.** The museum features the paintings of Howard Pyle, a Wilmington native and "father of American illustration," and his students—N. C. Wyeth, Frank Schoonover, and Maxfield Parrish. It also houses the largest American collection of 19th-century English pre-Raphaelite paintings and decorative arts and a children's participatory gallery. *2301 Kentmere Pkwy., Wilmington, DE 19806, tel. 302/571-9590. Admission: $4 adults, $3 seniors citizens, $2.50 children. Open Tues. 10-9, Wed.-Sat. 10-5, Sun. noon-5.*

10 In contrast to the opulent French-inspired du Pont homes is **Rockwood,** a quietly elegant English-style country house and a fine example of rural Gothic architecture. Built in 1851 by Joseph Shipley, a Quaker merchant, the house is now a museum filled with 17th- to 20th-century American, European, and Oriental decorative arts and furnishings. There is a guided tour of the mansion. *610 Shipley Rd., Wilmington, DE 19809, tel. 302/761-4340. Admission: $5 adults, $4 senior citizens, $1 children 5-16. Open Tues.-Sat. 11-3.*

Dining and Lodging

Dining It seems that while almost every restaurant in the Brandywine Valley serves what is called Continental-American cuisine, most also feature local specialties—fresh seafood from the Chesapeake Bay and dishes made with Kennett Square mushrooms.

Category	Cost*
Very Expensive	over $40
Expensive	$25–$40
Moderate	$15–$25
Inexpensive	under $15

*per person for a 3-course meal, without wine, tip, or tax (6%)

Lodging Many Brandywine Valley accommodations call themselves bed-and-breakfasts because they provide beds and serve breakfast, but they are far from the typical B&B—which is usually a room in a private home—and are more accurately characterized as inns or small hotels.

Unless otherwise indicated, all rooms have private bath and the hotel is open year-round.

Category	Cost*
Very Expensive	over $100
Expensive	$80–$100
Moderate	$65–$80
Inexpensive	under $65

double occupancy, without tax (6%)

Highly recommended restaurants and hotels in each price category are indicated by a star ★.

The following credit card abbreviations are used: AE, American Express; D, Discover; DC, Diners Club; MC, MasterCard; V, Visa.

Chadds Ford **Chadds Ford Inn.** Continental-American dishes such as grilled
Dining salmon in oatmeal crust and free-range game are featured in a lively former rest stop on the Wilmington-Philadelphia-Lancaster commerce route. Generous portions are served in a Colonial setting featuring candlelight, stone hearths, and Wyeth prints. This popular lunch spot is walking distance from the Brandywine River Museum. *Rte. 100 and U.S. 1, tel. 215/388–7361. Reservations advised. Dress: casual. AE, DC, MC, V. Sunday brunch. Expensive.*

Lodging **Brandywine River Hotel.** This small, modern, two-story hotel is across the highway from the Brandywine River Museum. Tasteful Queen Anne furnishings, classic English chintz, and florals create a homey feeling. Ten suites have fireplaces and Jacuzzis. Complimentary Continental breakfast and afternoon tea are served in a lovely dining room. *Rte. 100 and U.S. 1, Chadds Ford, PA 19317, tel. 215/388–1200. 40 rooms. AE, DC, MC, V. Very Expensive.*

Glen Mills **Sweetwater Farm.** A handsome 18th-century fieldstone farm-
Lodging house has been lovingly restored into a homey inn serving
★ hearty breakfasts. A shaded porch lined with rockers overlooks the 50-acre horse-farm; no other houses are in sight. Rooms have fresh flowers, fragrant potpourri, and reproductions of period furnishings, including some canopy beds. Rooms in the newer section (circa 1815) of the house are larger. *50 Sweetwater Rd., Glen Mills, PA 19342, tel. 215/459–4711. 6 rooms, 3 with private bath, and 5 cottages. Facilities: outdoor pool. Two-night minimum stay requested on weekends. AE, MC, V. Very Expensive.*

Kennett Square **Longwood Inn.** Live Maine lobsters, homemade crab cakes,
Dining Chesapeake seafood dishes, and mushroom specialties are served in a relaxed Williamsburg-style setting. The inn serves early-bird dinners; a good choice for lunch. *815 E. Baltimore Pike (U.S. 1), ½ mi south of Longwood Gardens, tel. 215/444–*

3515. Reservations suggested for dinner. Dress: informal. AE, DC, MC, V. Moderate.

Lodging **Longwood Inn.** This small, family-owned motel ½ mile south of Longwood Gardens offers affordable accommodations with simple, traditional furnishings. *815 E. Baltimore Pike, Kennett Square, PA 19348, tel. 215/444–3515. 27 rooms. Facilities: restaurant, lounge. AE, DC, MC, V. Moderate.*

Meadow Spring Farm. Anne Hicks's farmhouse is a gallery for her family's antiques, dolls, and teddy bears. Rooms have Amish quilts and televisions. A full country breakfast is served daily on the glassed-in porch. Children are welcome here. *201 E. Street Rd., Kennett Square, PA 19348, tel. 215/444–3903. 6 rooms, 4 with bath. Facilities: outdoor pool, hot tub in solarium, game room with pool table and Ping Pong, pond for fishing, farm animals. No credit cards. Moderate.*

Mendenhall **Mendenhall Inn.** Continental and American cuisine is served in
Dining this 1790s Quaker mill building with its old beams still intact. Crab imperial, prime rib, and game are featured. For lunch, request a table with a courtyard view; at Saturday dinner, ask for the Mill Room upstairs. *Rte. 52, 1 mi south of U.S. 1, tel. 215/ 388–1181. Reservations advised for lunch, required for dinner. Jacket and tie required, except in tavern. AE, DC, MC, V. Closed lunch Sun. Expensive.*

Lodging **Fairville Inn.** Halfway between Winterthur and Longwood
★ Gardens, Ole and Patti Retlev's inn offers bright, airy rooms furnished with Queen Anne and Hepplewhite reproductions. There's a main house, built in 1826; a remodeled barn; and a carriage house. Request a room in the back of the property, away from traffic. The main house has a striking living room with a large fireplace. The Fairville serves complimentary light breakfast and afternoon tea. Not suitable for children under 10. *Rte. 52 (Kennett Pike), Box 219, Mendenhall, PA 19357, tel. 215/388–5900, fax 215/388–5902. 13 rooms, 2 suites. AE, MC, V. Expensive–Very Expensive.*

Thornton **Pace One.** A 250-year-old barn with poplar beams and stone
Dining walls features country specialties such as pork chops stuffed with cornbread and sausage and marinated, broiled fish. Chocolate fondue and fudge cake head the list of tempting desserts. A friendly, casual spot. *Glen Mills and Thornton Rds., tel. 215/ 459–3702. Reservations advised. Dress: informal. AE, DC, MC, V. Closed lunch Sat. Expensive.*

West Chester **Dilworthtown Inn.** Fresh seafood from the Chesapeake, local
Dining quail and partridge, and smoked pheasant are among the en-
★ trées served at this inn. Vegetables and herbs are grown in the garden across the road. The wine cellar is stocked with over 14,000 bottles. *Old Wilmington Pike and Brinton's Bridge Rd., tel. 215/399–1390. Reservations advised. Jacket required. AE, DC, MC, V. Closed for lunch. Expensive.*

Wilmington **Green Room.** For years Philadelphians have trekked to Wil-
Dining mington to celebrate special occasions in the famous Hotel du
★ Pont restaurant. Classic French cuisine is served in Edwardian splendor under a gold-encrusted ceiling with massive Spanish chandeliers and high French windows. Harp music accompanies formal dinners. *Hotel du Pont, 11th and Market Sts., tel. 302/594–3100. Reservations advised. Jackets required. AE, DC, MC, V. Fri. and Sat. dinner only. Very Expensive.*

Lodging **Hotel du Pont.** The hotel is an elegant 12-story building with an old-world feel built in 1913 by Pierre-Samuel du Pont. The lobby has a spectacular gold-encrusted ceiling, polished marble walls, and carved paneling. Rooms feature antique reproductions and original art; request a newly renovated room. *11th and Market Sts., Wilmington, DE 19801, tel. 302/594–3100 or 800/441–9019. 216 rooms. Facilities: 2 restaurants serving French-Continental and American cuisine, lobby lounge, theater next door. AE, DC, MC, V. Very Expensive.*

Valley Forge

Valley Forge National Historical Park preserves the area where George Washington's Continental Army endured the bitter winter of 1777–1778. Although the park's 3,500 acres of rolling hills offer serenity and quiet beauty, it is doubtful that Washington enjoyed any peaceful nights as he struggled with the morale problems that beset his troops.

The army had just lost the battles of Brandywine, White Horse, and Germantown. While the British occupied Philadelphia, Washington's soldiers were forced to endure horrid conditions—blizzards, inadequate food and clothing, damp quarters, and disease. Many men deserted and, although no battle was fought at Valley Forge, 2,000 American soldiers died.

But the troops won one victory that winter—a war of the will. The forces slowly regained strength and confidence under the leadership of Prussian drillmaster Friedrich von Steuben. In June 1778, Washington led his troops away from Valley Forge in search of the British. Fortified, the Continental Army was able to carry on the fight for five years more.

For the day-tripper interested in early-American history, a visit to the monuments, markers, huts, and headquarters in Valley Forge National Historical Park, 20 miles from Center City, Philadelphia, is illuminating. If the weather is fine, consider renting a bicycle or packing a lunch and picnicking at one of three park sites. Other nearby attractions include Mill Grove, the home of naturalist John James Audubon; the studio and residence of craftsman Wharton Esherick; and The Court and The Plaza, one of the nation's largest shopping complexes.

If you stay overnight in Valley Forge, check the schedule for the **Valley Forge Music Fair** (Route 202, Devon 19133, tel. 215/644–5000). This theater-in-the-round presents top names in entertainment, with recent performances by Diana Ross, the Pointer Sisters, and Tom Jones. The **People's Light and Theater Company** (39 Conestoga Rd., Malvern 19355, tel. 215/644–3500), a pioneer of the regional theater movement, offers classics and modern productions throughout the year.

Getting Around

By Car Take the Schuylkill Expressway (I–76) west from Philadelphia to Exit 25 (Goddard Blvd.). Take Route 363 to North Gulph Road and follow signs to Valley Forge National Historical Park. Exit 25 also provides easy access to The Court and The Plaza shopping complex.

By Bus The **SEPTA** (tel. 215/580–7800) No. 125 bus leaves from 16th Street and John F. Kennedy Boulevard for King of Prussia Plaza. On weekdays, it continues on to Valley Forge National Historical Park. On Saturdays, transfer at the plaza to the No. 99 "Royersford" bus, which goes through the park. The No. 99 bus departs hourly. The No. 125 bus leaves from 16th and John F. Kennedy Boulevard in Center City starting at 5:30 AM, and departs from the park as late as 7:45 PM. It runs every ½-hour during rush hour, and hourly 9–4. There is no SEPTA transportation to Valley Forge on Sundays.

Guided Tours

The Valley Forge National Historical Park Bus Tour (tel. 215/783–5788) is a narrated minibus tour that originates from the park Visitor Center (Rte. 23 and N. Gulph Rd.). Passengers can alight, visit sites, and reboard. Tours are scheduled from June through September; times vary. Tours cost $5.50 for adults, $4.50 children 5–16, children under 5 free.

Important Addresses and Numbers

Tourist Information **Valley Forge Convention and Visitors Bureau** (Box 311, Norristown, PA 19404, tel. 215/278–3558 or 800/441–3549). Call or write for information packet.

Valley Forge Country Funline (tel. 215/275–4636) offers information about special events and exhibits 24 hours a day.

Exploring

Numbers in the margin correspond to points of interest on the Valley Forge map.

 Valley Forge National Historical Park, administered by the National Park Service, is the site of the 1777–1778 winter encampment of General George Washington and the Continental Army. Stop first at the Visitor Center for a 15-minute orientation film, exhibits, and a map for a 10-mile, self-guided auto tour of the park attractions. Stops include reconstructed huts of the Muhlenberg Brigade, and the National Memorial Arch, which pays tribute to those soldiers who suffered through the infamous winter. Other sites include the bronze equestrian statue on the encampment of General Anthony Wayne and his Pennsylvania troops; Artillery Park, where the soldiers stored their cannons; and the Isaac Potts House, which served as Washington's headquarters. From June through September, you can purchase an auto-tour cassette tape for $8 or rent a tape and player for $10.

The park contains 6 miles of paved trails for jogging or bicycling, and hiking trails. Visitors can picnic at any of three designated areas. A leisurely visit to the park will take no more than half a day. *Rtes. 23 and 363, Box 953, Valley Forge, PA 19481, tel. 215/783–1077. Admission to Washington's headquarters: $1 adults 17–61. Open daily 8:30–5. Closed Christmas.*

❷ The **Valley Forge Historical Society Museum** tells the Valley Forge story with military equipment and Colonial artifacts plus a large collection of items that belonged to Martha and George Washington. The nearby Chapel Cabin Shop sells homemade goodies such as Martha's 16-Bean Soup and blue-

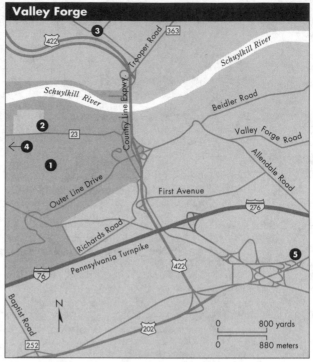

Valley Forge

barb jam. *Alongside the Washington Memorial Chapel on Rte. 23, tel. 215/783–0535. Admission: $1.50 adults, 50¢ children 2– 12. Open Mon.–Sat. 9:30–4:30, Sun. 1–4:30. Closed Thanksgiving, Christmas, New Year's Day, and Easter.*

3 **Mill Grove** was the first American home of Haitian-born artist and naturalist John James Audubon. Built in 1762, the house is now a museum displaying Audubon's major works, including reproductions, original prints, his paintings of birds and wildlife, and the double-elephant folio of his *Birds of America.* The attic has been restored to a studio and taxidermy room. The Audubon Wildlife Sanctuary has 4 miles of marked hiking trails along Perkiomen Creek. *Audubon and Pawlings Rds., Box 7125, Audubon, PA 19407, tel. 215/666–5593. Admission free. Museum open Tues.–Sat. 10–4, Sun. 1–4; grounds open Tues.–Sun. 7 AM–dusk. Closed Thanksgiving, Christmas, and New Year's Day.*

4 On the Horseshoe Trail, two miles west of Valley Forge park, is the **Wharton Esherick Museum,** the former home and studio of the "Dean of American Crafts." Best known for his sculptural furniture, Esherick shaped a new aesthetic in decorative arts by bridging art with furniture. The museum houses 200 samples of his work—paintings, woodcuts, furniture, and wood sculptures. The studio, in which everything from the light switches to the spiral staircase is hand-carved, is one of his monumental achievements. *Box 595, Paoli, PA 19301, tel. 215/ 644–5822. Admission: $5 adults, $3 children under 12. Open Sat. 10–5, Sun. 1–5 for hourly guided tours. Reservations required. Group tours weekdays. Closed Jan. and Feb.*

5 For lunch or an afternoon of browsing, head for the **Court and Plaza** at King of Prussia, one of the nation's largest shopping complexes. These two adjacent malls contain more than a dozen restaurants, 300 shops and boutiques, and a half-dozen major department stores, including Bloomingdale's and a stunning new branch of Philadelphia's own Strawbridge and Clothier. *Rte. 202 and N. Gulph Rd., tel. 215/265-5727. Open Mon.-Sat. 10-9:30, Sun. 11-5.*

Dining and Lodging

King of Prussia **Bocconcini.** Updated American and northern Italian special-
Dining ties (tortellini alla panna with prosciutto, mushrooms, and
★   cream) are served amid majestic marble columns and hanging vines interlaced on cherrywood ceiling beams. Italian desserts include spumoni, cannoli, and ricotta cheesecake. *Plaza Hotel at Valley Forge, N. Gulph Rd. and 1st Ave., tel. 215/265-1500. Reservations advised. Dress: casual. AE, DC, MC, V. Expensive ($25-$40).*

Kennedy Supplee Restaurant. New American cuisine is served in the seven dining rooms of a circa 1852 Italian Renaissance mansion overlooking Valley Forge National Historical Park. *1100 W. Valley Forge Rd., tel. 215/337-3777. Reservations advised. AE, DC, MC, V. No lunch weekends. Moderate-Expensive ($15-$40).*

Lily Langtry's Victorian Theater and Restaurant. This lavishly appointed Victorian-era restaurant/cabaret serves American and Continental dishes, but the campy Las Vegas-style entertainment—corny comedians, scantily clad showgirls, and some fine singers, dancers, and ice skaters—is the real draw here. *Sheraton Valley Forge Hotel, N. Gulph Rd. and 1st Ave., tel. 215/337-LILY. Reservations suggested. Jackets suggested. AE, DC, MC, V. Expensive ($25-$40).*

Lodging **The Plaza Hotel at Valley Forge.** The six-story Radisson, opened in early 1988, and the Sheraton Valley Forge flank the Valley Forge Convention Center and share several restaurants and nightclubs. Contemporary rooms here are minisuites with Jacuzzis for two and numerous telephones and TV sets. Excellent breakfast and champagne-dinner-theater package. *N. Gulph Rd. and 1st Ave., 19406, tel. 215/265-1500 or 800/333-3333. 160 rooms. Facilities: restaurant, dinner theater, comedy club, health club, outdoor pool. AE, DC, MC, V. Very Expensive (over $100).*

★   **Sheraton Valley Forge Hotel.** A bustling high rise catering to groups and couples escaping to Jacuzzi-equipped fantasy theme suites—a prehistoric cave, a wild-and-woolly jungle, the outer-space-like "Outer Limits." Excellent breakfast and champagne-dinner-theater package. *N. Gulph Rd. and 1st Ave., 19406, tel. 215/337-2000 or 800/325-3535. 326 rooms, including 72 fantasy suites. Facilities: restaurants, dinner theater, comedy club, health club, outdoor pool. AE, DC, MC, V. Very Expensive (over $100).*

Comfort Inn at Valley Forge. Spacious, modern rooms with king-size beds, three phones, VCR, stocked refrigerators, and remote control TV make this new five-story hotel a good buy. *550 W. DeKalb Pike (Rt. 202N), 19406, tel. 215/962-0700 or 800/228-5150. 121 rooms. Facilities: complimentary Continental breakfast, dining area with microwave and frozen foods. AE, DC, MC, V. Moderate ($65-$80).*

Reading

Reading (RED-ing), founded by William Penn's sons Thomas and Richard, was a 19th-century industrial city best known as the terminus of the Reading Railroad. Today, Reading has another claim to fame. It promotes itself as the "Outlet Capital of the World" and entices bargain hunters with promises of savings up to 80% off retail.

This method of merchandising began when local factories and mills started selling overruns and seconds to employees. Eventually, small stores sprang up inside the factories. About 10 million visitors a year, many coming in bus excursions from all over the East Coast, now visit some 300 outlets located within a 4-mile radius. The stores sell clothing for the whole family, pretzels, candy, luggage, jewelry, shoes, pet food, even tropical fish. A large number of outlets are grouped together in former factory complexes.

While bare floors and self service is the norm at most outlet stores, two upscale complexes have opened; Reading Station and Designers Place at the VF Outlet Village come complete with carpeting, fitting rooms, sales clerks, and classical music playing in the background. Designer labels, including Ralph Lauren, Oleg Cassini, Calvin Klein, Karl Lagerfeld, and Yves St. Laurent, are discounted.

It's easy to get caught up in the buying frenzy as you browse through racks marked $10 and under, but not all the buys are bargains. If an item is marked "irregular," look it over carefully. It may be fine or it might have holes in the sleeves. There is no sales tax on clothing in Pennsylvania.

Reading is an easy 75-minute drive from Philadelphia and the major outlets can be scanned in a day. Most outlet complexes have cafeterias or food courts. If you want another day to shop or sightsee, you have more overnight options since the success of the outlet stores has spawned revitalization of the local hotel and restaurant industries.

Sitting prettily atop Mt. Penn on Skyline Drive is the Pagoda, a seven-story building of Japanese design, which provides an expansive view of the city. Skyline Drive is a meandering road with miles of unspoiled vistas. The Daniel Boone Homestead, a renovation of the frontiersman's home, and the Mary Merritt Doll Museum, make good diversions after a shopping spree.

Getting Around

By Car Take the Schuylkill Expressway (I–76) west from Philadelphia to the Pennsylvania Turnpike. Go west to Exit 22, take I–176 north to U.S. 422 and then west into downtown Reading.

By Bus **Greyhound/Trailways** (tel. 215/931–4000) has frequent runs to the Intercity Bus Terminal, Third and Court streets, in Reading. Most buses make the trip in 90 minutes, although some locals take up to three hours. Check the schedule carefully.

Important Addresses and Numbers

Tourist Information **Reading & Berks County Visitors Information** (Factory Village Complex, Park Rd. and Hill Ave., Box 6677, Wyomissing, PA

19610, tel. 215/375–4085 or 800/443–6610) provides outlet maps and guides. Open Jan.–June, weekdays 9–5, Sat. 10–2; July–Dec., weekdays 9–7, Sat. 10–3, Sun. 10–2.

Exploring

Numbers in the margin correspond to points of interest on the Reading Environs and Reading maps.

If you can't wait to load up your shopping bag, stop at the **Manufacturers Outlet Mall** when you exit the Pennsylvania Turnpike in Morgantown (Exit 22). "MOM" looks like any modern suburban enclosed shopping mall and has 70 stores on one level including Van Heusen, Izod, Arrow, and London Fog. Attached to the mall is a 200-room Holiday Inn (tel. 215/286–3000) and indoor recreation center with pool. The food court serves lunch and dinner. *Exit 22, Pennsylvania Turnpike, Rtes. 23 and 10, tel. 215/286–2000. Open Mon.–Sat. 10–9, Sun. noon–5.*

The **VF Outlet Village** offers some of the best buys and the largest variety of goods in the city. Situated on what was once the world's largest hosiery mill, the complex originally sold surplus hosiery, sleepwear, and lingerie. Today it consists of nine major buildings on more than 900,000 square feet, with more than 75 outlets. The VF Factory Outlet store offers a vast selection of Lee jeans, women's sleepwear, and lingerie from Vanity Fair and Lollipop, and Jantzen and Jansport activewear at half price. Upstairs are Jonathan Logan and Capezio. Designers Place opened in 1993, with a three-story glass atrium, shopping amenities, and about 15 upscale outlets including Anne Klein, Perry Ellis, Carole Little, and Marithe & Francois Girbaud. *Park Rd. and Hill Ave., Wyomissing, tel. 215/378–0408. Food court. Shuttle buses take shoppers to and from the parking lot. Open weekdays 9–9, Sat. 9–6, Sun. 10–5.*

The **Reading Outlet Center** occupies a former silk-stocking mill in the heart of the city and now houses more than 70 shops on four floors plus stores in nearby buildings. An elevator and new signs now make getting around the store easier. Items for sale range from toys and cosmetics to sporting goods and wine. There's a Polo/Ralph Lauren outlet, Fashion Flair's Izod Lacoste clothes, Timberland, Gilligan & O'Malley, and Corning. Liz Claiborne occupies a new site nearby at 832 Oley Street. *801 N. 9th St., tel. 215/373–5495. Restaurant. Open Mon.–Thurs. 9:30–6, Fri. and Sat. 9:30–8, Sun. 11–5.*

A block away from the Reading Outlet Center, the smaller **Big Mill Outlet** is housed in a former shoe factory. Among the more than 20 stores are Gitano (sportswear), Delta Hosiery Mill Outlet, B.U.M. Equipment, Cross Colors, and Esprit. *8th and Oley Sts. tel., 215/378–9100. Elevator. Small food court. Open Mon.–Thurs. 9:30–6, Fri. 9:30–8, Sat. 9:30–7, Sun. 11–5.*

Outlets on Hiesters Lane is a grouping of three outlet buildings along one city block at the northern end of downtown Reading. Except for a linen outlet and the dinnerware at the Mikasa Factory Store, most stores sell coats, clothes, and shoes. There's Burlington Coat Factory Warehouse, Flemington Fashion Outlet, and the Sweater Mill. *Corner of Hiesters La. and Kutztown Rd., tel. 215/921–9394. Most stores are open Mon.–Sat. 9:30–5:30, Sun. noon–5.*

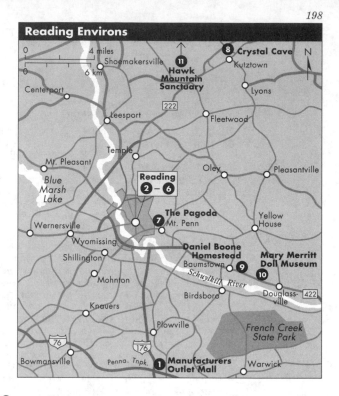

Reading Environs

0 4 miles
0 6 km

Shoemakersville
Centerport
Leesport
Temple
Mt. Pleasant
Blue Marsh Lake
Wernersville
Wyomissing
Shillington
Mohnton
Knauers
Plowville
Bowmansville
Penna. Tnpk.

11 Hawk Mountain Sanctuary
222
Fleetwood
Reading 2 – 6
Oley
7 The Pagoda Mt. Penn
Daniel Boone Homestead Baumstown **9**
Schuylkill River
Birdsboro
Douglass-ville
Warwick

8 Crystal Cave N
Kutztown
Lyons
Pleasantville
Yellow House
Mary Merritt Doll Museum 10
422
French Creek State Park

76   176   **1 Manufacturers Outlet Mall**

6 **Reading Station** bills itself as the "upscale outlet experience." This $23 million outlet complex is modeled after a turn-of-the-century Pennsylvania railroad village on the site of the former Reading Company railroad. The five buildings surrounding the courtyard display railroad memorabilia and house restaurants and about 90 factory outlet stores, including WestPoint Pepperell's Bed, Bath & Linens, Jones New York, Mondo Collection, and Brooks Brothers. *951 N. 6th St., tel. 215/478–7000. Open Mon.–Thurs. and Sat. 9:30–7, Fri. 9:30–9, Sun. 11–5.*

7 **The Pagoda,** a seven-story Japanese castle attached to the top of Mt. Penn by 10 tons of bolts, offers a panoramic view of the Reading area. Built in 1908 as a mountaintop resort, it underwent a $2 million renovation in 1993 and is now the home of the Berks Arts Council. Call to check on accessibility to the public. *Skyline Dr., tel. 800/443–6610.*

8 **Crystal Cave** 45-minute guided walking tours wind through illuminated stalactites and stalagmites in distinctive formations like the "ice cream cone," "totem pole," and innumerable others. *From Reading, take U.S. 222 north 15 mi to Kutztown exit, follow signs; tel. 215/683–6765. Admission: $7 adults, $4 children 4–11. Open daily 9–5, extended summer hours. Closed Dec.–Feb.*

9 The **Daniel Boone Homestead,** 10 miles east of Reading, is where the great frontiersman lived until the age of 16. The rebuilt homestead has been furnished to typify rural life in this part of the state. Offered are a half-hour house tour and unguided tours of the blacksmith shop, sawmill, and barn. *Daniel*

Big Mill Outlet, **4**
Outlets on Hiesters Lane, **5**
Reading Outlet Center, **3**
Reading Station, **6**
VF Factory Outlet Village, **2**

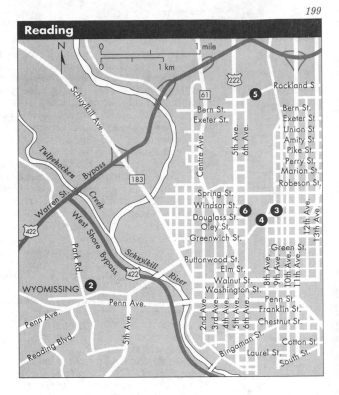

Boone Rd. off U.S. 422, tel. 215/582–4900. Admission: $4 adults, $3 senior citizens, $2 children 6–17, children under 6 free. Open Tues.–Sat. 9–5, Sun. noon–5. Closed Mon. except Memorial Day, Labor Day, and July 4.

⑩ It's a small world at the **Mary Merritt Doll Museum** where you'll find rare dolls—rag dolls, French bisque dolls, mechanical dolls, and more—crafted between 1725 and 1900. Also on display are toys, exquisitely fashioned miniature period rooms, and elaborate dollhouses. **Merritt's Museum of Childhood** has an eclectic collection of 18th-century Pennsylvania Dutch fraktur (hand-painted birth and marriage certificates), tin and iron toys, Colonial lighting devices, and early baby carriages. *Both on Rte. 422 in Douglassville, 1 mi east of Boone Homestead, tel. 215/385–3809. Admission: $3 adults, $2.50 senior citizens, $1.50 children 5–12, children under 5 free. Open Mon.–Sat. 10–5, Sun. 1–5. Closed major holidays.*

⑪ **Hawk Mountain Sanctuary,** a 2,200-acre refuge 28 miles north of Reading, is visited by more than 20,000 migrating raptors—hawks, bald eagles, ospreys, and falcons—each fall. In other seasons, you can spot songbirds, grouse, and white-tailed deer and other mammals; hike along the sometimes rocky trails; and picnic at a lookout offering a bird's-eye view of the spectacular scenery. Bring binoculars and proper footgear. No pets allowed. *Route 2, 8 miles west of Kempton, tel. 215/756–6961. Admission: $3 adults, $1.50 children 6–12. Visitor Center open daily, Dec.–Aug., 9–5; Sept.–Nov., 8–5. Closed Thanksgiving, Christmas, and New Year's Day.*

Dining

Joe's. This family-owned restaurant has attracted national attention for unusual dishes enriched by the exotic accents of wild and domestic mushrooms (cepes, morels, slippery jacks, woodblewits and boletes, among others), most of which are handpicked by the Czarnecki family. Wild mushroom soup is a don't-miss item. Jack Czarnecki wrote *Joe's Book of Mushroom Cookery*, the definitive mushroom cookbook. The wild game dishes include bear and antelope, and regional wines are featured. *7th and Laurel Sts., tel. 215/373–6794. Reservations requested on weekends. Dress: casual. DC, MC, V. Closed lunch. Closed Sun. and Mon. Very Expensive (over $40).*

The Peanut Bar. Free peanuts (throw the shells on the floor), video games, and good burgers and fries make this 1930s-style tavern and restaurant a fun outing. Besides such fun foods as Buffalo chicken wings and cheese balls, the chef serves up some gourmet meals, including Maryland crab cakes and Tandoori chicken. Beers from local breweries are featured. *332 Penn St., tel. 215/376–8500 or 800/515–8500. Reservations suggested. Dress: informal. AE, MC, V. Closed Sun. Moderate ($15–$25).*

Arner's. This chain of family restaurants has four locations all with the look and feel of spruced-up diners. The menu features American favorites with a Pennsylvania Dutch influence, such as pork chops, chicken pot pie, meatloaf, apple dumplings, and homemade pastries and pies. The bountiful salad bar and daily specials make this a hard-to-beat bargain. *9th and Exeter Sts., Reading, tel. 215/929–9795; Howard Blvd., Mt. Penn, tel. 215/779–6555; 1714 Bern Rd., Berkshire Mall, tel. 215/372–6101; 4643 Pottsville Pk., Tuckerton, tel. 215/926–9002. No reservations. Dress: informal. No credit cards. Inexpensive (under $15).*

Lodging

Sheraton Berkshire Inn. Recent renovations, including the addition of a striking Art Deco lobby and marble-tile floors, have made this an exceptionally attractive property. It's worth the extra $20 a night to upgrade from a standard room to an extra-large executive room in the tower. *U.S. 422 W, on Papermill Rd., Wyomissing 19610, tel. 215/376–3811 or 800/325–3535. 256 rooms, 4 bi-level suites. Facilities: 2 restaurants, nightclub, indoor pool, game room, fitness center. AE, DC, MC, V. Expensive–Very Expensive ($80–over $100).*

Inn at Reading. Housed in a well-kept, elegant complex, the inn's large rooms feature remote-control cable TV and traditional cherrywood furnishings, including some four-poster beds. Request a room close to the lobby. The Publick House restaurant serves excellent meals. *1040 Park Rd. and Warren St., Wyomissing 19610, tel. 215/372–7811. 250 rooms. Facilities: restaurant, live entertainment or DJ in nightclub, gift shop, outdoor pool, playground. AE, DC, MC, V. Expensive ($80–$100).*

Hampton Inn. This small hotel has stylish contemporary rooms but no dining or recreational facilities. The spacious King Special, just $5 more than a double, has a separate sitting area, king-size bed, and remote-control cable TV. Complimentary Continental breakfast is served. *1800 Papermill Rd., Wyo-*

missing 19610, tel. 215/374–8100 or 800/HAMPTON. 127 rooms. AE, DC, MC, V. Inexpensive (under $65).

Index

Fodor's Travel Guides

Available at bookstores everywhere, or call 1–800–533–6478, 24 hours a day.

U.S. Guides

Alaska

Arizona

Boston

California

Cape Cod, Martha's Vineyard, Nantucket

The Carolinas & the Georgia Coast

Chicago

Colorado

Florida

Hawaii

Las Vegas, Reno, Tahoe

Los Angeles

Maine, Vermont, New Hampshire

Maui

Miami & the Keys

New England

New Orleans

New York City

Pacific North Coast

Philadelphia & the Pennsylvania Dutch Country

The Rockies

San Diego

San Francisco

Santa Fe, Taos, Albuquerque

Seattle & Vancouver

The South

The U.S. & British Virgin Islands

The Upper Great Lakes Region

USA

Vacations in New York State

Vacations on the Jersey Shore

Virginia & Maryland

Waikiki

Walt Disney World and the Orlando Area

Washington, D.C.

Foreign Guides

Acapulco, Ixtapa, Zihuatanejo

Australia & New Zealand

Austria

The Bahamas

Baja & Mexico's Pacific Coast Resorts

Barbados

Berlin

Bermuda

Brazil

Brittany & Normandy

Budapest

Canada

Cancun, Cozumel, Yucatan Peninsula

Caribbean

China

Costa Rica, Belize, Guatemala

The Czech Republic & Slovakia

Eastern Europe

Egypt

Euro Disney

Europe

Europe's Great Cities

Florence & Tuscany

France

Germany

Great Britain

Greece

The Himalayan Countries

Hong Kong

India

Ireland

Israel

Italy

Japan

Kenya & Tanzania

Korea

London

Madrid & Barcelona

Mexico

Montreal & Quebec City

Morocco

Moscow & St. Petersburg

The Netherlands, Belgium & Luxembourg

New Zealand

Norway

Nova Scotia, Prince Edward Island & New Brunswick

Paris

Portugal

Provence & the Riviera

Rome

Russia & the Baltic Countries

Scandinavia

Scotland

Singapore

South America

Southeast Asia

Spain

Sweden

Switzerland

Thailand

Tokyo

Toronto

Turkey

Vienna & the Danube Valley

Yugoslavia

Special Series

Fodor's Affordables

Caribbean

Europe

Florida

France

Germany

Great Britain

London

Italy

Paris

Fodor's Bed & Breakfast and Country Inns Guides

Canada's Great Country Inns

California

Cottages, B&Bs and Country Inns of England and Wales

Mid-Atlantic Region

New England

The Pacific Northwest

The South

The Southwest

The Upper Great Lakes Region

The West Coast

The Berkeley Guides

California

Central America

Eastern Europe

France

Germany

Great Britain & Ireland

Mexico

Pacific Northwest & Alaska

San Francisco

Fodor's Exploring Guides

Australia

Britain

California

The Caribbean

Florida

France

Germany

Ireland

Italy

London

New York City

Paris

Rome

Singapore & Malaysia

Spain

Thailand

Fodor's Flashmaps

New York

Washington, D.C.

Fodor's Pocket Guides

Bahamas

Barbados

Jamaica

London

New York City

Paris

Puerto Rico

San Francisco

Washington, D.C.

Fodor's Sports

Cycling

Hiking

Running

Sailing

The Insider's Guide to the Best Canadian Skiing

Skiing in the USA & Canada

Fodor's Three-In-Ones (guidebook, language cassette, and phrase book)

France

Germany

Italy

Mexico

Spain

Fodor's Special-Interest Guides

Accessible USA

Cruises and Ports of Call

Euro Disney

Halliday's New England Food Explorer

Healthy Escapes

London Companion

Shadow Traffic's New York Shortcuts and Traffic Tips

Sunday in New York

Walt Disney World and the Orlando Area

Walt Disney World for Adults

Fodor's Touring Guides

Touring Europe

Touring USA: Eastern Edition

Fodor's Vacation Planners

Great American Vacations

National Parks of the East

National Parks of the West

The Wall Street Journal Guides to Business Travel

Europe

International Cities

Pacific Rim

USA & Canada

WHEREVER YOU TRAVEL, *H*ELP IS NEVER FAR AWAY.

From planning your trip to providing travel assistance along the way, American Express® Travel Service Offices* are always there to help.

Philadelphia

American Express Travel Service
615 Chestnut Street
Independence Mall Area
(215) 592-9211

American Express Travel Service
2 Penn Center Plaza
SE Corner 16th & JFK
(215) 587-2300

**For the office nearest you, call
1-800-YES-AMEX.**